CAREER CRIMINALS IN SOCIETY

CAREER CRIMINALS IN SOCIETY

MATT DeLISI
Iowa State University

SAGE Publications
Thousand Oaks ▪ London ▪ New Delhi

For information:

Sage Publications, Inc.
2455 Teller Road
Thousand Oaks, California 91320
E-mail: order@sagepub.com

Sage Publications Ltd.
1 Oliver's Yard
55 City Road
London EC1Y 1SP
United Kingdom

Sage Publications India Pvt. Ltd.
B-42 Panchsheel Enclave
Post Box 4109
New Delhi 110 017 India

Printed in the United States of America

Library of Congress Cataloging-in-Publication Data

DeLisi, Matt.
Career criminals in society / Matt DeLisi.
    p. cm.
Includes bibliographical references and index.
ISBN 1-4129-0553-2 (cloth: acid-free paper) — ISBN 1-4129-0554-0
    (pbk. : acid-free paper) 1. Recidivists. 2. Criminals. 3. Criminal
behavior, Prediction of. I. Title.
HV6049.D45 2005
364.3—dc22   2004019351

This book is printed on acid-free paper.

05   06   07   10   9   8   7   6   5   4   3   2   1

Acquiring Editor:	Jerry Westby
Editorial Assistant:	Vonessa Vondera
Production Editor:	Diana E. Axelsen
Typesetter:	C&M Digitals (P) Ltd.
Cover Designer:	Edgar Abarca

Contents

Preface

The actual writing of this manuscript was a relatively quick process, taking only about 3 months. However, *Career Criminals in Society* is, in many respects, the culmination of 10 years of my student, work, and academic life, and many people deserve thanks.

The best colleagues whom I have ever had the privilege to work with were my friends in the bond commissioner office in the 20th Judicial District in Boulder County, Colorado. With humor, intelligence, and good common sense, they encouraged my interest in, knowledge of, and acquaintanceship with high-rate criminal offenders. I would like to acknowledge Melissa Andrews, Laura Guzman, Cinnamon Jones, Kurt Miller, Dale Wetzbarger, Celia Wilson, and Gary York.

Three mentors guided me from a curious undergraduate to this point. The late Professor Arnold Goldstein taught me about juvenile delinquency and criminology when I was an undergraduate at Syracuse University. His courses remain the model for my own, and Dr. Goldstein showed me the importance of being fluent in the real and academic worlds of criminal justice. He was a wonderful man. Also at Syracuse, Professor William Coplin illustrated the link between policy and theory, provided my first criminological research opportunity, and believed that my chutzpah would someday lead somewhere good. Finally, Professor Robert Regoli was my dissertation chair, sometime coauthor, and advisor during my graduate study at the University of Colorado. From day 1, Bob treated me as his peer and offered good counsel on many topics.

Many others have benefited me with their scholarship, social commentary, or friendship. These include Gregg Barak, Mark Berg, Donna Bishop, Chet Britt, Pete Conis, John DiIulio, Bill Doerner, Dinesh D'Souza, Larry Elder, Del Elliott, David Farrington, Jewel Gatling, Michael Gottfredson, Robert Hare, Richard Herrnstein, Gertrude Himmelfarb, Michael Hindelang, Travis

Hirschi, Andy Hochstetler, Pete Iadicola, Patrick Krueger, John Laub, Seymour Lipset, Rolf Loeber, Joan McCord, John McWhorter, Walter Miller, Terrie Moffitt, Ted Nugent, David Olds, Bill O'Reilly, Joan Petersilia, Alex Piquero, Travis Pratt, Lee Robins, Angie Schadt, John Serdinak, Thomas Sowell, T. J. Taylor, Jackson Toby, Jay Thompson, Glenn Walters, James Q. Wilson, and Tom Winfree.

Thanks also to those who reviewed the manuscript: Ted Curry, University of Texas at El Paso; Elaine Gunnison, University of Nevada Las Vegas; Denise Huggins, University of Arkansas; Karen Dudash, Cameron University; William Doerner, Florida State University; and Craig T. Robertson, University of North Alabama. Jerry Westby at Sage Publications provided excellent guidance, faith, and a steadying presence while becoming both editor and friend.

Finally, I thank my family, especially my beautiful wife, Melissa, and our wonderful sons, Jamison and Landon. This is for you!

1

Introduction: Two Glimpses at the Career Criminal

Eugene Smith was well known among teachers and students for his consistently out of control behavior. Several teachers had already interrupted their class to take Eugene to the principal's office. Unfortunately, none of the punishments that school staff had assigned—such as staying after school, missing recess, going into the hall, standing in the corner, or calling home—seemed to make much difference to this fifth grader. Indeed, Eugene's parents seemed resigned to the belief that Eugene was simply "being a boy" and needed more self-control. A consensus among teachers was that Eugene's parents were partly to blame for his behavioral problems. When they did attend parent-teacher conferences, they were often indignant with teachers, suggesting that the majority of Eugene's troubles were the result of biased teachers who "had it in for Eugene." Eugene's older and younger brothers and sisters possessed the youthful orneriness common among children, especially schoolboys, but presented none of the problems of their increasingly infamous brother. Something was different about Eugene.

Whenever and wherever there was misbehavior, chances were good that Eugene was involved. Taunting and bullying other students, inappropriately touching female students, openly defying teachers and staff with profane language, smoking cigarettes, stealing other students' book bags, destroying school property, and the like were behaviors that Eugene had been committing since he was in kindergarten. Academically and behaviorally, Eugene was always the worst student in class, and he occupied the lowest math and reading groups. Clearly Eugene would not be considered cognitively gifted; however, the bulk of his academic problems seemed to be based on his basic refusal to perform schoolwork or participate in class. He could not stay on task, became frustrated when he had to sit at his desk, had difficulty paying attention, and liked to throw things at other students to disrupt them. Eugene simply hated school.

Always and everywhere, a dark cloud seemed to hover over Eugene Smith's head. It appeared that he did not have the most patient parents, and Eugene's behavior only served to exacerbate their frustration in dealing with him. Eugene's antipathy for school and lack of cognitive skills rendered each day a battle. Teachers and other students alternately empathized with Eugene's situation and expressed contempt for his constant interruptions and lack of consideration for others. The only thing that suited Eugene was misbehavior. Soon, it was the only thing he was known for.

The other children in Eugene's class and those who lived in his neighborhood had developed a tacit strategy in dealing with Eugene: Avoid him if possible. On the rare occasions when he could not be avoided, kids found it best to tolerate and placate him. The slightest provocation could send Eugene into fits, so other children tended to remain quiet, smile, and simply nod their heads to Eugene's latest banter—he was a notorious liar. Eugene made other children very uneasy because his behavior was unpredictable and sometimes frightening. Classmates did not hate Eugene; instead, most felt a profound sense of pity for him. However, all of the kids in school were afraid of him.

* * *

It was a crime that shocked the community. Three young men were found shot to death in a convenience store–gas station. Crime scene investigators indicated that two of the victims were store clerks who had been summarily executed after emptying the cash register and store safe. The other victim was a patron who unsuspectingly walked into the store during the commission of the robbery. Surveillance footage produced a clear picture of the assailant's face. Several eyewitnesses also reported that the gunman left the convenience store with a young woman who was identified as another store employee. The suspect abducted the victim and left the scene in her vehicle.

Seventy-three miles away and 90 minutes after the killings, the suspect's vehicle was spotted by highway patrol officers. In an attempt to elude the police, the suspect initiated a high-speed chase that involved officers from six local and state police agencies. Approximately 18 minutes later and after reaching speeds in excess of 110 miles per hour, the suspect crashed the vehicle into a concrete median support wall. Not wearing a seat belt, the suspect catapulted through the windshield of the vehicle and was killed instantly.

It took police and emergency medical personnel several hours to process the accident that occurred on the interstate, causing massive traffic congestion. Around this same time, a woman who was walking her dog in a rural area at the outskirts of town made a grisly discovery. The young woman who had been abducted during the convenience store robbery was found deceased near a thicket. She had been sexually assaulted and shot multiple times in the face and chest at close range.

When the day of carnage was over, authorities discovered the identity of the perpetrator, Michael Allen Garland. Garland, a 43-year-old machinist, was on parole after serving a 6-year sentence for burglary, grand theft, and cocaine possession convictions. With no fixed address, Garland frequently stayed at his mother's house, with friends, or in transient hotels. The Garland case received inordinate press attention and even made the national news. The families of four young victims and the community at-large attempted to come to grips with the senseless violence. The state department of corrections and parole board came under scrutiny for approving the release of an offender like Michael Garland and not appropriately monitoring him while on parole. These more immediate issues dominated the headlines and were the focus of print and television reporters.

Often omitted or buried in the back pages of news reports was the full extent of Garland's social and criminal history. Garland had a 29-year criminal record dating to the age of 14, when he was first institutionalized in the state boys' reformatory for several armed robbery convictions. Overall, Garland served more than a dozen prison sentences, most of them concurrently, in four states. A lifelong alcoholic and cocaine addict, Garland's arrest and conviction history included an array of offenses, such as larceny, auto theft, credit card fraud, burglary, drug possession, aggravated assault, and numerous probation and parole violations. His longest stint in prison was 11 years stemming from convictions in 1981 for armed burglary, armed robbery, assault with intent to kill, sexual abuse (reduced from armed rape), and felon in possession of a firearm. Never married, Garland had two children resulting from two common-law marriages. His formal education ended after eighth grade, but Garland acquired a machinist certificate in a prison vocational program and was episodically employed throughout his adult life.

The Life of Crime

These vignettes should sound familiar, for it is common for people to be exposed to career criminals through two general types of experiences. The first occurs during the elementary school years of childhood and relates to the unsavory bully who wantonly terrorizes property, pets, adults, and other children in the neighborhood. This bully, almost always a male, is the person whom your mother always warned you about. He is the type of person who preys upon the other kids in school, demands their lunch money, steals their clothes, and takes their basketball and kicks it afar. He does not do these things because he wants to play or necessarily even fit in, but because he simply wants to ruin others' play time. The bully seems angry about most things, is quick to lose his temper, and acts impulsively in all contexts, seemingly without a second thought. He also tends to do poorly in class, skip school, alienate himself from other children to the point where only other bullies will associate with him, and be well known for his delinquency. The bully usually has a stressful and often disadvantaged home life where one or both parents are absent, neglectful, generally uninvolved, and usually intoxicated.

The bully is the first kid in elementary school to use tobacco, drink alcohol, take drugs, and engage in sexual contact. He is also the first child to openly use verbal and physical defiance and resistance toward adult figures such as parents and teachers. Everyone who has contact with the bully, such as principals, teachers, parents, and other kids, offers the same general prognostication of his life trajectory: He will make a "career" of bad choices and bad behavior and probably end up, sooner or later, dead or in prison. Indeed, by middle school, the bully is known by the police and recurrently comes into contact with the juvenile court. By 9th or 10th grade, the bully becomes a memory, for he drops out of school, is institutionalized, or otherwise seems to disappear from conventional life. In fact, he does disappear into the subterranean criminal lifestyle. At this point, most people forever lose contact with the fledgling career criminal.

The second exposure to career criminals is vicarious and occurs later, usually in adulthood. This exposure is media driven, whereby citizens read about the criminal exploits of an incorrigible offender in the newspaper, watch the dramatic events of a high-speed police chase unfold on television, surf news on a criminal justice–related website, or hear the day's crime events on radio. Probably without realizing it or fully appreciating the implications of their experiences, many bear witness to the development path of the career criminal. The childhood memories of the school bully showcase a delinquent career prospectively. The vicarious media images capture the event that may serve as the culmination or termination of an offending career.

In some societies, the career criminal has proven to be an intriguing folk item. In different eras in nations such as the United States, England, Canada, and Australia, chronic and violent offenders have occasionally achieved some semblance of fame and have even become minor celebrities. Most citizens are familiar with the term and have even employed the it colloquially (e.g., "The Smith family sure has their hands full. Little Eugene is a career criminal in training."). What many people do not realize, however, is that the concept of the career criminal is one of grave importance and considerable criminological and legal meaning. More than a century of scientific research has indicated that the lion's share of crime that occurs in a society is committed by less than 10% of the population, the group commonly referred to as career criminals. More dramatic, upwards of 70% to 100% of the most severe forms of criminal behavior—predatory acts such as murder, rape, abduction, armed robbery, armed burglary or home invasions, and aggravated assault—are produced by this same 10%. Career criminals begin committing antisocial behavior before entering grade school and are versatile in that they engage in an array of destructive behaviors, offend at exceedingly high rates, and are less likely to quit committing crime as they age.

The policy implications of career criminals cannot be underestimated. Because they account for so much of the incidence of crime, the crime rate could effectively be cut in half by effectively controlling less than 10% of the offenders. Once more, a variety of other social ills, such as substance abuse, alcoholism, illegitimacy, unemployment, and government largesse could also be significantly reduced by successfully containing the worst offenders. Career criminals present the opportunity for policy makers and the criminal justice system to rid a large proportion of many social problems in one fell swoop. Unfortunately, efforts to prospectively identify or predict which offenders are likely to become career criminals have largely met with failure. For all of our criminological knowledge, we cannot confidently target the worst offenders without also misidentifying and inappropriately punishing offenders who do not pose the greatest risks. Thus, policies that seek to address and reduce the career criminal problem are rife with ethical and practical dilemmas.

Because crime is primarily the output of a small number of offenders, societal efforts to control crime should almost entirely focus on them. If societies were to devote their considerable resources toward preventing and neutralizing career criminals, they would experience dramatic reductions in crime per se, the fear of crime, and the assorted costs and collateral consequences of crime. Unfortunately, for a host of reasons that this book explores, a genuinely vigilant effort to prevent and control them has not yet been attempted, at least in the United States.

Chapter 2 explicates the social and behavioral science literature on career criminals and provides an overview of what is known about them. Historical examinations of career criminals, traditional methods of socially controlling them, and cross-cultural evidence of their misconduct are explored. Early criminological efforts such as biographical case studies and offender typologies are discussed and examined for their strengths and weaknesses. The contemporary criminal career marked by the publication in 1972 of Marvin Wolfgang and his colleagues' Philadelphia birth cohort study and its landmark findings are presented along with other important studies. More than any other piece of research, this landmark study established the empirical evidence that career criminals play a vital role in contributing to the total incidence of crime. An assortment of specific information is provided to frequently asked questions about the "worst" offenders: How many career criminals are there? What types of crimes do they commit? What are the parameters of their careers? Can they be effectively prevented or treated? Are career criminals and psychopaths the same phenomenon? What are the costs and consequences of career criminals? and Are American career criminals similar to chronic and violent offenders in places such as England, Germany, Colombia, Holland, Australia, China, Puerto Rico, Sweden, Denmark, New Zealand, and Finland?

Empirical questions often give rise to theoretical ones. What circumstances give rise to career criminals? Are they born? Are they made? Are they caused by some combination of forces of nature and nurture? These etiological questions are explored with two theoretical chapters, one devoted to a developmental, nurture perspective and the other devoted to a propensity-based, nature perspective. Chapter 3 explores the etiology of career criminals from the developmental perspective. This theoretical doctrine proffers that habitual criminals are the cumulative outcome of a variety of overlapping, age-graded, developmental processes. Thus, they dispute the notion that career criminality is the outcome of some amorphous, primordial condition. The chapter presents some of the major theories in the developmental camp and synthesizes their essential ideas. Additionally, the chapter demonstrates the usefulness of developmental theories by linking them to theoretically grounded prevention programs with proven track records of reducing problem behaviors among persons likely to be career criminals. These are viable, pragmatic policies that could meaningfully prevent future career offenders. For example, experimentally designed studies have shown that severely antisocial or quasi-psychopathic children have experienced significant reductions in antisocial behaviors with concomitant increases in conventional behaviors after treatment and intervention from medical and social service providers. This chapter, then, is focused on "front-end" policies that stress prevention, treatment, and amenability for meaningful change in the lives of severely antisocial persons.

Chapter 4 reviews the competing theoretical stance, which suggests that criminal propensity explains the various forms of antisocial behavior characteristic of career criminals. In varying degrees, propensity theorists acknowledge that much of the source of criminal propensity is genetic; however, these pathological traits interact and are often aggravated by environmental social conditions. Propensity theories broach some of the most controversial ideas in criminology because they speak directly to the issue of human nature. With their explicit focus on and documentation of the bad acts of career offenders, propensity theories raise the specter that dangerous criminals are, in whole or in part, evil. After reviewing the important propensity theories, the chapter also contains a synthesis of the debate between Michael Gottfredson and Travis Hirschi—creators of one of the major propensity perspectives, self-control theory—and their colleagues who advocate the longitudinal, career approach. Although their exchanges mostly pertain to methodological, analytical, and disciplinary issues, the debate centers on the more central issue of the very constitution of various types of offenders. The chapter concludes by postulating that some of the dissent between developmental and propensity theorists results from their differential investigation of two classes of offenders: career criminals and others. Moreover, a latent source of disagreement among criminologists relates explicitly to their ideological perception of criminals themselves and whether they are deserving of sympathy or vengeance.

Chapter 5 explores the more controversial aspects of career criminals and how these political fissures may contribute to the ineffective control of the nation's worst offenders. The central controversy stems from the difficulty in identifying which persons, even among groups of chronic delinquents, for example, will become career criminals. Indeed, most prediction instruments perform no better than chance, and many overpredict career criminality, that is, they falsely predict that nonchronic offenders will become chronic offenders. On scientific terms, criminologists are skeptical and leery of criminal justice policies that purport to predict future criminal conduct. The ethical quandaries about prediction and the continued inability of criminologists to devise accurate prediction instruments that can prospectively identify habitual offenders renders prevention even more crucial (discussed in Chapter 3).

Chapter 5 also explores how news media entities chronicle crime but frequently do not make an explicit connection to the contributions of career criminals. Moreover, some media accounts of career offenders are sympathetic in nature because career criminals themselves commonly had an extremely disadvantaged childhood. Additionally, the media can portray well-intentioned criminal justice policies such as recidivist or habitual offender statutes as draconian, costly, and unjust. This creates inconsistent images of the career criminal and complicates policy discussions to control crime. Two additional academic points, ideological in nature, also complicate our understanding of career criminals. Although peripheral to mainstream criminology, some scholars equivocate the empirical evidence of career criminals and instead proclaim that the nation's worst criminals are "social constructions," or figments of the imagination (and agenda) of conservative policy makers. Thus, there is a general notion that the most violent offenders are more hype than reality. Second, although the havoc wrought by career criminals has been well documented, some scholars seem to lack the fortitude to make the difficult but necessary judgments about controlling them. For example, the use of "get-tough" crime control policies such as three-strikes laws were generally maligned and hypothesized to have calamitous effects on the criminal justice system. However, subsequent research has shown that forecasts of the harm of the get-tough approach were erroneous.

Chapter 6 explores "back-end" policies that the police, courts, and corrections can and should do to effectively control career criminals. Many of these efforts are already in place and have produced modestly favorable results. For example, many agencies around the country have instituted serious or habitual offender comprehensive action programs (SHOCAP) policies to combat young habitual criminals, created specialized units to proactively target career recidivists, and enacted special prosecutorial bureaus to target the most chronic offenders. Furthermore, the chapter reviews four critical legal issues that relate to career criminals and that have been debated in the nation's courts: (a) the constitutionality of habitual offender statutes, (b) the proportionality of three-strikes legislation, (c) dangerousness and its prediction, and (d) the civil commitment of predatory sex offenders.

The debate between due process constitutionalists and crime control advocates has frequently centered on the most effective and democratic ways to identify and control career criminals. Some of the problems with the correctional system are highlighted vis-à-vis the inability to stop career criminals. The actual administration of criminal justice softens the punishment capacity of many well-intentioned policies. For example, many prison sentences are automatically reduced by 50% or more by good time, inmates sentenced to life imprisonment are routinely paroled, and the ultimate sanction, capital punishment, is used too infrequently to effectively neutralize career criminals. Finally, this chapter explores how the increased use of capital punishment could reduce and deter crime with an empirical illustration using a sample of habitual offenders. The chapter concludes with information from the Sentencing Project and a discussion of the dire problem of factually innocent offenders being sentenced to death and how the desire to stop chronic offenders may contribute to this.

Chapter 7 summarizes the book and presents two general sets of policy recommendations. First, the treatment effects of early-life prevention programs are nothing less than remarkable, yet prevention has histori-cally been marginalized by criminology. The prevention of career crimi-nals is possible with modest investments in the lives of families and children most at-risk for career criminality. Such a move requires an acknowledgment and political compromise from conservatives, who are usually ideologically opposed to social welfare. Second, whereas preven-tion clearly works, attempts to rehabilitate or treat adult career criminals have yielded little fruit. Just as we must commit to the humanistic policy of prevention, we must be equally strident in our commitment to meting out the appropriate punishments to career criminals. This necessitates incapacitation and condemnation. Here, liberals must desist from extend-ing any solicitude to the most violent among us. Without this political compromise and the attendant commitment to prevention and retributive justice, career criminals will continue to remain a social problem.

To date, most texts devoted to career criminals (and criminal careers generally) have been written with primarily one audience in mind—themselves. Undoubtedly, criminologists have provided a great service to the scientific community; indeed, it is they who have produced the knowledge base that appears herein. Unfortunately, these works have often failed to earnestly explore the more interesting political and philo-sophical issues pertaining to career criminals. Consequently, they missed an opportunity to demonstrate the salience of career criminals to members of our society. In this sense, my intention is to produce a book on career criminals that sheds the tacit academic code of political correctness and delves into some admittedly difficult substantive issues. My wish is that this approach engages faculty, students, and citizens alike and provides an opportunity for discussion, regardless of their occupational or ideological perspective.

The rationale behind such an approach is directly attributable to my previous work experience as a criminal justice practitioner, interviewing and interacting with thousands of criminal offenders. From 1995 to 2000, I was employed as a pretrial service officer or bond commissioner in Boulder County, Colorado. As a judicial officer, I interviewed arrestees to gather social and criminal history information for bond purposes. More than half of my work tenure was spent working the "graveyard" shift from approximately 10 p.m. to 8 a.m. During this experience, I commonly interacted with criminal defendants when they were admittedly in their worst condition, bewildered by their arrest and, often, extremely intoxicated. Obviously, the modal defendant was not a career criminal; indeed, the most common interviews were with persons arrested for failure to appear warrants for traffic violations, driving under the influence (DUI), and domestic violence.

Other interviews, those with career criminals, were qualitatively distinct from the majority of criminal defendants. Interpersonally, they took three forms. First, some career criminals, particularly if they had recently ingested narcotics and/or alcohol, were so combative and belligerent that they simply could not be interviewed. Instead, several sheriff deputies escorted them to an isolation cell in the disciplinary module of the jail. Having witnessed many of these visceral incidents, I can sadly offer that a handful of criminals were always in this condition.

Second, some career criminals interacted in a manner consistent with Cloward and Ohlin's retreatist subculture. These offenders' lives were ones of complete resignation and withdrawal from society, often via pathological addiction to alcohol and bizarre drugs such as paint or glue. Pronounced mental illness, particularly paranoid schizophrenia, was common among this group. Unlike the rancorous interaction of the first type, resigned career criminals would either nullify the bond interview altogether by sitting in silence with a vacant stare or simply and politely decline to participate.

The third type was, if nothing else, the most entertaining and, at times, even comical. These career criminals were completely oblivious to anything that transpired in their life, including recurrent interactions with the criminal justice system. Nothing seemed to concern them. An extremely talkative bunch, these offenders would often attempt to use their considerable verbal skills and audacity to influence the determination of bond. They brushed off all responsibility and had an excuse and exculpatory justification, believable only in their minds, for each arrest on their record.

Although clearly not pleased to be in jail and likely headed back to prison, these offenders were not generally disturbed by the criminal justice system. These qualities are well known to those who study and interact with habitual criminals; indeed, the glibness, egocentricity, pathological lying, refusal to assume responsibility, and attempts to manipulate are prototypical traits of psychopathy. Many of these qualities personify the theoretical ideas in Chapters 3 and 4.

A novel feature of this book is the inclusion of fictional criminal records that illustrate the offending patterns of career criminals. Although these people are not real, they are an amalgamation of 5 years of experience working with real offenders. Several important criminological points can be gleaned from the offender profile. The multiple aliases and other identifiers characterize an offender who uses deception when dealing with law enforcement and, more generally, an individual who is prone to excessive lying. The recorded criminal behavior is extensive and spans nearly 30 years. It contains an assortment of antisocial behaviors encompassing violent crimes, property crimes, drug offenses, traffic violations, and various incidents of noncompliance with the criminal justice system. The record illustrates the discontinuity and funnel-like effects of the criminal justice system: Many arrest charges are dismissed, rejected for filing, or discarded during plea arrangements with the prosecution. Although the offender is clearly no stranger to criminal punishment, there is little "truth-in-sentencing," and most incarcerations are short-lived. Finally, there appears to be no rhyme or reason to the offender's record, conduct appears to escalate then deescalate, and arrests appear intermittently. Such a feckless life illustrates the difficulty in predicting or forecasting what a chronic offender will do next. The profile in Box 1.1 typifies the modal career criminal that is described in considerable detail in Chapter 2.

Box 1.1   Career Criminal Profile

Name(s) Used

Alejandro Chapa	James Teebler
Alejandro Chapa-Gutierrez	Jaime Chapa
Alejandro Gutierrez	Chapa
Alex Chapa	Jaime Gutierrez
Alex Gutierrez	Jaime Martinez
Alex Santos-Martinez	Jaime Martinez-Gutierrez
Jimmy Santos	Jaime Alejandro
Alexander Martinez	James Alexander

Physical

Race:	W
Sex:	M
Height:	507
Weight:	165
Hair/Eyes:	BLK/BRO
Skin:	Med

Date(s) of Birth

062559	072559	082559	092559
122559	012559	062560	062561
062562	062563	062564	062565
062566	062567	062568	062569

Place(s) of Birth

Chihuahua, Mexico   TX   NM   AZ   CO   OK

Scars/Marks

SC L Arm/SC R Arm/SC Face/SC R Leg/SC L Leg/SC Chest/SC Abdomen/TAT Face/TAT Neck/TAT L Arm (Multiple)/TAT R Arm (Multiple)/TAT Back (Multiple)/TAT R Chest/TAT L Hand.

(Continued)

Box 1.1 (Continued)

Fingerprint Class

PM PI 15 PM 13
PM PM 15 PI 13
WU WU RS WU RS WU WU LS WU LS

1—Arrested or received 1974/10/10

Agency: Juarez Mexico Police Department
Charge 1: Burglary 1
Charge 2: Burglary 1
Charge 3: Poss Burg Tools
Charge 4: Ill Poss Firearm
Court: Dismissed

2—Arrested or received 1974/11/02

Agency: Juarez Mexico Police Department
Charge 1: Burglary 1
Charge 2: Burglary 2
Charge 3: Burglary 2
Charge 4: Ill Poss Firearm
Charge 5: Robbery by Force
Charge 6: Resist Arrest
Court: Charges 1-4 Dismissed
Charge 5: Guilty Plea
Charge 6: Guilty Plea
Sentence: Charges 5-6 Reformatory
Indeterminate to 4 Yrs

3—Arrested or received 1974/12/04

Agency: Northern Mexico Reformatory
Sentence: Indeterminate to 4 Yrs

4—Arrested or received 1976/01/01

Agency: Sheriff's Office, El Paso, Texas
Charge 1: Rob w/Firearm

Charge 2: Rob w/Firearm
Charge 3: Aggrav Menacing
Court: No Disposition

5—Arrested or received 1976/04/26

Agency: Oklahoma City Police Department
Charge 1: DUI
Charge 2: Unauth Use Vehicle
Charge 3: No Operator Insurance
Charge 4: Drive w/o Valid DL
Charge 5: Fugitive Other Jurisdiction
Court: Charges 1-4 Dismissed
Charge 5: Fugitive (Rob w/Firearm x2/Aggrav Menacing)
Extradition to El Paso, Texas

6—Arrested or received 1976/05/30

Agency: Sheriff's Office, El Paso, Texas
Charge 1: Rob w/Firearm
Charge 2: Rob w/Firearm
Charge 3: Aggrav Menacing
Charge 4: Flight to Avoid Prosecution
Court: Guilt Plea to All Charges
Sentence: 13 Yrs Texas DOC

7—Arrested or received 1976/07/01

Agency: Texas DOC
Sentence: 13 Yrs

8—Arrested or received 1982/01/15

Agency: Texas Dept. Parole and Probation
Charge 1: Release Conditional Parole 5 Yrs

9—Arrested or received 1983/03/15

Agency: Sheriff's Office, Denver, Colorado
Charge 1: Domestic Violence

(Continued)

Box 1.1 (Continued)

Charge 2: Aslt 3
Charge 3: Aslt 3
Charge 4: Child Abuse 2
Charge 5: Resist Arrest
Charge 6: Obstruct Police
Court: No Disposition

10—Arrested or received 1983/10/10

Agency: Denver Police Department
Charge 1: Domestic Violence
Charge 2: Poss Schedule II (Cocaine)
Charge 3: Poss Drug Paraph
Charge 4: Resist Arrest
Charge 5: Obstruct Police
Charge 6: Aslt on Police Off
Charge 7: Ex-felon Possess Weap
Court: Charge 1 Dismissed
Charge 2: Guilty Plea
Charge 3: Dismissed
Charge 4: Dismissed
Charge 5: Dismissed
Charge 6: Guilty Plea, Aslt 3
Charge 7: Guilty Plea, ccw
Sentence: 180 Dys Jail, Alc tx, $487 Fines

11—Arrested or received 1984/11/02

Agency: Sheriff's Office, Adams County, Colorado
Charge 1: DUI
Charge 2: No Operator Insurance
Charge 3: Drive w/o Valid DL
Charge 4: Criminal Impersonation/Fraud
Charge 5: Ex-felon Possess Weap
Court: Guilty at Trial
Charges 1-5
Sentence: 3 Yrs Co DOC

12—Arrested or received 1986/06/05

Agency: Phoenix Police Department
Charge 1: Burglary 1
Charge 2: Agg Robbery
Charge 3: Kidnap—No Ransom
Charge 4: Grand Theft
Charge 5: Burglary 2
Charge 6: Burglary 1
Charge 7: Agg Robbery
Charge 8: Kidnap—No Ransom
Charge 9: Agg Robbery
Charge 10: Burglary 1
Charge 11: Murder 2
Charge 12: Agg Robbery
Charge 13: Kidnap—No Ransom
Charge 14: Burglary 1
Charge 15: Rape 1
Charge 16: Agg Robbery
Charge 17: Burglary 2
Charge 18: Burglary 2
Charge 19: Grand Theft
Charge 20: Grand Theft
Charge 21: Fel Poss Firearm
Charge 22: Fel Poss Firearm
Charge 23: Fel Poss Firearm
Court: Guilty Plea
Murder 2
Burglary 1
Agg Robbery (x3)
Kidnap—No Ransom
Remain Charges Dismissed
Sentence: 60 Yrs State Prison AZ DOC

13—Arrested or received 2002/11/11

Agency: Arizona Dept. of Corrections

(Continued)

Box 1.1 (Continued)

Charge 1: Release Conditional Parole—Lifetime
Charge 2: Registry Violent Sexual Predator

14—Arrested or received 2002/12/31

Agency: Phoenix Dept. of Corrections
Charge 1: DUI
Court: No Disposition

SOURCE: National Crime Information Center, FBI Identification Record.

NOTE: This is a fictional profile; any similarity to a career criminal, living or dead, is purely coincidence.

2

The Empirical Evidence on Career Criminals

Officers in the criminal justice records bureau had an ingenious way of identifying and classifying career criminals: measuring how long it took for their rap sheet to print. Persons whose records took 10 minutes or more to print were likely habitual offenders. The largest National Crime Information Center (NCIC) record was from 13 states and took 37 minutes to print! Although this method clearly lacks scientific sophistication, records bureau officers were proud of the method's Aristotelian validity.

An important but largely unrecognized component of the criminal justice system, criminal records bureau officers recognized as fact the anecdotal claims that they have long heard among police officers: If they could arrest and detain a small amount of high-rate offenders, the entire city would experience a dramatic reduction in crime. There are several examples of this trend. Recently, a 22-year-old male was arrested after failing to pay his rent and storage fees at a local Rent-a-Garage unit. As the police investigated the unit, they discovered tens of thousands of dollars of stolen property, merchandise, cash, and drugs. Upon questioning, the defendant admitted to committing more than 120 commercial and residential burglaries over the past 8 months, thus single-handedly accounting for a wave of burglaries that had plagued the community. The defendant was currently on felony probation for burglary, theft, and credit card fraud and had an extensive juvenile record of similar crimes, including two commitments to juvenile correctional facilities.

Less serious in terms of crime severity were the activities of the group the records bureau referred to as the "park dwellers." The park dwellers were middle-aged males without a fixed address who slept, congregated, and simply lived in the city parks. Police were on a first-name basis with all 30 or so of these men after issuing dozens of summons for municipal violations, shoplifting, and subsequent failures to appear in court. The bulk of this group's criminal record included nuisance crimes that carried nominal punishments such as a weekend in jail. Because of the benign nature of many of their charges, transients accumulated epic criminal histories totaling hundreds of arrest charges. Records bureau clerks wondered what the costs generated by one transient offender were in terms of police resources, court costs, and associated jail expenditures. By their calculations, the average criminal career of one of the park dwellers cost the county approximately $3 million in criminal justice–related costs.

A final source of insight for the criminal records bureau was their shared location with the police dispatcher unit. This access meant that officers were privy to every emergency 911 call that occurred in the city. They would overhear the recurrent distressed calls from victims and witnesses. It seemed that a handful of neighborhoods and certain homes within those neighborhoods generated a disproportionately high number of calls for police and paramedics. Overall, the records bureau staff felt that, with a small number of exceptions, they lived in a generally safe community. Unfortunately, those few exceptions created most of the harm.

Introduction

Whether measured by the amount of time that elapses before a criminal record is printed, the total number of arrest charges on the criminal record, the volume of criminal episodes that an offender divulges, or the geographic concentration of 911 calls, this vignette suggests that crime is unevenly distributed across people and places. Indeed, one of the central points that students in criminal justice and criminology courses learn relates to the distribution or epidemiology of crime across social groups. Some groups simply commit more crime than others—for example, males commit more serious crimes than females, and adolescents commit more serious crimes than elderly persons. The same trend applies even when considering offending differences among and between criminal offenders. In terms of frequency, seriousness, and duration, criminals vary in their "productivity," and the "worst" across these parameters are career criminals. Fortunately, a fraction of offenders are career criminals. Unfortunately, this small fraction of offenders produces many negative consequences.

Over time, scholarly inquiries of habitual offenders have centered on their exceptional or rare characteristics. The earliest attempts accomplished this literally because they were case study, biographical accounts of individual persons. This evolved into typological studies that sought to categorize similar types of offenders into various groupings. Because criminals tend to be versatile in their behavior and commit assorted acts of delinquency, typologies did not fare well. Today, entire populations are surveyed and categorized according to their involvement in crime. Depending on the source of data, between 30% and 50% of people are involved in crime to some capacity. Fortunately, normal criminal involvement is short-lived, spans minor crimes, and ends as quickly as it begins. The exception is career criminals; their criminological story appears next.

Historical Background of Career Criminals

Referred to by a variety of monikers, including habitual criminals, chronic offenders, inveterate criminals, thugs, psychopaths, sociopaths, incorrigible delinquents, frequent offenders, and the like, career criminals are offenders for whom repeated violations of the law become a way of life. The term *career* is used to typify the longitudinal span of crimes and analogous deleterious behaviors, not to suggest that career criminals necessarily derive any remunerative value from their work. Over the years, various criteria such as serving a prior prison sentence, six prior felony convictions, five police contacts, 6 arrests, 9 arrests, 10 arrests, or even 30 arrests have been used to identify career criminals and quantify their offending.[1] The gold standard marker to delineate whether one is a habitual or career criminal is five or more police contacts or arrests. It is important to note that all of these measures consistently yield the same general finding: that a few contribute mightily to the crime problem.

Although American scholars and a largely American perspective have dominated the research in the area, it is important to note the universality of chronic and violent offenders. For example, Australian citizens recently celebrated the demise of a career criminal (the defendant was murdered by two other habitual criminals) who was implicated or charged with the majority of serious crimes occurring over a 20-year period. Like the fictional criminal record that appears in Chapter 1, this individual was repeatedly arrested and convicted of an assortment of serious crimes and served relatively brief stints in prison only to quickly recidivate upon release. In Canada, corrections officials are facing constant litigation from an incarcerated diagnosed psychopath with no less than 84 prior convictions for a plethora of violent, property, and public-order offenses. Also in Canada, an offender who recently pleaded guilty to 14 counts of robbery admonished the court to not view him as a bad person; rather, they should simply acknowledge that he is a person who has chosen to be a career criminal! New Zealand authorities recently snared a prolific fraud with more than 170 convictions on his criminal record. Finally, the most "international" career criminal scenario recently occurred in England, where authorities arrested two Venezuelan men who made a living by kidnapping and occasionally murdering British tourists who vacationed in the defendants' current home country of Spain.[2]

Career criminals have historically and contemporarily existed in many societies and are characterized by various stratification systems, economies, age structures, and ethnic compositions. For example, prior to the Common Era, historical figures such as the Athenian general Alcibiades were noted for a self-centered, impulsive, reckless, and violent disposition that matches the personality traits of today's worst offenders. Cultures as remote as rural Nigeria and northwest Alaska developed concepts, *aranakan* and *kunlangeta*, respectively, to describe the behavioral repertoire of males who were selfish, deceitful, globally irresponsible, uncooperative, full of malice, and thoroughly unwilling to peacefully coexist with others. Such men were extremely violent and indeed preyed upon others in the village.[3]

The historical lineage of the phenomenon of psychopathy similarly suggests that disparate societies have perennially struggled to deal with a small number of inveterate criminals who were immune from redemption and zealously committed to inflicting criminal harm. For instance, early in the 19th century, labels such as *manie sans delire* (insanity without delirium), "moral alienation of the mind with total perversion of moral faculties," and "moral insanity with deplorable defects in personality" were used to describe persons who today are diagnosed as psychopaths. The contemporary, definitive measure of psychopathy, the Psychopathy Checklist-Revised (PCL-R) created by North American scholar Robert Hare,[4] has been translated into Danish, French, German, Italian, Portuguese, Spanish, and Swedish so that medical, mental health, and criminal justice professionals in these countries can clinically diagnose the worst criminal offenders. Indeed, the predictive accuracy of the PCL-R has been replicated in Belgium, Canada, England, Finland, Germany, Holland, Portugal, Spain, and the United States, suggesting that psychopathic career criminals are an unfortunately common feature of societies.[5]

Consider this quotation from Judge Merritt Pinckney, who presided in the nation's seminal juvenile court in Cook County, Illinois:

> A child, a boy especially, sometimes becomes so thoroughly vicious and is so repeatedly an offender that it would not be fair to the other children in a delinquent institution who have not arrived at his age of depravity and delinquency to have to associate with him. On very rare and special occasions, therefore, children are held over on a mittimus to the criminal court.[6]

The criminality of the most active offenders is so pronounced, so aberrant, so unlike the delinquency of most offenders, that formal criminal justice systems have devised creative and at times draconian ways to control them. Efforts to socially control career criminals have included treatment approaches utilizing involuntary commitment to an asylum (a forerunner of civil commitment); vigilante and frontier approaches whereby problem offenders were tortured or summarily executed; creative approaches such as the British tradition of forced transportation of criminal offenders to remote locations such as Australia; and the contemporarily preferred method, incarceration. Chronic offenders are a long-standing concern of citizens and criminal justice practitioners; they would increasingly occupy the interest of criminologists as well.

Biographies and Typological Studies

Relatively early in the 20th century, criminologists began to investigate the life histories of career or professional criminals. These biographical studies were the forerunners of the current criminal career research paradigm. Works such as Clifford Shaw's *The Jack Roller: A Delinquent Boy's Own Story* (1930) and *The Natural History of a Delinquent Career* (1931), as well as Edwin Sutherland's *The Professional Thief* (1937), were crime memoirs that provided qualitative data from the criminal's perspective on criminal socialization processes, criminal associations, and the acquiring of criminal rationalizations, motives, and skills. These works conveyed the minutiae of criminal life in a way that was impossible for survey researchers to describe. Essentially, offender biographies, especially Shaw's work, showcased the resolute commitment among habitual delinquents to crime and other antisocial choices often in strident opposition to the conventional culture that was often viewed by the offenders as cruel and unfair to them. They showcased how the helter–skelter, day-to-day misdeeds of chronic offenders only served to further immerse them in negativity and forestall any semblance of conventional human development.

Today, most research of career criminals is quantitative; however, occasional qualitative pieces of research appear to provide context to the lives of habitual offenders. An important example is Neal Shover's *Great Pretenders*, a monograph based on in-depth interviews with persistent thieves. Like previous qualitative work, Shover's research discovered that the lives of chronic offenders were characterized by disorganization and malaise. Described as leading "lives of party," persistent offenders commit reciprocal acts of drinking, substance abuse, and crime while shunning the obligations and responsibilities that are external to their immediate social setting. Shover's work sheds light on the turning points in criminal careers (discussed extensively in Chapter 3) by illustrating that the seeming unpredictability of offending patterns waxes and wanes with the short-term needs and wants of persons immersed in a drugs and crime underworld.[7]

Unfortunately, biographical approaches were limited because they reflected what were perhaps the idiosyncrasies of an individual offender; therefore, they were not generalizable to the larger study of crime. Importantly, these monographs unearthed diverse offending patterns and implicitly hypothesized that there were different etiological causes for different types of criminal offenders. This idea led to the next stage in criminal career research, typological studies.

Typological studies sought to classify assorted criminals into discrete categories of offenders. Thus, they were a scientific attempt to match the conventional wisdom among police and other criminal justice practitioners that there existed distinct types of offenders. For example, many offenders are "normal" citizens who happen to occasionally get arrested for drunk driving but participate in no other forms of criminal conduct. As employed, functioning members of society, drunk drivers or DUI offenders are viewed as normative, regular people who are nominally criminal at best. In the same way, offenders who are repeatedly arrested for peeping into houses, exposing themselves in public, and other lewd acts are often viewed as an entirely different and therefore distinct offender type. In this sense, the sex offender is unlikely to be confused with the DUI offender.

A goal that has obvious implications for criminal justice policy is to create accurate typologies to identify the most troublesome offenders. If scholars could accurately identify and prosecute violent career criminals, then the criminal justice system could operate more efficiently. From approximately 1940 to 1970, some scholars developed assorted typologies of offenders and inmates. For example, Daniel Glaser identified 10 criminal patterns, including such groups as adolescent recapitulators, crisis-vacillation predators, and addicted performers, among others. Criminologist Don Gibbons developed a delinquent typology containing nine types, such as predatory gang delinquent, overly aggressive delinquent, female delinquent, and behavior problem delinquent. Gibbons's criminal typology contained 21 classifications, including such offender types as the professional theft, professional "heavy" criminal, professional "fringe" violator, aggressive rapist, violent sex offender, and opiate addict. Marshall Clinard and Richard Quinney organized offenders into nine types of criminal behavior systems: violent personal, occasional property, public order, conventional, political, occupational, corporate, organized, and professional.

These typologies left much to be desired, unfortunately. First, several of the labels were unclear as to what type of offender was being described. For example, what exactly was an adolescent recapitulator? Intuitively, what types of misconduct do crisis-vacillation predators engage in? Are these the same sorts of predatory acts that Clinard and Quinney's violent personal offender commits? Answers to these questions are not readily apparent. Second, the face validity of these typologies was weak if the classification of criminals was widely dependent on the classifier. If there were discrete criminal groups, how many were there? Based on these few examples, one does not know whether 9 or 21 is the appropriate number of criminal subtypes. Third, and perhaps most important, the typologies were limited because criminals tend to engage in a wide assortment of offenses, not a specific type of crime. In short, criminals are usually versatile or general in their offending practices, not specialized or specific. Consequently, it was likely that an individual offender met the criteria for multiple typologies and therefore was unable to be classified singularly (the importance of versatility/specialization is discussed later in this chapter). Overall, typologies were not widely adopted and, in the 1970s, ultimately fell out of favor among criminologists because they did not include mutually exclusive categories, were largely subjective, lacked comprehensiveness, and were unable to reliably differentiate offender types.[8]

Curiously, recent criminal career research is producing findings that are reminiscent of the typology era. A sophisticated data analysis method called semiparametric group-based or latent class analysis now exists. This method allows for the study of longitudinal data sets to compare discrete groups of offenders who are homogeneous within their grouping or trajectory but different from other groupings or trajectories. Scholars are identifying groups of offenders based on the shape of the offending trajectories over time. These groups have names such as nonoffenders, adolescence-peaked offenders, and low-rate, high-rate, and late-onset chronic offenders; classic desisters, moderate-rate desisters, and low-, moderate-, and high-rate chronic desisters; and "marginal lifestyle with versatile offending," "nonviolent property, especially burglary," and "aggressive property offending and wide-ranging car crime." Even today, there appears to be dissatisfaction with the substantive worth of these approaches. For example, Elaine Eggleston and her colleagues concluded that "there is always a danger when a particular methodology approaches hegemonic status within a field of inquiry. At such a point, questions are no longer asked and researchers unthinkingly apply the method of the day."[9] Despite advances in data analysis techniques, the easy compartmentalization of offender groups that typologies promise has yet to be realized.

The Modern Criminal Career Paradigm

The seminal work that established the contemporary understanding of career criminals was *Delinquency in a Birth Cohort* published by Marvin Wolfgang, Robert Figlio, and Thorsten Sellin in 1972. The study followed

9,945 males born in Philadelphia in 1945 who lived in the city at least from ages 10 to 18. The significance of this prospective, longitudinal birth cohort design was that it was not susceptible to sampling error because every male participant was followed. They found that nearly two thirds of the youth never experienced a police contact and that 35% of the population had. Based on this, we can be comforted to know that most people in a population are law-abiding to the extent that the police never contact them for deviant behavior. For the minority of persons who were actually contacted by police, the police contacts were rare occurrences occurring just once, twice, or three times. On the other hand, some youth experienced more frequent interaction with police. According to Wolfgang and his associates (1972), persons with five or more police contacts were chronic or habitual offenders. Of the nearly 10,000 boys, only 627 members, just 6% of the population, qualified as habitual offenders. However, the chronic 6% accounted for 52% of the delinquency in the entire cohort. Moreover, chronic offenders committed 63% of all Index offenses, 71% of the murders, 73% of the rapes, 82% of the robberies, and 69% of the aggravated assaults. Herein was the quantifiable evidence that a small minority of high-rate offenders was guilty of perpetrating the majority of all criminal acts in a population.

A second and improved study examined a cohort of persons born in Philadelphia in 1958. Conducted by Paul Tracy, Marvin Wolfgang, and Robert Figlio (1990), the second Philadelphia cohort contained 13,160 males and 14,000 females. Overall, the 1958 cohort committed crime at higher rates than the 1945 cohort and demonstrated greater involvement in the most serious forms of crime, such as murder, rape, robbery, and aggravated assault. However, roughly the same proportion of persons, 33%, experienced arrest prior to adulthood. Approximately 7% of the population members were habitual offenders and accounted for 61% of all delinquency, 60% of the murders, 75% of the rapes, 73% of the robberies, and 65% of the aggravated assaults. The 1958 Philadelphia birth cohort study is considered an improvement over the 1945 cohort because it contained males and females and spanned three times the population size that allowed for disaggregated analyses of various offender groups.

A classic data set that has experienced a renaissance of sorts is the Unraveling Juvenile Delinquency Study created by Sheldon and Eleanor Glueck in the early decades of the 20th century and resurrected by Robert Sampson and John Laub since about 1990. The study included 500 delinquent white males between the ages of 10 and 17 who had been committed to two Massachusetts correctional facilities: the Lyman School for Boys and the Industrial School for Boys. The Gluecks collected an array of data and created offender dossiers for each boy, including deviant and criminal history, psychosocial profile, family background, school and occupational history, and other life events such as marital and military history. The delinquent sample was matched on a case-by-case basis to 500 nondelinquent boys from the same area. Both samples were followed until age 32. The study design permitted researchers to examine the long-term effects of early life experiences on subsequent social and antisocial behavior.

The Gluecks' research and the more statistically sophisticated updates by Sampson and Laub produced some important findings. For example, an early onset of problem or antisocial behavior strongly predicted a lengthy criminal career characterized by high rates of offending and involvement in serious criminal violence. Indeed, the Gluecks used the phrase "the past is prologue" to capture the idea of the stability in behavior. However, the Gluecks also found that even high-rate offenders tended to reduce their offending after they passed through adolescence into early adulthood. Similarly, even serious offenders could desist from crime, and seemingly ignore their own criminal propensity, by participating in conventional adult social institutions such as marriage, work, and the military. The theoretical importance of these findings as they relate to stability and change in criminal careers appears prominently in Chapter 3.

Three other landmark criminal career data sets are the Dangerous Offender Project, the Cambridge-Somerville Youth Study, and the Racine, Wisconsin, birth cohorts. Under the guidance of Donna Hamparian, Simon Dinitz, John Conrad, and their colleagues, the Dangerous Offender Project examined the delinquent careers of 1,238 adjudicated youth born in Columbus, Ohio, between 1956 and 1960. Overall, these youth committed a total of 4,499 offenses, 1,504 crimes of violence, and 904 violent Index crimes. However, they found that even among violent juvenile offenders, a small minority (whom they dubbed the "violent few") accounted for the majority of crimes. Indeed, 84% of the youth were only arrested once for a violent crime as adolescents, and 13% experienced two arrests. The remaining 3% accumulated significantly more police contacts for violent crimes, ranging from 3 to 23 arrests.

Joan and William McCord used data from the Cambridge-Somerville Youth Study to examine the long-term effects of early childhood experiences on later criminality. The study contained 506 impoverished males born from 1925 to 1934 who had been treated for a variety of behavioral problems and tracked via official records until 1978. By age 50, approximately 30% of the males had been arrested, particularly those who were reared in broken homes characterized by parental conflict, parental criminality, and low levels of parental affection toward and supervision of the children. Like the Gluecks', the McCords' research illustrated the antecedent role of family strife and abuse in the development of habitual antisocial behavior.

Lyle Shannon selected 1942, 1949, and 1955 birth cohorts from Racine, Wisconsin, that yielded 1,352, 2,099, and 2,676 respondents, respectively, to examine criminal careers over time. Unlike the original Philadelphia birth cohort study, Shannon followed the birth cohorts well into adulthood to further explore continuity in criminal behavior. This included a follow-up of the 1942 cohort to age 30, the 1949 cohort to age 25, and the 1955 cohort to age 22. Like prior studies, Shannon's research found that a circumscribed cohort of chronic offenders committed the preponderance of offenses.[10]

A limitation of cohort studies is the reliance on official data, such as arrest records, that document only those crimes for which offenders were caught and therefore exclude the antisocial behaviors that did not result in arrest. To redress this limitation, criminologists at the RAND Corporation obtained self-reported criminal histories from prison inmates in California. Their analyses yielded some startling findings. Initial interviews with 49 incarcerated armed robbers suggested that serious criminals were extensively involved in crime. Indeed, the offenders admitted committing more than 10,500 crimes—an average of 20 serious crimes each year for approximately 20 years. A follow-up study examined the criminal careers of 624 male felons from five California prisons. Researchers found that about 25% of the inmates were hard-core career criminals who began getting arrested early in life, were firmly committed to a criminal lifestyle, and generally were undeterred and unthreatened by criminal justice system sanctions such as prison. The hard-core group among the prison inmates was responsible for 58% of the armed robberies, 65% of the auto thefts, and 46% of all acts of assault reported by the inmates. Indeed, Marcia and Jan Chaiken found that inmates in the 90th percentile of offending reported an average of 232 burglaries, 87 robberies, 13 assaults, 425 thefts, 206 acts of forgery, 258 acts of fraud, and 605 miscellaneous offenses per year! A more recent study by Jose Canela-Cacho and his colleagues indicated that incarcerated offenders commit crimes at rates in excess of 50 times the rate of the average street criminal.[11]

Unquestionably, the National Youth Survey is the definitive data source of self-reported criminal offending information. Initiated in 1976 by Delbert Elliott and his collaborators, the National Youth Survey is a prospective longitudinal study of the delinquency and drug use patterns of American youth. In total, the sample contains 1,725 persons from seven birth cohorts between 1959 and 1965, and multiple waves of data have been collected since the study's inception. Guided by Elliott's integrated theory that contains elements of differential association, strain, and control perspectives, the National Youth Survey has yielded plentiful information about the prevalence, incidence, correlates, and processes related to delinquency and other forms of antisocial behavior.

Career criminal information based on National Youth Survey data was generally concordant with information derived from studies employing official records. For most persons, involvement in crime generally and violence specifically was short-lived and limited in scope. Individual offending rates varied greatly. Delinquents tended to dabble in a mixed pattern of offenses, not focus on one type of crime. A small proportion of the sample was habitual in its delinquency. For example, approximately 7% of youth in the survey were serious career offenders, defined as persons who committed at least three Index offenses annually. These youth accounted for the vast majority of antisocial and violent behaviors in the sample and often committed many times the number of assaults, robberies, and sexual assaults than non–career offenders did. Perhaps most important, the National Youth Survey indicated that only 2% of those identified as self-reported career criminals were identified as such by using official records. This provided compelling evidence that career criminals engaged in exponentially more crime than their official records would indicate. Additionally, information from offender self-reports suggests that there might be more career offenders at large than previously thought. For example, later research using additional waves of data found that 36% of black males and 25% of white males aged 17 reported some involvement in serious violent offending.[12] Reconciling data sources and the magnitude of the career criminal problem is discussed later in this chapter.

Based in part on the concept and success of the National Youth Survey, the Office of Juvenile Justice and Delinquency Prevention created the Program on Research on the Causes and Correlates of Delinquency in 1986. The result was three prospective longitudinally designed studies: the Denver Youth Survey, Pittsburgh Youth Study, and Rochester Youth Development Study. The Denver Youth Survey is a probability sample of

1,527 youth living in high-risk neighborhoods in Denver, Colorado. Survey respondents included five age groups (7-, 9-, 11-, 13-, and 15-year-olds) and their parents interviewed between 1988 and 1992. By its design, the study would obtain longitudinal data covering the 7- to 26-year-old age span to examine the effects of childhood experiences and neighborhood disadvantage on problem behaviors. The Pittsburgh Youth Study contains 1,517 boys in Grades 1, 4, and 7 in public schools in Pittsburgh during the 1987-1988 school year. Data on delinquency, substance abuse, and mental health difficulties were obtained every 6 months for 3 years via interviews with the participants and their parents and teachers. The Rochester Youth Development Study contains 1,000 youth (75% male, 25% female) sampled disproportionately from high-crime neighborhoods. Interviews with multiple sources are ongoing to gather epidemiological data on criminal offending and related behaviors. Each study offered a "core measurement package" that provided official and self-reports of delinquent behavior and drug use, neighborhood characteristics, demographic characteristics, parental attitudes and child-rearing practices, attitudinal measures of school performance, peer and social networks, and views about committing crime.[13]

In sum, the panel studies from Denver, Pittsburgh, and Rochester provided a substantive glimpse into some of the nation's most crime-beleaguered communities and the youth who faced the multiple risks that unfortunately prevail there. More important, they produced nearly identical findings about the disproportionate violent behavior of chronic offenders. Between 14% and 17% of the youth were habitual offenders who accounted for 75% to 82% of the incidence of criminal violence. Like Delbert Elliott and his colleagues found with respondents from the National Youth Survey, researchers found that about 20% to 25% of adolescents in Denver, Pittsburgh, and Rochester tended to be "multiple-problem youth" who experienced an assortment of antisocial risk factors, such as mental health problems, alcoholism and substance abuse histories, and sustained criminal involvement. A small minority of youth were the most frequent, severe, aggressive, and temporally stable delinquent offenders. These youth, all of them male, were reared in broken homes by parents who themselves had numerous mental health and parenting problems. These boys were also noticeable by their impulsivity, emotional and moral insouciance, and total lack of guilt with which they committed crime; indeed, as children, they showed many of the characteristics of psychopathy.[14]

International Contributions

The primary European contribution to the contemporary study of criminal careers is the Cambridge Study in Delinquent Development, a prospective longitudinal panel study of 411 males born in London in 1952–1953. Originally conceptualized by Donald West in 1961, the study continues presently under the guidance of David Farrington. Now 50 years old, the study participants have been interviewed nine times between the ages of 8 and 46 with their parents participating in eight interviews. Unlike the American cohort studies, the Cambridge study uses convictions rather than police contacts or arrests as its unit of analysis; however, the results are consonant. For example, 37% of the sample had been convicted of some criminal offense, most commonly theft or burglary. Six percent of the sample, or 25 youth, were chronic offenders who accounted for 47% of all acts of criminal violence in the sample, including 59% of the robberies. Due to the richness of the Cambridge panel data, Farrington has published hundreds of articles and chapters on a variety of topics pertaining to chronic offenders, the criminal behavior of their siblings and parents, and the processes by which criminal behavior is transmitted from one generation to the next. In fact, David Farrington is the most prolific scholar in the area of criminal careers/career criminals, and his research appears throughout this book.

Several large-scale studies have been undertaken in the Scandinavian countries, the methodological details of which appear below. The Stockholm Project Metropolitan, under the direction of Per-Olof Wikstrom and Carl-Gunnar Janson, is a birth cohort study of 15,117 children born in Stockholm, Sweden, in 1953 who lived in the city until at least age 10. Interviews with teachers and parents have occurred periodically, in 1966 and 1968, and the study participants were followed up with official police records through 1983. Directed by David Magnusson and Hakan Stattin, the Orebro Project, also known as the Project on Individual Development and Environment, consists of 1,027 children born in 1955 who were surveyed at ages 13 and 15 and tracked by criminal records to age 30. These scholars have also surveyed two additional birth cohorts, persons born in 1950 and 1952. To compare criminal career trajectories in Sweden to Finland, Lea Pulkkinen and collaborators created the Jyvaskyla Longitudinal Study on Social Development. The study contains 196 boys and 173 girls who were born in Jyvaskyla, Finland, in 1959 and interviewed at ages 8, 14, 20, 27, and 32. A variety of published works produced similar findings across the two nations. For example, the onset of antisocial behavior was inversely related to involvement in an assortment of negative, aggressive, or criminal behaviors over the life span. That is, children who were the most aggressive at age 8 tended to be the "worst" criminals at all other ages. Moreover, the prevalence of aggression and antisocial behavior was sharply higher in males than females.[15] The characteristics of habitually deviant persons were nearly identical in Finland and Sweden.

In Denmark, Sarnoff Mednick initiated the Copenhagen Birth Cohort Studies that contained 28,879 men born in the city from 1944 to 1947, still living in Denmark in 1974, and tracked by police records until 1974. A second study containing extensive perinatal and criminal data examined 216 children born between 1959 and 1961 in Copenhagen and followed-up until age 22. Finally, the Danish Longitudinal Study under the direction of Britta Kyvsgaard is perhaps the most impressive data collection effort to date in the study of offending careers. Kyvsgaard's work includes a final sample of 333,742 persons containing 44,698 criminal offenders. In addition to their enormous scope, Danish studies also boast unrivaled data in terms of reliability and validity because of the accurateness and completeness of national registries. Although their study designs are unique, findings from Danish studies are not—they confirm findings from other parts of the world. Whereas most criminals have relatively paltry (e.g., only one arrest) offending careers, a small group of high-rate offenders amass scores of arrests and account for the majority of recidivism in Denmark.[16]

Asian and Australian/New Zealand researchers have also conducted criminal career research on various offenders from these continents. The Christchurch Health and Development Study features a sample of 1,265 children born in Christchurch, New Zealand, in 1977. Under the direction of David Fergusson, research participants were studied at birth, 4 months, 1 year, and annually until age 18. Utilizing data from the children, their mother, and teachers, researchers were able to identify various offender types that began to emerge from the cohort. Nearly half of the participants were nonoffenders, and most offenders engaged in a small number of offenses. However, 55 persons (4% of the sample) were chronic offenders characterized by an array of family, personality, and sociodemographic problems.[17] Another important study from this geographic area is the Dunedin Multidisciplinary Health and Human Development Study under the direction of Avshalom Caspi, Terrie Moffitt, Phil Silva, and their collaborators. A birth cohort of 1,037 persons born in 1972–1973 has yielded a plethora of epidemiological data from birth to age 30. One of the most important theoretical and empirical contributions to emerge from the study is Moffitt's developmental taxonomy. In short, the taxonomy identifies two archetypal groups of criminal offenders: the common and normative type, who engages in benign forms of delinquency (adolescence-limited offender); and the pathological type, who engages in assorted antisocial and criminal behaviors at high levels throughout the life span (life-course persistent offender).[18]

Somewhat different findings have emerged from examinations of offenders living in China. Before his death, American criminologist Marvin Wolfgang sought to replicate his Philadelphia birth cohort study using a birth cohort in China. Fortunately, other scholars continued the effort, resulting in a cohort of 5,341 persons born in the Wuchange District of Wuhan, China, in 1973. Amazingly, only 81 offenders emerged from the study, resulting in a prevalence rate of just 1.5%. Of these offenders, none was arrested more than twice, and the most common offense violations were for burglary, theft, and fighting. Although these prevalence estimates are exceedingly low compared to Western samples, comparisons of Chinese offenders and nonoffenders produced familiar information. Offenders were more self-centered and egocentric compared to nonoffenders, who espoused traditional, pro-community views. Furthermore, offenders were significantly likely to have negative peer relationships and more adverse family backgrounds, were less educated, had lower educational expectations, and seemed less attached to conventional society than persons who did not violate the law.[19] Additional studies employing Chinese offender samples also found a dearth of chronic offenders, especially compared to those who appear in the extant literature. However, even in the Chinese context, repeat offenders, though rare, tended to commit the most serious forms of crime and led lives characterized by malaise and disorganization.[20]

Career Criminal Characteristics

Exceptionality and Disproportionate Criminal Involvement

Fortunately, career criminals are the exception, not the rule. As the aforementioned studies indicate, most persons are generally law-abiding citizens who never come into contact with the criminal justice system. Prevalence estimates for involvement in delinquency range from approximately 30% when using official records to about 50% when using self-reports. Of these persons who either report involvement in criminal behavior or have been arrested for alleged violations of legal statutes, most will lead rather paltry criminal careers. Their criminal or antisocial behavior is generally short-lived, includes benign or relatively nonserious offenses, and dissipates as they transition from adolescence to adulthood. However, a small number of offenders, often less than 10% of an entire population, are career criminals who account for the bulk of crime, especially serious, violent crimes, in a population.[21]

It is important to note that the career criminal effect is not an artifact of the type of data source used (e.g., official or self-reports). Using official and self-reports from the Seattle Social Development Project, David Farrington and his colleagues concluded that

> in both court records and self-reports, a small fraction of the sample (the "chronic offenders") accounted for half of all the offenses . . . there was a significant overlap between chronic offenders identified in court referrals and chronic offenders identified in self-reports. Therefore, to a considerable extent, self-reports and court referrals identified the same people as the worst offenders.[22]

There are several examples of skewness in the offending distribution, indicating that a small percentage of offenders accounted for the majority of offenses. In Sweden, Stattin and Magnusson found that 5% of the participants recorded 41% of all convictions and 62% of all arrests. Lyle Shannon studied the offending patterns of three birth cohorts born in Racine, Wisconsin, in 1942, 1949, or 1955. For the 1942 cohort, 1% of the males accounted for 29% of the felony offenses. Moreover, 3% of the males in the 1949 cohort were responsible for 50% of the felonies, and 6% of the males born in 1955 accounted for 70% of the felony offenses. Interestingly, this trend persists even when examining offending careers occurring in prison. Using a sample of 1,005 inmates, Matt DeLisi found that a small cadre of inmates accounted for 100% of the murders, 75% of the rapes, 80% of the arsons, and 50% of the aggravated assaults occurring in the correctional facilities of a southwestern state in the United States. Overall, the rule of thumb is that less than 10% of criminals in a population commit more than 50% of all crime and anywhere from 60% to 100% of the most serious forms of crime such as murder, rape, and kidnapping. This characterizes offenders across the United States and in countries such as Canada, China, Denmark, England, Finland, Germany, Israel, New Zealand, and Sweden.[23]

Demographic Characteristics

Sex

That career criminals are almost always male is inarguable. Males are significantly more likely than females to become chronic, habitual, or career criminals in addition to being diagnosed with oppositional defiant disorder, attention deficit hyperactivity disorder, antisocial personality disorder, or psychopathy. Samples of offenders who have been convicted of the most serious forms of violence—such as murder, kidnapping, and sexual offenses—are constituted almost entirely by male criminals. Similarly, some prototypical traits of psychopathy (e.g., the use of physical cruelty toward people and animals; the use of weapons with intent to inflict serious injury; and the propensity to bully, threaten, or intimidate others) are almost exclusively limited to males.[24] Regardless of research design or source of data, males commit diverse forms of crime at higher rates and for longer periods of time than females do. The evidence for the disproportionate male versus female involvement in crime is omnipresent. Nationally, about 75% of all arrestees are male, and in most states, 9 out of 10 inmates are men. Among the 3,581 prisoners in the United States who were awaiting execution in 2001, only 51 were women.

Despite the clear sex differences in criminal involvement, it is important to recognize that habitual female offenders do exist, and a variety of scholars have empirically documented chronic antisocial behavior among women. Like their male counterparts, female career criminals tend to commit an array of criminal offenses over their life span and are plagued by overlapping mental health and substance abuse problems. Drug problems are so acute that the offending careers of women are best characterized by arrests for forgery, fraud, and prostitution—relatively quick and inexpensive ways to obtain money to purchase illicit drugs. Prior to and during their criminal careers, female offenders often have more extensive victimization experiences, especially sexual victimization, than males.[25] Although some differences exist between female and male career criminals, their commonality is an enduring and tenacious involvement in various forms of crime and assorted behaviors. However, female career criminals are one order of magnitude, or 10 times, less common than male career criminals.[26]

Race and Ethnicity

Unlike the relationship between sex and career criminality, the link between race, ethnicity, and habitual offending is equivocal and more open to interpretation.[27] Much research conducted in the United States has found that racial minorities, such as African Americans and Hispanics, were more likely than whites to be career criminals. There is compelling evidence for such a conclusion. In the 1945 Philadelphia birth cohort study, sharp differences existed across racial groups for chronic offender status. Just 3% of whites were chronic offenders, whereas 14.4% of nonwhites (the majority of whom were black) were chronic offenders. Thus, blacks were 4.5 times more likely than whites to demonstrate habituation in criminal behavior. Moreover, blacks had a significantly greater involvement than whites in the most serious forms of violence, such as homicide, rape, robbery, and aggravated assault. The respective prevalence rates of the violent Index offenses per 1,000 cohort subjects for blacks were 4.8%, 13.1%, 59.6%, and 62.4%. The commensurate white prevalence rates were significantly lower, at 0%, 0.9%, 2.8%, and 5.5%. These data suggested that, ceteris paribus, racial minorities, especially blacks, were much more likely than whites to be career delinquents involved in serious criminal violence.[28]

Of course, career criminals are not merely an issue of blacks and whites because other racial and ethnic group members also commit crime. Kimberly Kempf-Leonard and her colleagues (2001) used data from the 1958 Philadelphia birth cohort to examine various offender types by race and ethnicity. They found that among white delinquents, 12% were chronic offenders, 9.5% were serious and chronic offenders, and 4.1% were violent and chronic offenders. Comparatively, 21.1% of black delinquents were chronic offenders, 18.4% were serious and chronic offenders, and 13.7% were violent and chronic offenders. The respective prevalence estimates for Hispanic delinquents were 15% for the chronic group, 12.8% for the serious and chronic group, and 6.4% for the violent and chronic group. The Philadelphia birth cohort design was replicated using a 1970 birth cohort from the San Juan, Carolina, and Bayamon police districts in Puerto Rico. Although the levels of delinquency in Puerto Rico were much lower than in the Philadelphia studies, similarities did emerge in that chronic recidivists accounted for a disproportionate share of delinquency and violence. Dora Nevares and colleagues' racial analysis was operationalized using skin color for three groups: nonwhites, whites, and Triguenos. They found that among delinquents, nonwhites (16%) and Triguenos (11%) were more likely than whites (9%) to demonstrate habitual criminality. Similarly, Lyle Shannon's examination of 6,127 persons in the 1942, 1949, and 1955 Racine birth cohorts found that blacks and Chicanos (original nomenclature) were disproportionately more likely than whites to engage in chronic and serious criminal offending.[29]

Recall, however, that studies from the United States and around the world have been used to produce the scientific literature on career criminals. Many of these studies contained samples with exclusively white research participants. Irrespective of the racial composition of the sample, the traits and behaviors of the most active offenders were consistently found. In other words, career criminals, *regardless of race or ethnicity*, tended to be males who initiated their offending career in childhood or early adolescence and continued it well into middle adulthood. They engaged in an assortment of antisocial behaviors (e.g., violent, property, public-order, and drug crimes) at exceedingly high levels, often at the expense of their own development in family, educational, and work endeavors. The replication of these findings suggests that a small cadre of statistically aberrant criminals is an empirical reality that ostensibly transcends race and ethnicity.[30]

Age

All types of criminal offenders tend to decrease their level of criminal offending as they age. The "age-crime curve" indicates that delinquency emerges in early adolescence, peaks at about age 17, and then declines sharply upon adulthood. From age 20 onward, the involvement in crime approaches zero. Some have argued that the age-crime curve is invariant and cannot be explained by social factors or any causal variables. It simply "is." Because criminal involvement is peaking for persons aged 15, 16, or 17, serious and violent juvenile offenders are a national priority.

Although an inverse relationship characterizes age and crime, one should not conclude that adults are uninvolved in criminal offending. To the contrary, adults account for 70% of all arrests in the United States. It is simply the case that not all offenders desist from offending upon reaching adulthood (although most do). Others continue to run afoul of the law at various rates. For example, a 50-year-old chronic offender is likely to be less violent and dangerous than he was at age 18, but he is clearly more dangerous than persons who were never chronic offenders.

The strong effect of age on crime has important implications for criminological theory and research. The changing involvement in crime across the life course is central to the developmental theories that appear in Chapter 3. Furthermore, the meaning of the age-crime relationship as it relates to conducting criminological research constituted the heated academic debates of the 1980s and appears in Chapter 4.

Onset, Versatility, and Seriousness/Dangerousness

Inextricably related to the age-crime effect is onset. Onset is the emergence of antisocial behavior and the initiation of a criminal career. Onset exerts a strong, negative effect on the duration, seriousness, and extremity of the criminal career. In other words, the earlier one demonstrates serious antisocial behavior, whether or not they are arrested, the worst his or her criminal career will be. In a comprehensive review of the subject, Rolf Loeber and Tom Dishion concluded, "Almost without exception, the early behaviors of the youths that are predictive of delinquency remain predictive at a later age." Thus, persons who were first arrested during childhood or adolescence are likely to be more serious criminal offenders than individuals whose arrest onset occurred at age 30.[31]

If one were to survey the life history of a 60-year-old career criminal, one would likely find that the offender was also a juvenile delinquent and seriously antisocial child. As children, early-starting criminals were found to be troublesome, dishonest, daring, impulsive, and poorly tempered. They had multiple conduct problems, were especially difficult to govern or discipline, and performed poorly in school. Even in elementary school, early starters committed an assortment of delinquent offenses that seemed to portend a sustained career of wayward conduct. These behavioral problems foreshadow more serious criminal behavior during early adolescence, and most chronic offenders were first arrested at the beginning of their adolescence. Early-starting offenders have been found to be among the most versatile and dangerous criminals. Indeed, a recent study found that offenders who are first arrested at age 14 were significantly likely to be chronic offenders who committed more serious crimes at the highest rates.[32] The theoretical significance of onset will be discussed further in Chapters 3 and 4. Indeed, how one interprets the meaning of the onset effect speaks to one's conceptualization of human behavior and the etiology of criminal behavior.

One of the more widespread misconceptions in popular culture is the idea of the specialized career criminal, an offender who exclusively focuses on committing one specific type of offense. Several incarnations of the specialized offender exist, such as the serial killer, kleptomaniac, and pyromaniac. However, even a cursory analysis of the offending patterns of these defendants demonstrates that they commit an array of offenses. For example, serial killers almost always commit abduction or kidnapping to control their victim. Furthermore, serial killers commonly rape and/or rob their victims. Thus, a serial killer could just as easily and accurately be labeled a serial kidnapper, serial rapist, or serial robber. Because of this, criminals are more apt to be versatile or general, not specialized, in their offending patterns. In his classic *Delinquent Boys*, Albert Cohen quipped, "A generalized, protean 'orneriness,' not this or that specialized delinquent pursuit seems best to describe the vocation of the delinquent."[33]

Interestingly, some in academia also seem attached to the concept of specialized criminals and have made it a recurrent research item. As Michael Gottfredson and Travis Hirschi suggested, "In spite of years of tireless research motivated by the belief in specialization, no credible evidence of specialization has been reported." To be sure, scholars have found modest statistical evidence of offenders who recurrently engaged in similar types of offending, such as auto theft, armed robbery, and narrow clusters or violent or property crime.[34] However, affirmative evidence of specialization is heavily statistical in nature, and its substantive meaning is often unclear. For example, consecutive arrests for the same crime constitute specialization even if all other arrests in the offender's history are for different crimes. Thus, 10% of an offender's criminal record might demonstrate specialization, but this implies that 90% of the record does not. Chester Britt addressed this issue directly in his assessment of the specialization literature: "A double standard is used; specialization is imputed when offenders are not shown to be completely versatile in their offending, yet the reverse is not held to be true." Overwhelmingly, researchers have found that criminals are generalists who commit an array of offenses, not specialists who fixate on one type of crime. This holds true even for sex offenders, arsonists, and nonviolent drug offenders.[35]

Career criminals are the persons most likely to engage in the most serious or dangerous forms of criminal behavior. In this sense, the most dire and frightening forms of crime—murder, armed robbery, abduction and rape, and armed burglary—are principally their domains. Following this logic, it is very unlikely for nominal criminal offenders, that is, persons who are arrested only once in their lifetime, to commit serious felonies. Unfortunately, a primary manner that researchers have attempted to quantify this with is by studying the progression, specifically the escalation, of offending from benign forms of crime to more serious forms. Again, escalation research relies on fairly sophisticated analytical techniques that have been largely unhelpful in understanding whether escalation patterns exist. For example, although it is commonly the case that offenders progress from status offending (e.g., truancy, running away) to public-order and property offending (e.g., vandalism, shoplifting) to violent offending (e.g., assault and robbery), obviously not all career criminals fit this pattern.[36]

A more straightforward and potentially fruitful way to assess the seriousness and dangerousness of offenders is to examine their criminal justice system involvements, particularly their prison history. By definition, felony convictions and imprisonment reflect the seriousness of the underlying criminal conduct. Indeed, career criminals spend a large part of their lives on probation, in jail, on bond, in prison, on parole, and generally in police custody. A seminal study by Joan Petersilia, Peter Greenwood, and Marvin Lavin in 1978 used interview data of 49 habitual offenders incarcerated in California. On average, these offenders reported committing more than 200 serious crimes per year. Comparing their self-reported criminal involvement to their rap sheets, Petersilia and her colleagues calculated that only 3% to 20%, depending on the offense, of the serious crimes committed by habitual offenders resulted in arrest. Over careers that lasted 21 years on average, habitual offenders served a considerable amount of time, approximately half of their career, in jail or prison. More recent research replicated these findings. The most serious types of offenders, particularly those who have been convicted of murder, rape, or kidnapping, generate criminal records that span 25 years or more and average four separate commitments to prison. Those offenders in the 90th percentile in criminal offending amassed more than 30 felony convictions and more than 20 stints in prison.[37]

Summary: The Universality of Career Criminals

Consider the following passage:

> There is evidently a large class of habitual criminals—who live by robbery and thieving and petty larceny—who run the risk of comparatively short sentences with comparative indifference. They make money rapidly by crime, they enjoy life after their fashion, and then, on detection and conviction, serve their time quietly with the full determination to revert to crime when they come out. . . . When an offender has been convicted a fourth time or more he or she is pretty sure to have taken to crime as a profession and sooner or later to return to prison. We are, therefore, of opinion that further corrective measures are desirable for these persons. When under sentence

they complicate prison management—when at large they are responsible for the commission of the greater part of the undetected crime . . . they are a nuisance to the community. To punish them for the particular offense is almost useless, the real offense is the willful persistence in the deliberately acquired habit of crime.

This paragraph clearly resonates with today's political climate about crime control. However, the quotation comes from a British House of Commons report on crime dated from 1895.[38] Nevertheless, the profile that it depicts is equivalent to today's career criminal. Across more than a century of research, this has not changed much.

Career criminals have existed across epochs, cultures, and ethnic populations. They are not merely an American problem, nor are they limited to whites and blacks. Instead, within dramatically different societies such as China, Israel, Sweden, Denmark, Puerto Rico, New Zealand, and England exists an archetypal person who demonstrates pronounced antisocial behavior from childhood tantrums and defiance to assorted acts of delinquency to disparate forms of crime. Often, this person is likely to have substantial substance abuse and mental health problems, in addition to an almost pathological unwillingness to participate in conventional roles at home, school, and work. Career criminals are exceedingly damaging people.

If career criminals are consistent features of modern societies, then is it right to assert that their pathology has its roots in culturally specific factors, such as culture, economics, or racial composition? Moreover, because career criminals appear in societies that are heterogeneous and homogenous, is it again questionable to suggest that their behavior is necessarily produced by inequalities in a differentiated social system? Academicians have engaged in sometimes fierce debates about the etiology of career criminals and the theoretical perspective that best explains them. In short, they have attempted to explain whether career criminals are born bad or turned into bad people. Chapter 3 explores the latter point with the emphasis on human development and its assumption of a malleable human nature.

Notes

1. Petersilia, J., & Honig, P. (1980). *The prison experience of career criminals*. Santa Monica, CA: RAND Corporation; Morris, N. (1951). *The habitual criminal*.

Westport, CT: Greenwood Press; Wolfgang, M. E., Figlio, R. M., & Sellin, T. (1972). *Delinquency in a birth cohort.* Chicago: University of Chicago Press; Hamparian, D. M., Schuster, R., Dinitz, S., & Conrad, J. (1978). *The violent few: A study of dangerous juvenile offenders.* Lexington, MA: Lexington Books; Hirschi, T. (1969). *Causes of delinquency.* Berkeley: University of California Press; Wolfgang, M. E., Thornberry, T. P., & Figlio, R. M. (1987). *From boy to man, from delinquency to crime.* Chicago: University of Chicago Press; Tillman, R. (1987). The size of the "criminal population": The prevalence and incidence of adult arrest. *Criminology, 25,* 561-579; DeLisi, M. (2001). Extreme career criminals. *American Journal of Criminal Justice, 25,* 239-252.

2. References appear in order: Hedge, M. (2002, May 2). Career criminal Pierce finally finds his "perfect alibi." *AAP Newsfeed,* Melbourne, Australia. Retrieved October 1, 2003, from http://web.lexis-nexis.com/universe/document?_m=dc38ee235386; Sands, A. (2002, November 9). Condo loses court motion to halt disciplinary action. *The Ottawa Citizen,* p. D1; Canadian Press. (2002, February 21). "I'm not bad—just a career criminal," robber tells judge. *Victoria Times Colonist,* p. A8; Fisher, D. (2003, March 2). Anti-terror laws snare notorious career criminal. *The Sunday Star-Times* (Auckland, New Zealand), p. A6; Narain, J. (2003, March 28). The men accused of murdering Britons on house hunt; South American "career criminals" appear in court after discovery of bodies. *London Daily Mail,* p. 37. Retrieved October 2, 2003, from http://web.lexis-nexis .com/universe/document?_meb9c62646d1

3. For explorations of the history of career criminals and other criminally dangerous persons, see Black, D. W., & Larson, C. L. (1999). *Bad boys, bad men: Confronting antisocial personality disorder.* New York: Oxford University Press; Murphy, J. M. (1976). Psychiatric labeling in cross-cultural perspective: Similar kinds of disturbed behavior appear to be abnormal in diverse cultures. *Science, 191,* 1019-1028; Cooke, D. J. (1998). Psychopathy across cultures. In D. J. Cooke, A. E. Forth, & R. D. Hare (Eds.), *Psychopathy: Theory, research, and implications for society* (pp. 13-45). London: Kluwer Academic Publishers; Kramer, R. C. (1982). From "habitual offenders" to "career criminals": The historical construction and development of criminal categories. *Law & Human Behavior, 6,* 273-293.

4. Not all scholars are as praiseworthy of Hare's psychopathy measure; indeed, some have found that broader measures such as the Level of Service Inventory–Revised are more effective. See Gendreau, P., Little, T., & Goggin, C. (1996). A meta-analysis of the predictors of adult offender recidivism: What works! *Criminology, 34,* 575-607; Gendreau, P., Goggin, C., & Smith, P. (2002). Is the PCL-R really the "unparalleled" measure of offender risk? A lesson in knowledge cumulation. *Criminal Justice and Behavior, 29,* 397-426. For a spirited reply, see Hemphill, J. F., & Hare, R. D. (2004). Some misconceptions about the Hare PCL-R and risk assessment: A reply to Gendreau, Goggin, and Smith. *Criminal Justice and Behavior, 31,* 203-243. Indeed, there are other measures of psychopathy and related

pathological conditions that are also effective in predicting recidivism and violent. These include the traditional psychiatric diagnostic categories of conduct disorder and oppositional defiant disorder that appear in the *Diagnostic and Statistical Manual of Mental Disorders* published by the American Psychiatric Association, the Minnesota Multiphasic Personality Inventory psychopathic deviate scale, the Level of Service Inventory—Revised, the Antisocial Process Screening Device, the Child Psychopathy Scale, the Youth Psychopathic Traits Inventory, and other diagnostic batteries.

5. Arrigo, B. A., & Shipley, S. (2001). The confusion over psychopathy (I): Historical considerations. *International Journal of Offender Therapy & Comparative Criminology, 45,* 325-344 (see pp. 328-329); Hare, R. D., Clark, D., Grann, M., & Thornton, D. (2000). Psychopathy and the predictive validity of the PCL-R: An international perspective. *Behavioral Sciences & the Law, 18,* 623-645.

6. Original quotation from 1911, cited in Tanenhaus, D. S. (2000). The evolution of transfer out of the juvenile court. In J. Fagan & F. Zimring (Eds.), *The changing borders of juvenile justice: Transfer of adolescents to the criminal court* (pp. 13-43). Chicago: University of Chicago Press.

7. Shover, N. (1996). *Great pretenders: Pursuits and careers of persistent thieves.* Boulder, CO: Westview Press.

8. For examples of typological approaches, see Clinard, M., & Quinney, R. (1973). *Criminal behavior systems.* New York: Holt, Rinehart, & Winston; Gibbons, D. C., & Garrity, D. L. (1962). Definitions and analysis of certain criminal types. *Journal of Criminal Law, Criminology, & Police Science, 53,* 27-35; Gibbons, D. C. (1988). Some critical observations on criminal types and criminal careers. *Criminal Justice & Behavior, 15,* 8-23; Glaser, D. (1972). *Adult crime and social policy.* Englewood Cliffs, NJ: Prentice Hall. Reviews of the methodological and substantive weaknesses of typological studies appear in Bursik, R. J., Jr. (1989). Erickson could never have imagined: Recent extensions of birth cohort studies. *Journal of Quantitative Criminology, 5,* 389-396; Gibbons, D. C. (1975). Offender typologies: Two decades later. *British Journal of Criminology, 15,* 140-156.

9. D'Ungar, A. V., Land, K. C., McCall, P. L., & Nagin, D. S. (1998). How many latent classes of delinquent/criminal careers? Results from mixed Poisson regression analyses. *American Journal of Sociology, 103,* 1593-1630; Francis, B., Soothill, K., & Fligelstone, R. (2004). Identifying patterns and pathways of offending behavior: A new approach to typologies of crime. *European Journal of Criminology, 1,* 47-87; Eggleston, E. P., Laub, J. H., & Sampson, R. J. (2004). Methodological sensitivities to latent class analysis of long-term criminal trajectories. *Journal of Quantitative Criminology, 20,* 1-26 (quotation from p. 24).

10. Hamparian, D. M., Schuster, R., Dinitz, S., & Conrad, J. (1978). *The violent few: A study of dangerous juvenile offenders.* Lexington, MA: Lexington Books; McCord, J. (1978). A thirty-year follow-up of treatment effects. *American Psychologist, 32,* 284-289; McCord, J. (1979). Some child-rearing antecedents of

criminal behavior in adult men. *Journal of Personality and Social Psychology, 37*, 1477-1486; McCord, J., & McCord, W. (1958). The effects of parental role model on criminality. *Journal of Social Issues, 14*, 66-75; McCord, J., & McCord, W. (1959). A follow-up report on the Cambridge-Somerville Youth Study. *Annals of the American Academy of Political and Social Science, 322*, 89-96; Shannon, L. W. (1988). *Criminal career continuity: Its social context.* New York: Human Services Press; Shannon, L. W. (1991). *Changing patterns of delinquency and crime: A longitudinal study in Racine.* Boulder, CO: Westview Press.

    11.   Petersilia, J., Greenwood, P. W., & Lavin, M. (1978). *Criminal careers of habitual felons.* Santa Monica, CA: RAND Corporation; Peterson, M. P., Braiker, H. B., & Polich, S. M. (1980). *Doing crime: A survey of California prison inmates.* Santa Monica, CA: RAND Corporation; Chaiken, J. M., & Chaiken, M. R. (1982). *Varieties of criminal behavior.* Santa Monica, CA: RAND Corporation; Canela-Cacho, J. A., Blumstein, A., & Cohen, J. (1997). Relationship between the offending frequency (lambda) of imprisoned and free offenders. *Criminology, 35*, 133-175.

    12.   Dunford, F. W., & Elliott, D. S. (1984). Identifying career offenders using self-reported data. *Journal of Research in Crime and Delinquency, 21*, 57-86; Elliott, D. S. (1994). Serious violent offenders: Onset, developmental course, and termination— the American Society of Criminology 1993 presidential address. *Criminology, 32*, 1-21; Elliott, D. S., Huizinga, D., & Morse, B. (1986). Self-reported violent offending: A descriptive analysis of juvenile violent offenders and their offending careers. *Journal of Interpersonal Violence, 1*, 472-514.

    13.   Summary reviews of these studies appear in Thornberry, T. P., Huizinga, D., & Loeber, R. (1995). The prevention of serious delinquency and violence: Implications from the program of research on the causes and correlates of delinquency. In J. C. Howell, B. Krisberg, J. D. Hawkins, & J. J. Wilson (Eds.), *Serious, violent, and chronic juvenile offenders* (pp. 213-237). Thousand Oaks, CA: Sage; Loeber, R., & Farrington, D. P. (Eds.). (1998). *Serious and violent juvenile offenders: Risk factors and successful interventions.* Thousand Oaks, CA: Sage.

    14.   Elliott, D. S., Huizinga, D., & Menard, S. (1989). *Multiple problem youth: Delinquency, substance use, and mental health problems.* New York: Springer-Verlag; Huizinga, D., Loeber, R., Thornberry, T. P., & Cothern, L. (2000, November). *Co-occurrence of serious and violent juvenile offending and other problem behaviors.* Washington, DC: U.S. Department of Justice, Office of Justice Program, Office of Juvenile Justice and Delinquency Prevention; Loeber, R., et al. (2001). Male mental health problems, psychopathy, and personality traits: Key findings from the first 14 years of the Pittsburgh Youth Study. *Clinical Child and Family Psychology Review, 4*, 273-297.

    15.   Brennan, P., Mednick, S., & John, R. (1989). Specialization in violence: Evidence of a criminal subgroup. *Criminology, 27*, 437-453; Hamalainen, M., & Pulkkinen, L. (1995). Aggressive and non-prosocial behaviors as precursors of criminality. *Studies on Crime and Crime Prevention, 4*, 6-21; Pulkkinen, L., et al. (2000). Child

behavior and adult personality: Comparisons between criminality groups in Finland and Sweden. *Criminal Behavior & Mental Health, 10,* 155-169; Stattin, H., & Magnusson, D. (1991). Stability and change in criminal behavior up to age 30. *British Journal of Criminology, 31,* 327-346; Stattin, H., Magnusson, D., & Reichel, H. (1989). Criminal activity at different ages: A study based on a Swedish longitudinal research population. *British Journal of Criminology, 29,* 368-385.

16.   Kyvsgaard, B. (2003). *The criminal career: The Danish longitudinal study.* Cambridge, UK: Cambridge University Press.

17.   Fergusson, D. M., Horwood, L. J., & Nagin, D. S. (2000). Offending trajectories in a New Zealand birth cohort. *Criminology, 38,* 525-552.

18.   Moffitt, T. E. (1993). "Life-course persistent" and "adolescence-limited" antisocial behavior: A developmental typology. *Psychological Review, 100,* 674-701; Moffitt, T. E., Caspi, A., Rutter, M., & Silva, P. A. (2001). *Sex differences in antisocial behavior: Conduct disorder, delinquency, and violence in the Dunedin longitudinal study.* Cambridge, UK: Cambridge University Press.

19.   Friday, P. C., Ren, X., Weitekamp, E., & Leuven, K. U. (2003). *Delinquency in a Chinese birth cohort, final report.* Washington, DC: U.S. Department of Justice, National Institute of Justice.

20.   Chu, M. (2002). Incarcerated Chinese men: Their life experiences and criminal onset. *British Journal of Criminology, 42,* 250-266; Liu, J., Messner, S., & Liska, A. (1997). Chronic offenders in China. *International Criminal Justice Review, 7,* 31-45.

21.   Blumstein, A., Cohen, J., Roth, J., & Visher, C. (Eds.). (1986). *Criminal careers and "career criminals."* Washington, DC: National Academy Press; DeLisi, M. (2001). Extreme career criminals. *American Journal of Criminal Justice, 25,* 239-252; Howell, J. C., B. Krisberg, J. D. Hawkins, & J. J. Wilson. (Eds.). (1995). *Serious, violent, and chronic juvenile offenders.* Thousand Oaks, CA: Sage.

22.   Farrington, D. P., et al. (2003). Comparing delinquency careers in court records and self-reports. *Criminology, 41,* 933-956 (quotation from p. 953).

23.   Shannon, L. W. (1991). DeLisi, M. (2003). Criminal careers behind bars. *Behavioral Sciences & the Law, 21,* 653-669.

24.   DeLisi, M. (2001), see note 1; Cruise, K. R., Colwell, L. H., Lyons, P. M., & Baker, M. D. (2003). Prototypical analysis of adolescent psychopathy: Investigating the juvenile justice perspective. *Behavioral Sciences & the Law, 21,* 829-846.

25.   Danner, T. A., Blount, W. R., Silverman, I. J., & Vega, M. (1995). The female chronic offender: Exploring life contingency and offense history dimensions for incarcerated female offenders. *Women & Criminal Justice, 6,* 45-65; DeLisi, M. (2002). Not just a boy's club: An empirical assessment of female career criminals. *Women & Criminal Justice, 13,* 27-45; Maxwell, S., & Maxwell, C. (2000). Explaining the "criminal careers" of prostitutes within the nexus of drug use, drug selling, and other illicit activities. *Criminology, 38,* 787-810; Warren, M., & Rosenbaum, J. (1987). Criminal careers of female offenders. *Criminal Justice & Behavior, 13,* 393-418.

26. DeLisi, M. (2002), ibid.; Moffitt, T. E., Caspi, A., Rutter, M., & Silva, P. A. (2001). *Sex differences in antisocial behavior* (pp. 214-225). Cambridge, UK: Cambridge University Press.

27. Especially in the United States, the disproportionate minority representation among serious, violent, and career criminals is closely linked with another sociological variable: social class. Because minorities, particularly African Americans, are more likely than whites to live in extremely poor neighborhoods, their life chances are severely limited vis-à-vis persons living in neighborhoods characterized by higher socioeconomic status. Involvement in crime and official sanctioning by the criminal justice system exacerbates the social class deprivation. Dubbed variously as concentrated disadvantage, truly disadvantaged, cumulative disadvantage, or structural disadvantage, theoretical and empirical research suggests that crime and labeling from official social control agents "trigger exclusionary processes that have negative consequences for conventional opportunities . . . leading to increased involvement in crime due to the negative effect of intervention on educational attainment and employment" (Bernburg & Krohn, 2003, p. 1287). Generally, see Bernburg, J. G., & Krohn, M. D. (2003). Labeling, life chances, and adult crime: The direct and indirect effects of official intervention in adolescence on crime in early adulthood. *Criminology, 41,* 1287-1318; Pager, D. (2003). The mark of a criminal record. *American Journal of Sociology, 108,* 937-975; Sampson, R. J., & Laub, J. H. (1997). A life-course theory of cumulative disadvantage and the stability of delinquency. *Advances in Criminological Theory, 7,* 133-162.

28. Elliott, D. S. (1994). Serious violent offenders: Onset, developmental course, and termination. The American Society of Criminology 1993 Presidential Address. *Criminology, 32,* 1-21. Hamparian, D. M., et al. (1978). *The violent few: A study of dangerous juvenile offenders.* Lexington, MA: Lexington Books; Loeber, R., & Farrington, D. P. (Eds.). (1998) *Serious and violent juvenile offenders: Risk factors and successful interventions.* Thousand Oaks, CA: Sage; Piquero, A. R., & Buka, S. L. (2002). Linking juvenile and adult patterns of criminal activity in the Providence cohort of the National Collaborative Perinatal Project. *Journal of Criminal Justice, 30,* 259-272; Piquero, A. R., MacDonald, J. M., & Parker, K. F. (2002). Race, local life circumstances, and criminal activity. *Social Science Quarterly, 83,* 654-670.

29. Kempf-Leonard, K., Tracy, P. E., & Howell, J. C. (2001). Serious, violent, and chronic juvenile offenders: The relationship of delinquency careers types to adult criminality. *Justice Quarterly, 18,* 449-478; Nevares, D., Wolfgang, M. E., & Tracy, P. E. (1990). *Delinquency in Puerto Rico: The 1970 birth cohort study.* New York: Greenwood Press; Shannon (1991). *Changing patterns of delinquency and crime: A longitudinal study in Racine.* Boulder, CO: Westview Press.

30. It is important that two very different conclusions not be convoluted. First, career criminals are a static feature of human society, regardless of race or ethnicity. However, this point does not obfuscate that there are dramatic racial and ethnic differences in criminal offending and victimization in most societies, especially

the United States. For example, Pallone and Hennessy (1999) found that young minority males perpetrated criminal violence and had violence inflicted on them at levels that ranged from 10 to 30 times their representation of the national (U.S.) population.

31. Loeber, R., & Dishion, T. (1983). Early predictors of male delinquency: A review. *Psychological Bulletin, 94,* 68-99. A classic study that speaks to this is the 22-year longitudinal study of more than 600 youth from New York conducted by L. R. Huesmann and his colleagues (1984). They found considerable behavioral stability by comparing aggression levels when participants were age 8 to life outcomes when the participants were age 30. These included the correlations between age 8 aggression and age 30 aggression ($r = .30$), spousal abuse ($r = .27$), criminal convictions ($r = .24$), crime seriousness ($r = .21$), and self-rated physical aggression ($r = .29$). All of these relationships were significant at the $p < .001$ level. In relation to the effects of onset, they concluded, "What is not arguable is that aggressive behavior, however engendered, once established, remains remarkably stable across time, situation, and even generations within a family." Huesmann, L. R., Eron, L. D., Lefkowitz, M. M., & Walder, L. O. (1984). Stability of aggression over time and generation. *Developmental Psychology, 20,* 1120-1134 (p. 1133).

32. Dean, C. W., Brame, R., & Piquero, A. R. (1996). Criminal propensities, discrete groups of offenders, and persistence in crime. *Criminology, 34,* 547-575; DeLisi, M. (2004). *Zeroing in on early arrest onset: Results from a population of extreme career criminals.* Unpublished manuscript, Department of Sociology, Iowa State University, Ames; Piquero, A. R., & Chung, H. L. (2001). On the relationship between gender, early onset, and the seriousness of offending. *Journal of Criminal Justice, 29,* 189-206; Piquero, A., Paternoster, R., Mazerolle, P., Brame, R., & Dean, C. W. (1999). Onset age and offense specialization. *Journal of Research in Crime and Delinquency, 36,* 275-299; Farrington, D. P. (1997). Human development and criminal careers. In M. Maguire, R. Morgan, & R. Reiner (Eds.), *The Oxford handbook of criminology* (pp. 361-408). Oxford, UK: Oxford University Press; Farrington, D. P. (2000). Psychosocial predictors of adult antisocial personality and adult convictions. *Behavioral Sciences & the Law, 18,* 605-622.

33. Cohen, A. K. (1955). *Delinquent boys: The culture of the gang.* New York: The Free Press (p. 30).

34. For examples, see Blumstein, A., Cohen, J., Das, S., & Moitra, S. D. (1988). Specialization and seriousness during adult criminal careers. *Journal of Quantitative Criminology, 4,* 303-345; Brennan, P., Mednick, S., & John, R. (1989). Specialization in violence: Evidence of a criminal subgroup. *Criminology, 27,* 437-453; Britt, C. L. (1996). The measurement of specialization and escalation in the criminal career: An alternative modeling strategy. *Journal of Quantitative Criminology, 12,* 193-222; Bursik, R. J., Jr. (1980). Dynamics of specialization in juvenile offenders. *Social Forces, 58,* 850-864; Schwaner, S. L. (1998). Patterns of violent specialization: Predictors of recidivism for a cohort of parolees. *American Journal of*

Criminal Justice, 23, 1-17; Schwaner, S. L. (2000). "Stick 'em up, buddy": Robbery, lifestyle, and specialization within a cohort of parolees. *Journal of Criminal Justice, 28,* 371-384.

35.   Britt, C. L. (1994). Versatility. In T. Hirschi & M. Gottfredson (Eds.), *The generality of deviance* (pp. 173-192). New Brunswick, NJ: Transaction; DeLisi, M. (2003). The imprisoned nonviolent drug offender: Specialized martyr or versatile career criminal? *American Journal of Criminal Justice, 27,* 167-182; Mazerolle, P., Brame, R., Paternoster, R., Piquero, A., & Dean, C. (2000). Onset age, persistence, and offending versatility: Comparisons across gender. *Criminology, 38,* 1143-1172; Piquero, A. (2000). Frequency, specialization, and violence in offending careers. *Journal of Research in Crime and Delinquency, 37,* 392-418; Simon, L. M. J. (2000). An examination of the assumptions of specialization, mental disorder, and dangerousness in sex offenders. *Behavioral Sciences & the Law, 18,* 275-308; Stickle, T. R., & Blechman, E. A. (2002). Aggression and fire: Antisocial behavior in firesetting and nonfiresetting juvenile offenders. *Journal of Psychopathology and Behavioral Assessment, 24,* 177-193.

36.   For a review, see Tracy, P. E., & Kempf-Leonard, K. (1996). *Continuity and discontinuity in criminal careers.* New York: Plenum.

37.   Petersilia, J., Greenwood, P. G., & Lavin, M. (1978). *Criminal careers of habitual felons.* Washington, DC: U.S. Department of Justice, Law Enforcement Assistance Administration, National Institute of Law Enforcement and Criminal Justice; DeLisi, M. (2001), *supra,* note 12.

38.   House of Commons. (1895). *Report of the Committee on Prisons.* London: Author.

3

Developmental Theory and Its Application

Family and friends could not understand what was happening to Darius Schumacher. Ever since losing his job with the Board of Education, Darius seemed to be a completely different person. Once happy and upbeat, Darius had sunk into the doldrums and was very unpleasant to be around. Only a social drinker before the layoff, Darius was now drinking daily, and his behavior was becoming more and more unpredictable and erratic. His wife and children suffered along with him during his layoff. Secretly, they hoped that this period of his life would be brief.

Unfortunately, things went from bad to worse when Darius was arrested. Local police officers pulled Darius over after he was observed driving along the double-yellow centerline on a major thoroughfare. Upon contact with the officers, Darius was thoroughly incoherent, unsteady on his feet, and verbally abusive. Just after he was administered a portable breath test, which registered a whopping blood alcohol content of .278, Darius became increasingly uncooperative with the officers. He disputed the reading of the portable breath test and insisted that he had not been drinking. Their verbal commands to him went unheeded. As the officers began to place Darius in handcuffs to be arrested for drunk driving, he became physically combative and resistive. Consequently, the officers used force when handcuffing Darius and placing him in the backseat of the police vehicle. They informed him that an additional felony charge of resisting a law enforcement officer with violence would be added.

The fallout from the arrest was extensive. Once he sobered, Darius was ashamed, embarrassed, and devastated to have been arrested and detained in jail. This was his first arrest, and the financial strain of hiring an attorney was especially difficult since he was not working. His wife and children were also saddened and ashamed that their husband/father had caused this. Picking Darius up from jail was particularly difficult for his family, as was the notice in the police blotter of the local paper that Darius Schumacher had been severely intoxicated and combative with police. It seemed that all of their neighbors, friends, and acquaintances were aware of the incident, which made it even more stressful to deal with. It was as if the single event of losing his job had radically altered Darius's life.

Overview of Developmental Theory

Developmentally inclined criminologists take as their null hypothesis that antisocial behavior has to develop and is not simply the manifestation of some underlying or primordial condition. Rather than attribute career criminality to the pathologies of the individual, the developmental perspective points to life experiences that mold individuals and send them along trajectories or pathways. As the introductory vignette portrays, the circumstances of Darius's life seemed to cause his problems—and once these problems were initiated, they tended to snowball. As Daniel Nagin and Raymond Paternoster have suggested, the

observed correlation between past and future behavior is not based on the predictive power of the initial distribution of criminal propensity or conventional opportunities and characteristics of the population. It is instead based upon the fact that *some actions have dynamically increased the subsequent probability of crime by weakening previous inhibitions or strengthening previous incentives for criminal activity*.[1]

As conventional wisdom and common sense would indicate, early family life is essential to the social and antisocial development of an individual. In their influential general theory of crime, Michael Gottfredson and Travis Hirschi acknowledged that there is a "belief of the general public (and those who deal with offenders in the criminal justice system) that 'defective upbringing' or 'neglect' in the home is the primary cause of crime."[2] Overwhelmingly, decades of research have shown that the dysfunctional family is the environment that cultivates chronic criminality. A variety of factors including family size, degree of parental affection toward the child, level of supervision and monitoring of the child, parental involvement in deviance, parental aggressiveness and temper, and parental mental health have been found to be antecedent predictors of serious criminal behavior. Indeed, in comparing the offending careers of respondents from the Cambridge Study in Delinquent Development and the Pittsburgh Youth Study, David Farrington and Rolf Loeber found that the family-related risk factors for chronic offenders were nearly identical across two continents.

Moreover, retrospective analyses of serious delinquents and career criminals discovered that their childhoods were characterized by alternately harsh, punitive, overly lax, or neglectful parenting; parental rejection; and assorted forms of child abuse and maltreatment. For example, Robin Weeks and Cathy Spatz Widom found that 68% of incarcerated male felons in New York reported some form of childhood victimization. Generally speaking, the worse the victimization was, the worse the subsequent criminal career. Felons incarcerated for violent crimes reported significantly more physical abuse than nonviolent felons, and violent sexual predators reported the highest prevalence of childhood physical and sexual abuse. In sum, Janna Haapasalo and Elina Pokela examined several of the longitudinal studies reviewed in Chapter 2 and consistently found that family violence begets many problems, including the cultivation of what will become chronic criminal careers.[3]

Unlike the neoclassical stance of static theories that is explored in Chapter 4, the developmental perspective consults an array of theoretical perspectives from an assortment of disciplines, including early childhood development, developmental psychology, differential association, social learning, social control, strain, and labeling theories. This multidisciplinary approach has been crucial to establishing that home environments characterized by various degrees of abuse and neglect, erratic monitoring, cold affection, inconsistent or nonexistent disciplining,

---

Box 3.1   Risk Factors for Child Delinquency and Subsequent
                   Career Criminality

Child Factors

Difficult temperament
   Impulsive behavior

Hyperactivity
   (occurring with
   disruptive behavior)

Impulsivity

Substance use

Aggression

Early onset disruptive
   behaviors

Withdrawn behaviors

Low intelligence

Lead toxicity

Peer Factors

Association with delinquent
   siblings

Association with
   delinquent peers

Rejection by peers

School Factors

Poor academic performance

Old for grade

Weak bonding to school

Low educational aspirations

Low school motivation

Attends dysfunctional school

Neighborhood Factors

Neighborhood
   disadvantage/poverty
Disorganized
   neighborhoods

Availability of weapons
   practices
Poor supervision

Family Factors

Parental antisocial or
   delinquent behaviors

Parental substance abuse

---

coercion, and authoritarianism place children at risk for a myriad of problem behaviors.

As shown in Box 3.1, children exposed to these environments embody a variety of risk factors. Interpersonally, they tend to be hyperactive, fidgety, and prone to outbursts. As a result, they have a very difficult time staying on task and paying attention in school, a behavioral pattern that seriously jeopardizes their educational attainment. Teachers have described "problem children" as cheating, crafty, cruel, disobedient,

---

Box 3.1 (Continued)

Parents' poor child-rearing	Teenage motherhood
Media portrayal of violence	Parental disagreement on child discipline
Poor communication	Single parenthood
Physical punishment	Large family size
Poor parent-child relations	High turnover of caretakers
Parental physical and/or sexual abuse	Low family socioeconomic status
Parental neglect	Unemployed parent
Maternal depression	Poorly educated mother
Mother's smoking during pregnancy	Family access to weapons (especially guns)

SOURCE: Adapted from Loeber, R., & Farrington, D. P. (2001). The significance of child delinquency. In R. Loeber & D. P. Farrington (Eds.), *Child delinquents: Development, intervention, and service needs* (pp. 1-24). Thousand Oaks, CA: Sage.

---

impudent, lying, boredom-prone, and rude.4 Children who demonstrated these and other interpersonal characteristics were significantly likely to engage in criminal behavior well into adulthood.5 Indeed, severely adverse family environments can help engender the emotional deficiencies demonstrated by some of the worst chronic offenders—psychopaths. Sabine Herpertz and Henning Sass have suggested that children with poor emotional conditioning fail to appreciate the consequences of their actions, leading to a deficit of avoidance behavior. This emotional detachment compromises the child's ability to experience feelings such as guilt, which can inhibit violent impulses. Additionally, the emotional void contributes to underarousal or chronic boredom, leading to the need for inappropriate sensation-seeking.[6]

This chapter reviews some of the major developmental theories used in the study of career criminals, as well as some of the research that provides empirical support for the theories. Afterward, successful prevention efforts that are rooted in developmental theories are discussed.

Patterson's Coercion Theory

Beginning in the mid-1950s, Gerald Patterson and his colleagues at the Oregon Social Learning Center developed one of the earliest developmental models to study delinquent careers. Overall, Patterson suggested that parental monitoring behaviors determined a child's social and academic wherewithal. The appropriate inculcation of social skills influenced adolescent successes (e.g., strong attachment to school) and failures (e.g., resultant association with delinquent peers). Patterson was one of the first scholars to differentiate the two general classes of offenders: those whose onset occurred early in life and those whose onset occurred later in life. Early starters were exposed to inept, coercive, or authoritarian parenting. These experiences instilled an overall negativity or personal malaise that facilitated rejection by conventional peers, academic strife, anger, low self-esteem, and mental health problems such as depression. As early as fourth grade, these youth were identifiable for their academic failure and were especially prone to associate with (similarly situated) delinquent peers. Early starters often experienced an arrest or police contact by age 14 and were most likely to engage in chronic criminality.[7]

By comparison, chronic criminality was not expected from late starters—persons whose onset of delinquent involvement occurred after age 14. Late starters were normative delinquents who were particularly prone to the influences of delinquent peers if their parents poorly monitored their behavior. Indeed, for late-starting, "normal" delinquents, the significant relationship between delinquent peer association and delinquency is so robust that it has been found to mediate other known correlates of crime such as socioeconomic status. Patterson's theory has enjoyed a great deal of empirical support, and his approach has proven crucial in demonstrating the contributions of families and peers in producing delinquent behavior.[8]

Moffitt's Developmental Taxonomy

Like Patterson's work, Terrie Moffitt's developmental taxonomy posited that there were two discrete types of delinquents: adolescence-limited and life-course persistent offenders. Adolescence-limited offenders constitute the lion's share of delinquents; indeed, nearly 90% of offenders are this type. According to Moffitt, adolescence-limited offenders are able to stifle any antisocial impulses that they may have and are therefore generally law-abiding citizens. However, as their name implies, adolescence-limited offenders engage in delinquency for a brief period during their teen years. The impetus driving their deviance is the ambiguity of puberty and adolescent development. During this life phase, youth often have difficulty grappling with quickly changing expectations and responsibilities that are a function of age, such as obtaining a driver's license, dating, working, the demands of peer relationships, and the overall angst of being a teenager. By observing the delinquent behavior of serious delinquents, a process Moffitt refers to as social mimicry, adolescence-limited offenders ascertain that a certain level of autonomy and adult reinforcement comes from "bad" behavior. Indeed, recognition of their emerging adult status is the primary motivation for delinquent behavior. As such, their delinquency encompasses benign, low-level offenses such as underage use of alcohol, marijuana use, shoplifting, and vandalism that serve to push adult status. Indeed, a recent empirical assessment of adolescence-limited offenders found that, as theorized by Moffitt, they engaged in rebellious but not violent forms of delinquency during the difficult stages of puberty.[9]

Life-course persistent offenders have received much more empirical attention because they are the most threatening to society. Like adolescence-limited offenders, the delinquency of life-course persistent offenders develops, albeit along a different trajectory. According to Moffitt, two types of neuropsychological defects, verbal and executive functions, give rise to an assortment of antisocial behaviors. Verbal functions include reading ability, receptive listening, problem-solving skill, memory, speech articulation, and writing—in short, verbal intelligence. Executive functions relate to behavioral deportment, such as inattention, hyperactivity, and impulsivity. Children with these neuropsychological deficits are restless, fidgety, destructive, and noncompliant, and employ violent outbursts in lieu of conversation. Such a profile clearly matches the behavioral repertoire of children with attention deficit hyperactivity disorder (ADHD). Empirical evidence demonstrates that 80% of the variation in ADHD is explained by biological or genetic factors.[10]

Two additional, concomitant circumstances disadvantage children who demonstrate some traits of life-course persistent offenders. First, children are likely to resemble their parents in terms of temperament, personality, and cognitive ability. Thus, the parents of life-course persistent offenders are themselves poorly tempered, impulsive, and prone to use violence to resolve disputes, a cycle that further exacerbates the effects of neuropsychological defects. Second, life-course persistent offenders are raised in home environments that are often impoverished by material, social, and health standards. A host of pre- and perinatal factors influence ADHD and the antisocial syndrome that life-course persistent offenders embody. These factors include exposure to alcohol, nicotine, and other illicit substances during pregnancy; obstetric care; low birth weight; and complications during delivery. Health factors co-occur with social variables related to family structure, family processes, and involvement in conventional activities. Indeed, a substantial literature indicates that childhood material disadvantage and troublesome home environments are closely linked.[11]

Once thrust into impoverished circumstances, the life-course persistent offender continually behaves poorly and faces consequences that narrowly limit the options for future success. As Moffitt stated in the original conceptualization of the taxonomy, the behavioral repertoire of the life-course persistent offender is limited to negativity and rejection, and the continuity in his behavior reflects this. Scholars have found that life-course persistent offenders often suffered adverse childhoods, demonstrated an array of problematic and antisocial behaviors, and generally led lives of crime and involvement with the criminal justice system.[12] Their pathology was pronounced at all stages of life.

Sampson and Laub's Age-Graded Theory of Informal Social Control and Cumulative Disadvantage

The dominant developmental theoretical perspective is Robert Sampson and John Laub's age-graded theory of informal social control. Their thesis is that informal social controls—such as involvement in family, work, and school—mediate structural context and explain criminal involvement, even in the face of the underlying level of criminal propensity. Like static theorists, Sampson and Laub acknowledge that individuals differ in their underlying criminal propensity and in how likely they are to place themselves in troublesome or criminogenic situations. Unlike others, they acknowledge that individuals garner variable amounts of social capital from informal social control networks; this social capital, in turn, explains the continuity in antisocial behaviors across various life stages. Persons with low social capital (and past criminal involvement) mortgage their future life chances—a process referred to as the cumulative continuity of disadvantage. On the other hand, prosocial adult social bonds or turning points can "right" previously deviant pathways such as juvenile delinquency, unemployment, and substance abuse and place an individual onto a trajectory toward more successful outcomes. Unlike the static theories that are criticized for being overly simplistic and deterministic, Sampson and Laub's theory stresses that change or dynamism characterizes criminal careers because even the most active offender desists over the life course. For instance, 60-year-old criminals are not as active and violent as they were at age 17. Theories must, then, be able to account for these changes.[13]

Sampson and Laub's thesis has received a great deal of attention and spawned additional research programs across the United States. Their own research applies modern statistical methods to the archival data of 500 officially defined delinquents and a matched sample of 500 nondelinquents originally collected by Sheldon and Eleanor Glueck. Overall, they have found that family processes (e.g., the amount of maternal supervision, parental discipline style, and attachment to parents) are among the most robust predictors of chronic criminality. These family variables largely mediated background social class factors and predicted delinquency even when considering the antisocial dispositions of children and their parents.[14] Even though Sampson and Laub's theory stressed the importance of proximal adult sociality, they did not ignore the profound implications of childhood antisocial behavior. Indeed, they found that childhood antisociality was predictive of an array of deviance in adulthood; however, these relationships were rendered spurious once adult social bonds were considered. In their words, "Adult social bonds not only have important effects on adult crime in and of themselves, but help to explain the probabilistic links in the chain connecting early childhood differences and later adult crime."[15]

Several scholars have developed and tested life-course models based on Sampson and Laub's theoretical ideas. Using data from an ongoing panel study of 451 Iowa families, Ronald Simons and his colleagues examined the effects of association with deviant peers, socioeconomic status, parenting techniques, and oppositional/defiant disorder on delinquency. They found that late starters, who represent the preponderance of persons engaging in delinquency after age 14, followed a developmental sequence. Specifically, they found that antisocial adolescents who were in strong marriages were significantly less involved in crime than their peers who were single or in problematic marriages. They argue for "consideration of the manner in which peer friendships, as well as other social relationships, may operate to amplify or moderate the antisocial tendencies fostered by ineffectual parental behavior."[16] Similarly, others have found that the salience of criminal propensity measured by childhood and adolescent misconduct tended to disappear once the effects of family, school, and peers were considered. This suggests that informal social control networks are more important than latent traits of deviance in explaining delinquency.[17]

Thornberry's Interactional Theory

Terence Thornberry's interactional theory is another important developmental approach. From Thornberry's perspective, it is vital for academicians to recognize that all human behavior occurs in the context of some social interaction. Social interaction affects everyone and is complex, overlapping, and multidirectional, or reciprocal. In terms of criminological research, scholars need to be cognizant that although independent variables such as association with delinquent peers may predict delinquency-based dependent variables, dependent variables can also influence and predict independent variables. For example, children who are attached to their parents are likely to harbor conventional values and beliefs (of course, provided that the parents are not inculcating antisocial values and beliefs) and thus be committed to school. Over time, a serious commitment to school will bolster the child's support of conventional beliefs and solidify relationships with parents who, at the same time, are pleased with their child's commitment to school. Alternately, children who are not committed to school are likely to weaken their relationship with their parents and are even more likely to initiate or strengthen relationships with peers who are also not committed to school. The processes of prosociality and antisociality are constantly in flux, overlapping, and in the process of development.[18]

These ideas have subsequently been supported empirically with data from the Rochester Youth Development Study, a panel study of middle-school children from Rochester, New York. As conceptualized, school and family bonding variables were found to predict delinquency, which in turn weakened school and family bonding.[19] Once involvement in delinquency has begun, its interactional effects are often difficult for youth to overcome. Delinquent behavior and association with delinquent peers have a synergistic effect whereby antisocial or delinquent beliefs become increasingly important to the youth. In other words, their delinquent beliefs and persona become hardened, further impacting what types of people delinquent youth are willing to associate with. For this reason, desisting from crime is a process, not a discrete event, whereby offenders gradually transition from a social network centered on delinquency to one centered on conventional behavior. Most important for developmental theory, these assorted research findings demonstrate that one's involvement in social institutions such as family, school, and work is directly, indirectly, and variably related to delinquency. Moreover, they indicate that there is substantial behavioral change and responsiveness to parents, peers, and social institutions *within* individuals as they pass through adolescence.[20]

Social Development Model

Since 1981, Richard Catalano, David Hawkins, Joseph Weis, and other researchers at the University of Washington have been conducting the Seattle Social Development Project, a prospective longitudinal panel study of 808 respondents who were enrolled in fifth grade in 1985 from 18 Seattle public elementary schools. The panel study is informed by their social development model, which claims that the causes of delinquency are complex, multifaceted, and ultimately the outcome of an individual's journey along overlapping pro- and antisocial paths. The social development model is rooted in the integrated theoretical traditions of differential association, social control, and social learning and focuses on four specific periods of development: preschool, elementary school, middle school, and high school. According to the theory, socializing agents such as family, school, peers, and others teach and inculcate "good" and "bad" behaviors to children. At each and every stage of development, children demonstrate or are faced with risk and protective factors toward delinquency. The social development model asserts that four constructs constitute the socialization processes occurring via the above social institutions: opportunities for involvement in activities and interactions with others, the degree of involvement and interaction, the skills to participate in these involvements and interactions, and the reinforcement forthcoming from performance in activities and interactions.[21]

An interesting feature of the social development model is its explicit focus on developmental processes across various stages of childhood development for all types of persons. In other words, the theory views antisocial behavior and the risks for it generally and not prescriptively for high-risk or pathological groups. Consequently, some of the empirical tests of the social development model are slightly at odds with the claims of other developmental theories. For example, researchers have found that the theory is applicable or generalizable to males, females, and children from divergent social class backgrounds.[22] Although it is well known that these groups have differential involvement in antisocial offending and victimization, the processes by which they are exposed to or protected from delinquency reflect commonality, not difference, in development. Similarly, scholars have found that children in whom onset occurred at different ages nevertheless followed similar developmental patterns toward violent behavior at adulthood. In support of the theory, it suggests that proximal developmental patterns of normal youthful development and not the independent effect of onset are more salient to the prediction of delinquency. Overall, the social development model has a systemic quality that speaks to the delinquencies and conventional behaviors of many social groups.[23] Moreover, the theory is heavily geared toward delinquency prevention, and its authors have painstakingly identified the mechanisms by which social institutions and socialization agents promote healthy (e.g., protective factors) and maladaptive (e.g., exposure to risk factors) development.

To summarize, several research programs around the country have developed and tested models that promulgate a developmental perspective. This approach, steeped in the social learning/differential association tradition, questions the deterministic or ontogenetic nature of static theory. Instead, it suggests that offending careers develop and change over time and are susceptible to the effects of normal social processes (e.g., marriage, employment, the military), regardless of an individual's underlying criminal propensity. Both pro- and antisocial developments are contingent on the interconnections between early family development (e.g., parenting styles, punishment, and monitoring), social and academic success, and peer associations. Exposure to adverse family environments is inversely related to the risk for chronic delinquency. Overall, the developmental perspective is more complex, theoretically integrative, and amenable to the rehabilitative goals of policy.

Developmental Theory in Action: A Review of Some Successful Prevention Policies

It is frequently the case that adult career criminals were themselves exposed to severe abuses and deprivation from very early in life. Indeed, some public sentiment is characterized by a "What did we expect?" belief about the effects of early life abuses on subsequent violence and criminal behavior. This leads many observers to wring their hands in resignation, convinced that nothing can be done to stem the actions of habitual criminals. Fortunately, this is not the case. For example, Mark Lipsey recently reviewed the literature on programs that target serious delinquents, concluding that

> the average effect on the recidivism of serious juvenile offenders of those interventions studied is positive, statistically significant, and, though modest, not trivial . . . this evidence shows that optimal combinations of program elements have the capability to reduce recidivism by 40-50 percent, that is, to cut recidivism rates to nearly half of what they would be without such programming.[24]

Over the past few decades, several prevention studies have produced promising and oftentimes staggering results in reducing recidivism and related antisocial behaviors among children and youth who either were already on a career criminal trajectory or embodied multiple risk factors for engaging in a life of crime. Moreover, the external validity of these studies is bolstered by their experimental designs whereby participants are randomly assigned to experimental or control groups. Treatment effects produced by such designs are sounder methodologically and less susceptible to errors related to research design, sample composition, and measurement.

Although some developmental theorists, such as Sampson and Laub, acknowledge the idea of individual criminal propensity, they are more likely to view the onset of antisocial behavior as a product of social processes, not the ineluctable manifestation of some innate pathology. Thus, the reason that youth begin to demonstrate wayward behavior is negative conditions in their home life. For this reason, prevention efforts seek to create, instill, cultivate, and enable conventional attitudes, beliefs, and behaviors in the lives of antisocial youth and their families while reducing, denying, or destroying antisocial attitudes, beliefs, and behaviors. Most of the studies targeted poor, single, adolescent mothers and their families because they demonstrated the most risk factors. The goal of prevention, in short, is to promote protective factors and extinguish risk factors.

As previously mentioned, the social development model used by researchers at the University of Washington is noteworthy because its theoretical rationale is explicitly connected to prevention efforts.

Recalling the risk factors in Box 3.1, the strategy of this model is to provide healthy beliefs and clear standards for behavior in families, schools, and the community toward the promotion of healthy (i.e., non-criminal) behavior in children. Community institutions that are dedicated to healthy, conventional behavior can provide the motivation that youth need to protect them from exposure to risk. Children who are bonded to those who hold healthy beliefs do not want to threaten that bond by behaving in ways that would jeopardize their relationships and investments.[25] Empirically, this approach appears to work. David Hawkins, Richard Catalano, and their colleagues employed this multipronged approach by using the Catch Them Being Good program on a sample of 458 first graders from 21 classes across eight schools in the Seattle area. Children were randomly assigned to the full-treatment group (receiving interventions from Grades 1 through 6), late-intervention group (receiving interventions in Grades 5 and 6), or control group and followed until adulthood. Predictably, youth receiving social support were significantly less involved in delinquency, substance abuse, and related deviance.[26]

Although a multi-institutional approach is needed for successful prevention efforts, it is clear that the most important social institution for the production of pro- and antisocial values, beliefs, and behaviors is the family. School and community effects are ancillary to what transpires in the lives of children from the prenatal stage to early childhood. Given space constraints, some of the model treatment and prevention programs geared specifically toward the family are reviewed here.[27]

Strategies That Help to Forestall Career Criminality

Perhaps the most famous prevention study that demonstrated the long-term effects of early life interventions on a high-risk sample is the Nurse-Family Partnership program that was supervised by David Olds and his colleagues. The Olds Study, as it is commonly referred to, used a sample of 400 women and 315 infants who were born in upstate New York between April 1978 and September 1980. The mothers in the sample posed a variety of risk factors for their children to adopt delinquency. All were unmarried, 48% were younger than age 15, and 59% lived in poverty. Via random assignment to four groups receiving various social services, the comprehensive experimental group received 9 home visits during pregnancy and 23 home visits from nurses from birth until the child's second birthday. Control participants received standard but less comprehensive prenatal care. All groups were followed up 15 years later. The results were impressive in the reduction of a variety of problem behaviors associated with chronic delinquency. Compared to those in the control group, boys who were in the treatment groups had a lower incidence of running away, accumulated significantly fewer arrests and convictions, accrued fewer probationary sentences and subsequent violations, had fewer lifetime sexual partners, and had a lower prevalence of smoking, alcoholism, and casual alcohol use. In short, the experiment offered compelling evidence that early-life interventions teaching parents the skills they need to raise healthy children were achievable.[28]

The Nurse-Family Partnership program is one of the model prevention programs in the country and is part of the Blueprints for Violence Prevention Program at the Center for the Study and Prevention of Violence at the University of Colorado at Boulder. The Blueprints for Violence Prevention Program is a national violence prevention initiative that identifies programs that meet the most scientifically rigorous standards of program effectiveness. They have found that the nurse visits in the Olds Study resulted in 79% fewer verified reports of child abuse and neglect; 31% fewer subsequent births and increased intervals between births; a 30-month reduction in the receipt of Aid to Families with Dependent Children, a social welfare subsidy; 44% fewer maternal behavioral problems due to substance abuse; 69% fewer maternal arrests; and 56% fewer child arrests. Most impressive from a policy perspective, the costs of the program, approximately $3,200 per family annually, were recouped by the child's fourth birthday.[29]

Additional studies have also proved effective in promoting healthy and conventional behaviors and reducing criminal behaviors in at-risk infants and toddlers. The Syracuse University Family Development Research Project offered weekly home visits that contained nutritional, health, child-care, human services, and educational resources to low-income families from pregnancy until the elementary school years of the children. Sixty-five families constituted the experimental group and 54 families were in the control group. Children in the treatment group were significantly less likely to be involved in the juvenile and criminal justice systems than youth from the control group. Specifically, they were nearly four times less likely to garner delinquency convictions, and the prevalence of chronic delinquency among boys was reduced by nearly 50%.[30]

The High/Scope Perry Preschool Project targeted poor, African American 3- and 4-year-olds who scored between 60 and 90 on IQ tests. The study employed 121 children, 58 of whom were randomized to the intervention group and 63 of whom were assigned to the control group. Children in the treatment group received weekly home visits from preschool teachers, who provided educational programming while parents received informational and emotional support to increase their parenting skills. Parents also participated in monthly meetings to follow up on the educational curriculum being provided. Follow-ups occurred until the child's 27th birthday. Across an array of outcome measures, the treatment participants enjoyed significantly healthier and more successful lives than those in the control group. Children who received early intervention had greater academic success based on grades and standardized tests, were less likely to repeat a grade level or require special education instruction, were more likely to graduate high school and be employed, and were less likely to receive welfare. Moreover, youth in the treatment group were five times less likely to be arrested, in addition to being five times less likely to become a chronic criminal offender.[31]

In addition to the successes of prevention programs that target infants, toddlers, and their families, other studies have also proved effective at reducing antisocial behavior among children with pronounced behavioral problems. Like the aforementioned studies, these programs are multifaceted and offer treatments not only to the antisocial child but also to the parents, other family members, and teachers. Unlike the other studies, which seek to promote protective factors among those who face multiple risk factors, these programs face the uphill challenge of reducing antisocial behavior that has already been observed. One of the best at accomplishing this is the Incredible Years Parent, Teacher, and Child Training Series developed by Dr. Carolyn Webster-Stratton. The Incredible Years is a comprehensive social competence program that treats conduct problems in children aged 2 to 8. In six randomized trials, aggression and conduct problems have been reduced by 60% among the participating children and families. Other promising outcomes were increased academic competence and achievement, increased sociability and friendship-making skills, anger management and problem solving, and increased empathy among previously problem youth.[32] In fact, the Incredible Years program is one of the model prevention programs in the United States.[33]

Multisystemic Therapy (MST) is a family- and community-based treatment program that seeks to address the multiple-problem needs of seriously antisocial youth aged 12 to 17. Like all of the theories described in this chapter, the multisystemic approach views individuals as nested within a complex network of interconnected systems that encompass family, peer, school, and neighborhood domains. The major objective of MST is to empower parents and youth with the skills and resources needed to surmount risk factors and capitalize on protective opportunities. These empowerments include strategic family therapy, structural family therapy, behavioral parent training, and cognitive behavior therapies over a 4-month period. Despite the difficulties inherent in treating seriously antisocial people, preliminary evaluations of MST have shown 25% to 70% reductions in rearrest and 47% to 64% reductions in out-of-home placements. Additionally, serious juvenile offenders often experience fewer mental health problems. Because mental health problems contribute to substance abuse, MST can also help in addressing substance abuse. At a cost of a mere $4,500 per youth, MST has been ranked as the country's most cost-effective program targeting serious juvenile offenders.[34]

Early intervention efforts have not been limited to the United States, of course. For example, Richard Tremblay and his collaborators examined the effects of parent and child training on the emergence of antisocial behavior using participants from the Montreal Longitudinal-Experimental Study. From a sample of 319 kindergarten males with severely disruptive behavior, 96 boys from 46 families received 2 years of school-based social skills training while their parents received a home-based program that included instruction on monitoring their child's behavior, effective reinforcement and punishment strategies, family crisis management, and other skills. The remaining boys and their families were placed in control groups. Behavioral ratings for all youth were secured from teachers, peers, mothers, and the boys themselves, with follow-up for 3 years. Treated boys manifested 50% less physical aggression in school, had less serious school adjustment problems, reported fewer delinquent behaviors, and were more likely to be in age-appropriate classrooms than control boys.[35]

Across cultures, parenting of infants and toddlers is the most important factor in producing either healthy and functioning children or unhealthy and antisocial children. Consequently, Nurturing Parenting Programs (NPPs) have been implemented in several countries across Europe and South America, in addition to Canada, Mexico, and Israel. Within the United States, NPPs have been developed to reach the potentially special needs of Hmong, African American, and Hispanic families. The NPPs

---

Box 3.2   Summary of Program Benefits

Outcome Variable	Benefits
Delinquency/crime	Savings to criminal justice system Tangible and intangible costs to crime victims avoided (e.g., medical care, damaged and lost property, lost wages, lost quality of life, pain, suffering) Tangible and intangible costs to family members of crime victims avoided (e.g., funeral expenses, lost wages, lost quality of life)
Substance abuse	Savings to criminal justice system Improved health

---

target families at risk for abuse and neglect, families identified by local social service providers as abusive or neglectful, families in recovery for alcohol and other drug abuse, parents incarcerated for crimes against society, and adults seeking to become adoptive or foster parents. An evaluation conducted by the National Institute of Mental Health examined the effectiveness of NPPs among 121 abusive adults and 150 abused children from Indiana, Minnesota, Ohio, Pennsylvania, and Wisconsin. They found that 93% of the adults successfully modified their previously abusive parenting techniques. Only 7% failed the program and committed new acts of child abuse. Overall, parents reported being more empathetic to their child's needs and development and also showed improvements on cognitive ability, enthusiasm, self-assurance, and self-confidence. After treatment, parents reported reduced incidence of anxiety, radical behavior, and having a poor attitude. Similarly, formerly abused children improved their self-image, happiness, and expectations of conventional parenting. That is, they learned that abuse was wrong and not a tolerable aspect of childhood. As a whole, the families were more cohesive, expressive, organized, harmonious, and moral after the NPP. Undoubtedly, healthier families reduce the likelihood that early home environments will be characterized as abusive breeding grounds for multiple problem behaviors.[36] A summary of the benefits of these programs appears in Box 3.2.

Box 3.2 (Continued)

Education	Improved educational output (e.g., high school completion, enrollment in college or university)
	Reduced schooling costs (e.g., remedial classes, support services)
Employment	Increased wages (tax revenue for government)
	Decreased use of welfare services
Health	Decreased use of public health care (e.g., fewer visits to hospital and clinic)
	Improved mental health
Family factors	Fewer childbirths to at-risk women
	More parental time spent with children
	Fewer divorces and separations

SOURCE: Adapted from Welsh, B. C. (2001). Economic costs and benefits of early developmental prevention. In R. Loeber & D. P. Farrington (Eds.), *Child delinquents: Development, intervention, and service needs* (pp. 339-354). Thousand Oaks, CA: Sage.

Summary

Developmental theories showcase the dynamism that characterizes human lives. They recognize, quantify, and seek to explain the often dramatic, within-individual changes in antisocial behavior across various points of life. In this sense, individuals can serve as their own controls while gauging the effects that the social world has on their conduct. Developmental theories do not ignore constitutional factors such as criminal propensity or stable traits such as aggression. To the contrary, they use these very constructs, frequently interpreted as static characteristics, to demonstrate the changeability of behavior and its susceptibility to context. Thus, an array of scholars employing data from various local and national data sets have found that human development events, turning points, short-term life events, or local life circumstances are often more meaningful explanations of crime than prior record, criminal propensity, or level of self-control.[37] Mundane processes such as going to bed at a reasonable hour to wake up early for work, enrolling in and attending school, initiating a romantic relationship, or getting married (particularly when the partner does not drink, use drugs, or engage in crime) provide the incremental structures whereby the informal social controls specific to these adult responsibilities take effect. These contexts and processes shape, harness, or reduce whatever impulses, criminal or otherwise, we have. John Laub and Robert Sampson once wrote that adult lives were not merely settings within which predetermined lives were played out.[38] Indeed, life is development and change.

Development begins at conception; thus, it is never too early to intervene in the lives of those who suffer from multiple risk factors for chronic delinquency or who already use antisocial behavior as their typical mode of conduct. This encompasses many domains. Prenatal and obstetric care is critical for all mothers, especially teenagers with few resources and little social support. Parenting infants and toddlers is challenging and has endless implications, not the least of which is sending a youth along a trajectory with healthy and antisocial opportunities. When schools, peer networks, neighbors, and other social institutions are on board, the mission of rearing healthy children, not deviant ones, is more likely to be achieved. When successful, the lives of today's defiant and violent children can be saved for the greater good; when unsuccessful, the lives of today's defiant and violent children likely degenerate, and they become tomorrow's career criminals.

Notes

1. Nagin, D. S., & Paternoster, R. (2000). Population heterogeneity and state dependence: State of evidence and directions for future research. *Journal of Quantitative Criminology, 16,* 117-144.

2. Gottfredson, M. R., & Hirschi, T. (1990). *A general theory of crime.* Stanford, CA: Stanford University Press (p. 97).

3. Farrington, D. P., & Loeber, R. (1999). Transatlantic replicability of risk factors in the development of delinquency. In P. Cohen & C. Slomkowski (Eds.), *Historical and geographical influences on psychopathology* (pp. 299-329). Mahwah, NJ: Lawrence Erlbaum; Weeks, R., & Widom, C. S. (1998). Self-reports of early childhood victimization among incarcerated adult male felons. *Journal of Interpersonal Violence, 13,* 346-361; Haapasalo, J., & Pokela, E. (1999). Child-rearing and child

abuse antecedents of criminality. *Aggression and Violent Behavior, 4,* 107-127. For explicit investigations of the family effects, criminal transmission, and crime, see Farrington, D. P. (1989). Early predictors of adolescent aggression and adult violence. *Violence & Victims, 4,* 79-100; Farrington, D. P., & West, D. J. (1993). Criminal, penal, and life histories of chronic offenders: Risk and protective factors and early identification. *Criminal Behavior & Mental Health, 3,* 492-523; Juby, H., & Farrington, D. P. (2001). Disentangling the link between disrupted families and delinquency. *British Journal of Criminology, 41,* 22-40; Nagin, D. S., Pogarsky, G., & Farrington, D. P. (1997). Adolescent mothers and the criminal behavior of their children. *Law & Society Review, 31,* 127-162; Pogarsky, G., Lizotte, A. J., & Thornberry, T. P. (2003). The delinquency of children born to young mothers: Results from the Rochester Youth Development Study. *Criminology, 41,* 1249-1286.

4. McCord, J. (2000). Developmental trajectories and intentional actions. *Journal of Quantitative Criminology, 16,* 237-253.

5. For example, see Farrington, D. P. (2000). Psychosocial predictors of adult antisocial personality and adult convictions. *Behavioral Sciences & the Law, 18,* 605-622; Herrnstein, R. J. (1995). Criminogenic traits. In J. Q. Wilson & J. Petersilia (Eds.), *Crime* (pp. 39-63). San Francisco: ICS Press.

6. Herpertz, S. C., & Sass, H. (2000). Emotional deficiency and psychopathy. *Behavioral Sciences & the Law, 18,* 567-580.

7. Patterson, G. R. (1986). Performance models for antisocial boys. *American Psychologist, 41,* 432-444; Patterson, G. R. (1995). Coercion as a basis for early age of onset for arrest. In J. McCord (Ed.), *Coercion and punishment in long-term perspectives* (pp. 81-105). New York: Cambridge University Press; Patterson, G. R., & Southamer-Loeber, M. (1984). The correlation of family management practices and delinquency. *Child Development, 55,* 1299-1307.

8. Patterson, G. R., & Dishion, T. J. (1985). Contributions of families and peers to delinquency. *Criminology, 23,* 63-79; Patterson, G. R., DeBaryshe, B. D., & Ramsey, E. (1989). A developmental perspective on antisocial behavior. *American Psychologist, 44,* 329-335; Patterson, G. R., & Yoerger, K. (1995). Two different models for adolescent physical trauma and for early arrest. *Criminal Behavior & Mental Health, 5,* 411-423.

9. Nagin, D. S., Farrington, D. P., & Moffitt, T. E. (1995). Life-course trajectories of different types of offenders. *Criminology, 33,* 111-139; Piquero, A. R., & Brezina, T. (2001). Testing Moffitt's account of adolescence-limited delinquency. *Criminology, 39,* 353-370; McCabe, K. M., Hough, R., Wood, P. A., & Yeh, M. (2001). Childhood and adolescent onset conduct disorder: A test of the developmental taxonomy. *Journal of Abnormal Child Psychology, 29,* 305-316.

10. Moffitt, T. E. (1990). Juvenile delinquency and attention deficit disorder: Boys' development trajectories from age 3 to age 15. *Child Development, 61,* 893-910; Pratt, T. C., Cullen, F. T., Blevins, K. R., Daigle, L., & Unnever, J. D. (2002). The relationship of attention deficit hyperactivity disorder to crime and delinquency: A meta-analysis. *International Journal of Police Science & Management, 4,* 344-360.

11.   Farrington, D. P., Barnes, G., & Lambert, S. (1996). The concentration of offending in families. *Legal and Criminological Psychology, 1,* 47-63; Henry, B., Moffitt, T. E., Robins, L., & Earls, F. (1993). Early family predictors of child and adolescent antisocial behavior: Who are the mothers of delinquents? *Criminal Behavior & Mental Health, 3,* 97-118; Henry, B., Caspi, A., Moffitt, T. E., & Silva, P. A. (1996). Temperamental and familial predictors of violent and nonviolent criminal convictions: Age 3 to age 18. *Developmental Psychology, 32,* 614-623; Loeber, R., & Farrington, D. P. (2000). Young children who commit crime: Epidemiology, developmental origins, risk factor, early interventions, and policy implications. *Developmental and Psychopathology, 12,* 737-762; Maughan, B., Pickles, A., Rowe, R., Costello, E. J., & Angold, A. (2000). Developmental trajectories of aggressive and non-aggressive conduct problems. *Journal of Quantitative Criminology, 16,* 199-221. Robins, L. N., & O'Neal, P. (1958). Mortality, mobility, and crime: Problem children thirty years later. *American Sociological Review, 23,* 162-171; Robins, L. N., & Wish, E. (1977). Childhood deviance as a developmental process. *Social Forces, 56,* 448-473.

12.   For example, see DeLisi, M. (2001). Scaling archetypal criminals. *American Journal of Criminal Justice, 26,* 77-92; Gibson, G. L., Piquero, A. R., & Tibbetts, S. G. (2001). The contribution of family adversity and verbal IQ to criminal behavior. *International Journal of Offender Therapy and Comparative Criminology, 45,* 574-592; Kratzer, L., & Hodgins, S. (1999). The typology of offenders: A test of Moffitt's theory among males and females from childhood to age 30. *Criminal Behavior & Mental Health, 9,* 57-73; Krueger, R. F., Schmutte, P. S., Caspi, A., Moffitt, T. E., Campbell, C., & Silva, P. A. (1994). Personality traits are linked to crime among men and women: Evidence from a birth cohort. *Journal of Abnormal Psychology, 103,* 328-338. Krueger, R. F., Caspi, A., & Moffitt, T. E. (2000). Epidemiological personology: The unifying role of personality in population-based research on problem behaviors. *Journal of Personality, 68,* 967-998; Moffitt, T. E., Lynam, D., & Silva, P. A. (1994). Neuropsychological tests predicting persistent male delinquency. *Criminology, 32,* 277-300; Piquero, A. R. (2001). Testing Moffitt's neuropsychological variation hypothesis for the prediction of life-course persistent offending. *Psychology, Crime & Law, 7,* 193-215.

13.   Sampson, R. J., & Laub, J. H. (1993). *Crime in the making: Pathways and turning points through life.* Cambridge, MA: Harvard University Press; Sampson, R. J., & Laub, J. H. (2003). Life-course desisters? Trajectories of crime among delinquent boys followed to age 70. *Criminology, 41,* 555-592.

14.   Laub, J. H., & Sampson, R. J. (1988). Unraveling families and delinquency: A reanalysis of the Gluecks' data. *Criminology, 26,* 355-380; Sampson, R. J., & Laub, J. H. (1994). Urban poverty and the family context of delinquency: A new look at structure and process in a classic study. *Child Development, 65,* 523-540.

15.   Laub, J. H., & Sampson, R. J. (1993). Turning points in the life course: Why change matters to the study of crime. *Criminology, 31,* 301-326 (p. 320); see also Sampson, R. J., & Laub, J. H. (1990). Crime and deviance over the life course: The salience of adult social bonds. *American Sociological Review, 55,* 609-627.

16. Simons, R. L., Wu, C., Conger, R. D., & Lorenz, F. O. (1994). Two routes to delinquency: Differences between early and late starters in the impact of parenting and deviant peers. *Criminology, 32,* 247-276 (p. 269).

17. Simons, R. L., Johnson, C., Conger, R. D., & Elder, G. (1998). A test of latent trait versus life-course perspectives on the stability of adolescent antisocial behavior. *Criminology, 36,* 901-927; Warr, M. (1998). Life-course transitions and desistance from crime. *Criminology, 36,* 183-216; Wright, B. R. E., Caspi, A., Moffitt, T. E., & Silva, P. A. (1999). Low self-control, social bonds, and crime: Social causation, social selection, or both? *Criminology, 37,* 479-514; Wright, B. R. E., Caspi, A., Moffitt, T. E., & Silva, P. A. (2001). The effects of social ties on crime vary by criminal propensity: A life-course model of interdependence. *Criminology, 39,* 321-352. A Canadian perspective on the developmental control perspective appears in Ouimet, M., & Le Blanc, M. (1996). The role of life experiences in the continuation of the adult criminal career. *Criminal Behavior & Mental Health, 6,* 73-97.

18. Thornberry, T. P. (1987). Toward an interactional theory of delinquency. *Criminology, 25,* 863-892.

19. Thornberry, T. P., Lizotte, A. J., Krohn, M. D., Farnworth, M., & Jang, S. J. (1991). Testing interactional theory: An examination of reciprocal causal relationships among family, school, and delinquency. *Journal of Criminal Law and Criminology, 82,* 3-35.

20. Bushway, S. D., Thornberry, T. P., & Krohn, M. D. (2003). Desistance as a developmental process: A comparison of static and dynamic approaches. *Journal of Quantitative Criminology, 19,* 129-153; Jang, S. J. (1999). Age-varying effects of family, school, and peers on delinquency: A multilevel modeling test of interactional theory. *Criminology, 37,* 643-686; Ireland, T. O., Smith, C. A., & Thornberry, T. P. (2002). Developmental issues in the impact of child maltreatment on later delinquency and drug use. *Criminology, 40,* 359-400; Thornberry, T. P., Lizotte, A. J., Krohn, M. D., Farnworth, M., & Jang, S. J. (1994). Delinquent peers, beliefs, and delinquent behavior: A longitudinal test of interactional theory. *Criminology, 32,* 47-83.

21. Catalano, R. F., & Hawkins, J. D. (1996). The social development model: A theory of antisocial behavior. In J. D. Hawkins (Ed.), *Delinquency and crime: Current theories* (pp. 149-197). New York: Cambridge University Press; Hawkins, J. D., & Weis, J. G. (1985). The social development model: An integrated approach to delinquency prevention. *Journal of Primary Prevention, 6,* 73-97.

22. Fleming, C. B., Catalano, R. F., Oxford, M. L., & Harachi, T. W. (2002). A test of the generalizability of the social development model across gender and income groups with longitudinal data from the elementary school developmental periods. *Journal of Quantitative Criminology, 18,* 423-439.

23. Ayers, C. D., Williams, J. H., Hawkins, J. D., Peterson, P. L., Catalano, R. F., & Abbott, R. D. (1999). Assessing correlates of onset, escalation, de-escalation, and desistance of delinquent behavior. *Journal of Quantitative Criminology, 15,* 277-306; Hartwell, S. W. (2000). Juvenile delinquency and the social development model: The retrospective accounts of homeless substance abusers. *Criminal Justice Policy*

Review, 11, 217-233; Herrenkohl, T. I., Huang, B., Kosterman, R., Hawkins, J. D., Catalano, R. F., & Smith, B. H. (2001). A comparison of social development processes leading to violent behavior in late adolescence for childhood initiators and adolescent initiators of violence. *Journal of Research in Crime and Delinquency, 38,* 45-63; Huang, B., Kosterman, R., Catalano, R. F., Hawkins, J. D., & Abbott, R. D. (2001). Modeling mediation in the etiology of violent behavior in adolescence: A test of the social development model. *Criminology, 39,* 75-108.

24.   Lipsey, M. W. (1999). Can intervention rehabilitate serious delinquents? *Annals of the American Academy of Political and Social Science, 564,* 142-166 (p. 163).

25.   Hawkins, J. D., Catalano, R. F., & Brewer, D. D. (1995). Preventing serious, violent, and chronic juvenile offending: Effective strategies from conception to age 6. In J. C. Howell, B. Krisberg, J. D. Hawkins, & J. J. Wilson (Eds.), *Serious, violent, & chronic juvenile offenders* (pp. 47-60). Thousand Oaks, CA: Sage (p. 51).

26.   Hawkins, J. D., von Cleve, E., & Catalano, R. F. (1991). Reducing early childhood aggression: Results of a primary prevention program. *Journal of the American Academy of Child and Adolescent Psychiatry, 30,* 208-217; Hawkins, J. D., Catalano, R. F., Kosterman, R., Abbott, R., & Hill, K. G. (1999). Preventing adolescent health risk behaviors by strengthening protection during childhood. *Archives of Pediatrics and Adolescent Medicine, 153,* 226-234.

27.   For exhaustive reviews of intervention programs geared toward school, family, and community implementation, see Greenwood, P. W. (2002). Juvenile crime and juvenile justice. In J. Q. Wilson & J. Petersilia (Eds.), *Crime: Public policies for crime control* (pp. 75-108). Oakland, CA: ICS Press; Howell, J. C., Krisberg, B., Hawkins, J. D., & Wilson, J. J. (Eds.). (1995). *Serious, violent, & chronic juvenile offenders.* Thousand Oaks, CA: Sage; Loeber, R., & Farrington, D. P. (Eds.). (1998). *Serious & violent juvenile offenders: Risk factors and successful interventions.* Thousand Oaks, CA: Sage; Mihalic, S., Irwin, K., Elliott, D. S., Fagan, A., & Hansen, D. (2001). *Blueprints for violence prevention.* Washington, DC: U.S. Department of Justice, Office of Justice Programs, Office of Juvenile Justice and Delinquency Prevention.

28.   Olds, D., Henderson, C., Cole, R., Eckenrode, J., Kitzman, H., Luckey, D., Pettitt, L., Sidora, K., Morris, P., & Powers, J. (1998). Long-term effects of nurse home visitation on children's criminal and antisocial behavior: 15-year follow-up of a randomized controlled trial. *Journal of the American Medical Association, 280,* 1238-1244.

29.   Olds, D., Hill, P., Mihalic, S., & O'Brien, R. (1998). *Blueprints for violence prevention, book seven: Prenatal and infancy home visitation by nurses.* Boulder, CO: Center for the Study and Prevention of Violence.

30.   Lally, J. R., Mangione, P. L., & Honig, A. S. (1988). The Syracuse University family development research project: Long-term impact of an early intervention with low-income children and their families. In D. R. Powell (Ed.), *Advanced in applied developmental psychology* (Vol. 3, pp. 79-104). Norwood, NJ: Ablex.

31. Berrueta-Clement, J. R., Schweinhart, L. J., Barnett, W. S., Epstein, A. S., & Weikart, D. P. (1984). *Changed lives: The effects of the Perry Preschool Program on youths through age 19.* Ypsilanti, MI: High/Scope; Schweinhart, L. J., Barnes, H. V., & Weikart, D. P. (1993). *Significant benefits: The High/Scope Perry Preschool Project through age 27.* Ypsilanti, MI: High/Scope.

32. For a comprehensive review of the program's history and treatment results, see Webster-Stratton, C. (2000). *The Incredible Years training series.* Washington, DC: U.S. Department of Justice, Office of Justice Programs, Office of Juvenile Justice and Delinquency Prevention.

33. Mihalic, S., Irwin, K., Elliott, D. S., Fagan, A., & Hansen, D. (2001). *Blueprints for violence prevention.* Washington, DC: U.S. Department of Justice, Office of Justice Programs, Office of Juvenile Justice and Delinquency Prevention (pp. 5-6).

34. Henggeler, S. W., Mihalic, S. F., Rone, L., Thomas, C., & Timmons-Mitchell, J. (1998). *Blueprints for violence prevention, book six: Multisystemic therapy.* Boulder, CO: Center for the Study and Prevention of Violence.

35. Tremblay, R. E., et al. (1992). Parent and child training to prevent early onset of delinquency: The Montreal Longitudinal-Experimental Study. In J. McCord & R. Tremblay (Eds.), *Preventing antisocial behavior: Interventions from birth through adolescence* (pp. 117-138). New York: Guilford.

36. Bavolek, S. J. (2000, November). *The nurturing parenting programs.* Washington, DC: U.S. Department of Justice, Office of Justice Programs, Office of Juvenile Justice and Delinquency Prevention.

37. Horney, J., Osgood, D. W., & Marshall, I. H. (1995). Criminal careers in the short-term: Intra-individual variability in crime and its relation to local life circumstances. *American Sociological Review, 60,* 655-673; Laub, J. H., Nagin, D. S., & Sampson, R. J. (1998). Trajectories of change in criminal offending: Good marriages and the desistance process. *American Sociological Review, 63,* 225-238; Osgood, D. W., Johnston, L. D., O'Malley, P. M., & Bachman, J. G. (1988). The generality of deviance in late adolescence and early adulthood. *American Sociological Review, 53,* 81-93; Piquero, A. R., MacDonald, J. M., & Parker, K. F. (2002). Race, local life circumstances, and criminal activity. *Social Science Quarterly, 83,* 654-670; Uggen, C. (2000). Work as a turning point in the life course of criminals: A duration model of age, employment, and recidivism. *American Sociological Review, 67,* 529-546; Warr, M. (1998). Life-course transitions and desistance from crime. *Criminology, 36,* 183-216.

38. Laub & Sampson (1993, p. 305), see note 15; also see Dannefer, D. (1984). Adult development and social theory: A paradigmatic reappraisal. *American Sociological Review, 49,* 100-116.

4

The Challenges Posed
by Propensity Theory

Isidro "Johnny" Baca was simply the worst criminal that most of
the staff at the supermaximum-security prison had ever seen.
Baca transferred to the state's most secure facility for his role in
one of the worst prison riots in the state's history. A longtime
member of the Hispanic street gang *Gamberros del Sur*
(Southside Thugs), Baca was convicted of the attempted murder
of three prominent African American gang leaders during a
power struggle over narcotics sales in the facility. Following the
attack, the prison population became embroiled in increased
acts of violence that fissured along inter- and intraracial strife
and gang divisions. Six days after Baca's original attack, the
entire state prison system was ordered on 24-hour lockdown.
The days of violence claimed the lives of nine inmates. Several
hundred inmates and 22 staff members suffered various injuries,
and the correctional facility sustained $8 million in damages.
Baca was sentenced to 150 years imprisonment at the state's
supermax facility for the attempted killing. Prior to the event,
Baca had amassed 119 official violations for fighting, extortion,
weapons possession, threatening staff, arson, rioting, organizing

a security threat group, and a slew of additional acts of non-compliance. Correctional officers always had to shackle Baca's hands and legs whenever he was transported within the facility, and his supervision required no less than five staff members. Officers in the supermax module that housed him estimated that the annual overtime costs for the custodial supervision of Baca alone exceeded $100,000.

Johnny Baca's criminal career began as a 7-year-old when he was removed from public school for fondling four girls in his kindergarten classroom. Home schooling was not an option because Johnny's parents were abusive and tended not to monitor Johnny and their six other children, so the assistant principal tutored him until he could be placed in the special education program beginning in third grade. Standardized tests placed Johnny in the 5th percentile for verbal intelligence and the 15th percentile for mathematics. After placement in special ed, Johnny's problems continued; however, they did not affect the majority of the other students. He was the only elementary school student to receive an out-of-school suspension for bringing a knife to school, and his other delinquencies included assorted acts of bullying, smoking cigarettes, drinking wine, and theft. At age 12, Johnny was placed in a juvenile facility for participating in several commercial burglaries with his older brothers. Released after 8 months, Johnny had attended middle-school classes for only 6 weeks when he was arrested for auto theft, joyriding, possession of a firearm, and narcotics possession. This case resulted in a 2-year commitment to the State Training School for Boys. While detained, Johnny's incorrigibility only worsened. He was repeatedly cited for refusing to obey institutional rules, flooding his cell, sexually assaulting other boys, fighting, smoking, weapons possession, and the like. Additional charges increased the 2-year commitment, and administrators had the option of supervising Johnny until his 21st birthday. Instead, they released him once he turned age 18.

From his release from juvenile prison to his present age of 41, Baca has been arrested 78 times, totaling more than 300 arrests charges in six states across the United States. Like many chronic offenders, Baca was savvy enough to recognize the benefits of pleading guilty to various felonies and serving time in prison.

How could this be a savvy move? Every time Baca plead guilty, numerous additional charges were dismissed, and the prison sentences were almost always served concurrently. Consequently, Baca amassed several relatively brief sentences between 1 and 4 years for robbery, burglary, theft, drug, and weapons convictions. His most serious convictions and length of time served was a 9-year stint in a Colorado prison stemming from a 60-year sentence for second-degree murder, aggravated robbery, aggravated sexual assault, and kidnapping. A previous murder arrest, resulting from the killing of a fellow gang member at a Phoenix, Arizona, bar, was dismissed. Baca performed moderately well on parole. He quickly secured employment in construction and roofing, and although he was no stranger to substance abuse, he was never pathologically addicted to narcotics. For these reasons, parole officers often had little reason to violate Baca's sentence, regardless of their suspicions about his continued involvement in crime. In sum, Baca was convicted of 40 felonies and served 14 separate confinements during his criminal career.

Overview of Propensity Theories as They Relate to Career Criminals

The late Richard Herrnstein once wrote,

> It would be an overstatement to say "once a criminal always a criminal," but it would be closer to the truth than to deny the evidence of a unifying and long-enduring pattern of encounters with the law for most serious offenders.[1]

This quotation conveys the rationale underlying static, general, or propensity explanations of career criminality and seems to accurately describe persons like Johnny Baca in the vignette. A few points of clarification about the theories in this chapter are in order because these terms (e.g., *static*, *general*, *propensity*) are often used interchangeably and thus, imprecisely. Something is *static* if it is fixed, stationary, or nonchanging. *General* means widely applicable and not specific. *Propensity* is an innate inclination or tendency. Taken together, these rubrics typify criminological explanations that view recurrent problem behavior as manifestations of some individual-level pathology that remains stable within an individual across social settings and circumstances. More pointedly, this theoretical perspective asserts that career criminals have been flawed since childhood and that their multifaceted acts of wayward behavior are, quite simply, demonstrative of their inherent "badness."

Scholars who advocate this approach are often criticized and even caricaturized for advancing crudely deterministic explanations of criminal behavior.[2] To the contrary, static theories are often explicitly developmental in their description of the processes that give rise to serious antisocial behavior. However, some propensity theorists are willing to acknowledge that much variation of the etiology of career criminality is unexplained. In doing so, general theorists set themselves up for the criticism that their theories are limited and potentially problematic.

Two features of propensity theory clearly resonate with a politically conservative ideology and its policy leanings. Indeed, the putative conservatism of some of these theories is the primary reason why they are so controversial. First, like developmental theories, propensity arguments point to early-life family processes as the primary cause of crime. In this sense, theoretical foes are in agreement that various abuses in the family help to produce persons who will someday be career criminals. However, unlike the developmental camp that is sanguine about the crime-reduction efforts of policies such as prevention, propensity theorists view the family as a difficult-to-reach area for public policy. For reasons related to civil libertarianism and public labeling, some in the propensity camp are resigned to the belief that the government is unable to meaningfully intervene in early-life family processes. Second, propensity theorists have a more cynical view of career criminals. Theories in the current chapter view career criminals as individuals with a negative disposition and high propensity for crime. This characterization emerges early in life and does not meaningfully change. Getting married, enrolling in an educational program, and finding a job will not turn the lives of career criminals around. To the contrary, career criminals will consistently marry someone who is not good for them, will lack the tenacity to stay in school, and will quit their job after 1 month. Attachments to conventional society are fleeting and carry no rehabilitative weight.[3]

Such a strong view not only typifies views of career criminals but cuts to the very issue of conducting this type of research in the first place. This chapter reviews the main arguments that view career criminality in general, propensity, or static terms; explicates the debate between Michael Gottfredson and Travis Hirschi, advocates of the current view, and Alfred

Blumstein, Jacqueline Cohen, David Farrington, and their allies who support the developmental, career view; and offers some new and additional challenges that propensity theories pose.

The Implicit and Explicit Role of Psychopathological Conditions

There has been a recurrent tendency for scholars to gravitate toward the concept of psychopathy to illuminate criminality that is so apparent at such an early age that it appears to be innate. First conceptualized as "insanity without delirium" by Phillipe Pinel in 1801, psychopathy defines a particularly virulent type of career criminal who engages in predatory and other forms of crime without conscience or remorse. Throughout the 19th and 20th centuries in the United States, the United Kingdom, and Germany, a variety of scholars documented a pejorative group of offenders noted for their pronounced involvement in crime.[4] In part because of the ideological baggage related to the study of psychopathy, scholars often broached the phenomenon of psychopathology carefully. For example, the seminal criminal career research of Sheldon and Eleanor Glueck frequently unearthed the presence of a small group of pathological offenders who committed more than their proportionate share of crime. As early as 1930, Glueck and Glueck acknowledged the existence of an intellectual debate that still occurs today, namely the tenability of offenders who seem to embody an innate form of destructive criminality. In their words,

> It is fashionable to criticize the use of this concept on the grounds that it is the "waste basket" of psychiatry . . . until such time as the peculiar personality and conduct groups comprised in the psychopathic category are more carefully defined and distinguished, we can only utilize the diagnosis found in the records.[5]

Empirically, the Gluecks found that psychopathy was an important variable in differentiating delinquents from nondelinquents. Specifically, they found that 7.3% of persons in a delinquent sample versus 0.4% in the control sample were psychopathic offenders—persons described as "openly destructive and antisocial or asocial" and "less amenable than the neurotic to therapeutic or educative efforts."[6] Other researchers produced findings that mirrored the contemporary profile of psychopathic offenders.

For instance, David Levy described a group of persons noted for their early onset of antisocial behavior, chronic offending, "unmodifiability," or imperviousness to treatment, a pathologically void emotional life. Harrison Gough's early research on the sociology of psychopathy described an individual who was impulsive, grossly irresponsible, self-centered, and morally bankrupt, and cared little for others. Similarly, Lee Robins and Patricia O'Neal concluded that

> a relatively circumscribed segment of the population [is] distinguished by a life-long failure to conform to the social mores . . . it seems probable that criminal activities are more frequently only one expression of a grossly disturbed life pattern of which transiency, violence, and unstable family relations, as well as crime, are typical. Even as children, these boys engaged in antisocial behavior in most contexts, were thoroughly irresponsible, and showed neither concern for their actions nor remorse for the persons whom they affected.[7]

The seminal study of psychopathy as it is contemporarily understood is Hervey Cleckley's *The Mask of Sanity* published in 1941. Cleckley identified a constellation of 16 interpersonal traits and characteristics that constituted the core of the psychopath's profile and behavior. Some of these included superficial charm coupled with good intelligence, complete lack of neurotic emotions and manifestations, pathological lying, egocentricity, incapacity for empathy, global irresponsibility, and lack of guilt or shame, especially in the use of antisocial and violent behavior. Since 1965, Robert Hare furthered the study of psychopathy with the creation of his Psychopathy Checklist–Revised (PCL-R). The PCL-R is composed of an interpersonal/affective traits component (Factor 1) and a social deviance component (Factor 2). Factor 1 contains 8 items: glibness/superficial charm, grandiose sense of self-worth, pathological lying, conning/manipulative, lack of remorse or guilt, shallow affect, callous/lack of empathy, and failure to accept responsibility. Factor 2 contains 12 items: need for stimulation/proneness to boredom, parasitic lifestyle, poor behavioral controls, early behavioral problems, lack of realistic long-term goals, impulsivity, irresponsibility, juvenile delinquency, revocation of conditional release, promiscuous sexual behavior, many short-term marital relationships, and criminal versatility. During diagnostic interviews with professional clinicians, participants are scored 0, 1, or 2 on the 20 items. Most scholars use 30 as the minimum threshold for psychopathy.[8]

Much has been learned about psychopathy and psychopathological conditions, as these constructs relate to criminal careers and career

between a mother experiencing birth complications, her subsequent rejection of her child, and that child's subsequent violent behavior. A cohort of 4,269 males born in Denmark was used to evaluate this hypothesis. Birth complications such as prolonged labor, breech delivery, preeclampsia, umbilical cord problems, and the like interacted with maternal rejection (e.g., out-of-home placement for the child) to predict violent behavior. In fact, only 4% of the birth cohort experienced these early risk factors; however, they accounted for nearly 20% of all violent crimes committed by the cohort. A recent review of the literature indicated that studies that employed biological and social variables explained far greater variation in violent behavior than studies that utilized exclusively social variables.[17] Indeed, the biosocial approach, such as that pioneered by Raine's work, is quickly becoming a visible paradigm in criminology.

Viewing psychopathology as a clinical disorder is not without controversy, however. According to Raine,

> Free will is better conceptualized as a dimension than as a dichotomy and there are strong social and biological pressures beyond the individual's control which, to some degree at least, strongly shape the person's antisocial behavior; consequently, such offenders can be viewed in part as not being entirely responsible for their actions.[18]

By logical extension, career criminals who suffered from this clinical disorder could not be held legally responsible for their conduct because it was involuntary and nonvolitional. The slippery slope that this creates has not been explored nearly as much as the theoretical relationships between biology and social explanations of crime. In fact, a study by Grant Harris and his colleagues resoundingly rejected Raine's clinical disorder theory by using a sample of 868 violent offenders housed at a maximum-security psychiatric hospital. Harris and his associates used structural equation modeling and found that psychopathy and neurodevelopmental insults were not interrelated but distinct predictors of violence. They also found that antisocial parenting was related to both factors but had no direct effect on criminal violence. Taken together, the authors concluded that psychopathology was an independent, chosen life strategy that was profoundly related to criminal violence. Because psychopathy was independent of the neurodevelopmental factors that would suggest it was a clinical disorder, they disconfirmed Raine's thesis.[19]

Wilson and Herrnstein's
Crime and Human Nature

In 1985, James Q. Wilson and the late Richard Herrnstein published the immodestly titled *Crime and Human Nature: The Definitive Study of the Causes of Crime*. Although it is one of the most widely cited books in criminology, it is often misinterpreted in two concomitant ways: It is not a theory, and, hence, it is not a biological theory of crime. Instead, it is a sprawling synthesis of many theoretical perspectives across academic disciplines. It incorporates rational choice theory from economics, operant conditioning theory from psychology, and an assortment of sociological theories that invoke the importance of social institutions such as family, school, and community in predicting criminal behavior. Wilson and Herrnstein used these literatures to attempt to explain the

> differences in the frequency with which persons break the law are associated with differences in the rewards of crime, the risks of being punished for a crime, the strength of internalized inhibitions against crime, and the willingness to defer gratifications, and then to ask what biological, developmental, situational, and adaptive processes give rise to these individual characteristics.[20]

The book is an exhortation to criminologists to acknowledge the importance of constitutional and social factors when attempting to explain criminal behavior. To Wilson and Herrnstein, genetic factors were crucial to the explanation of crime; however, they were just one piece of the puzzle. The authors fully acknowledged that genetic predispositions could be activated or suppressed by local life circumstances and situational exigencies. By establishing the fact that individuals differ at birth in the degree to which they are at risk for criminality, Wilson and Herrnstein were similar to other scholars discussed in the current and previous chapters who noted the salience of assorted bio- and psychosocial risk factors for crime. Nevertheless, their multidisciplinary approach was at times crudely caricatured as a simple, deterministic, quasi-biological theory of crime.[21]

Perhaps Wilson and Herrnstein were criticized for their insistence on an individual-level explanation of criminal behavior. In their words,

> Whatever factors contribute to crime—the state of the economy, the competence of the police, the nurturance of the family, the availability of drugs, the quality of the schools—they must all affect the behavior of *individuals*, if they

are to affect crime. If people differ in their tendency to commit crime, we must express those differences in terms of how some array of factors affects their individual decisions.[22]

A strict focus on individual-level characteristics as the primary cause of crime stands in direct opposition to the viewpoint of sociologists who tend to view crime in structural terms. Whether one supported or disagreed with *Crime and Human Nature* or its authors, the book's lasting contribution is that it helped to steer criminology from a discipline almost exclusively based in sociology to one that incorporated phenomena from multiple disciplines. The current paradigm—one that without controversy stresses human development and the interaction between biological and social factors, and employs a life-course perspective—owes a debt of gratitude to Wilson and Herrnstein. To them, it was obvious that constitutional factors and early life environments were related, even causally related, to mysterious constructs like criminal propensity. Noting that approximately 5% of the offenders accounted for more than half of the crime in any population, they argued that clearly it was time to look within these individuals to uncover their common criminogenic traits.

Finally, Wilson and Herrnstein were unequivocal in framing the criminal offender as an agent endowed with free will. From this perspective, chronic criminals *chose* to offend and conduct their lives in a destructive fashion. Moreover, these scholars, particularly Wilson, were unique in their confident assertion that the career criminals among us were simply evil people, evidenced by their recurrent tendency to inflict harm, violence, and despair upon others. Years earlier, Wilson had stated that "evil people exist" and should be separated from the majority of citizens, who are good. Thus, Wilson and Herrnstein were willing to stand in moral judgment and openly condemn the pathology of the worst criminals.[23]

Gottfredson and Hirschi's
A General Theory of Crime

Unquestionably, the theory that has had the greatest recent impact on the discipline of criminology, let alone criminal career research, is the self-control theory articulated by Michael Gottfredson and Travis Hirschi in their *A General Theory of Crime* published in 1990. According to the authors, "Theories of crime lead naturally to interest in the propensity of individuals committing criminal acts";[24] consequently, they proffer that low self-control is the individual-level variable that best explains crime and analogous behaviors. The etiology of self-control occurs during parental socialization from birth to about age eight, when peers begin to supplant parents as socialization agents. According to the theory, ineffective parental socialization occurs when parents fail to monitor their child's behavior, fail to acknowledge their child's deviance, and fail to appropriately sanction their child's deviance. Ineffective parents—persons who are unable or unwilling to instill these conventional traits in their children—produce children who prefer immediate gratification of their personal desires; pursue simple tasks rather than activities that require tenacity; value physical rather than verbal or cognitive experiences; enjoy quick returns instead of long-term investments on marriage and relationships, educational attainment, and occupational careers; are employed in low-skilled versus academic endeavors; and are self-centered and generally insensitive to the feelings of others. Conversely, effective parents have a greater investment in their offspring and tend to rear children who are more capable of delaying gratification, more understanding of the immediate and potentially long-term consequences of their choices and behavior, more willing to accept restraints on their activity, and more considerate of others.

Once established, one's level of self-control is relatively stable. Therefore, children who were ineffectively parented are placed at a considerable disadvantage compared to youth who were socialized more effectively. According to Gottfredson and Hirschi,

> People who lack self-control will tend to be impulsive, insensitive, physical (as opposed to mental), risk-taking, short-sighted, and nonverbal, and they will tend therefore to engage in criminal and analogous acts. Since these traits can be identified prior to the age of responsibility for crime, since there is considerable tendency for these traits to come together in the same people, and since the traits tend to persist through life, it seems reasonable to consider them as comprising a stable construct useful in the explanation of crime.[25]

It is no coincidence that deviance and other personal problems generally and consistently characterize specific individuals.

Several critiques were levied against self-control theory for theoretical, methodological, and ideological reasons, primarily relating to the authors' polemical delivery and the theory's audacious scope.[26] Empirically, the relationship between low self-control and various antisocial outcomes has been nothing short of spectacular. Dozens of studies have explicitly tested the theory and found that low self-control was predictive of failure in family relationships, dating, attachment to church, educational attainment, and occupational status; risky traffic behaviors; work-related deviance; having criminal associates and values; residing in a neighborhood perceived to be disorderly; and noncompliance with criminal justice system statuses. Moreover, persons with low self-control are significantly more likely to engage in drinking alcohol; substance abuse; smoking; gambling; violent, property, white-collar, and nuisance offending, and they are more likely to be victimized.[27] Finally, Travis Pratt and Frank Cullen reviewed 21 studies that included 17 independent data sets, nearly 50,000 individual cases, and 126 self-control estimates of crime. They found that self-control with an overall effect-size of .20 was one of the strongest individual-level correlates of crime. They concluded that "future research that omits self-control from its empirical analyses risks being misspecified."[28]

The Gottfredson and Hirschi Critiques

In the years before the publication of their general theory, Michael Gottfredson and Travis Hirschi published a series of papers that were caustically critical of the emerging criminal career paradigm. The subtext and, at times, the actual statements in their work revealed the elements of the self-control theory that would emerge later. In their first paper, Hirschi and Gottfredson presented the age-crime curve as a brute social fact. According to them, across settings, epochs, and types of data, involvement in crime rises steadily in middle adolescence, peaks at age 17 or 18, and then declines sharply and asymptotically thereafter. The authors also advanced that the age-crime curve was invariant in that it could not be explained by other phenomena. Theories that attempted to utilize demographic or other sociological constructs to explain a natural fact were in error.

From this perspective, high-rate and low-rate offenders followed the same general pattern of offending. Thus, even high-rate offenders desisted from crime and were generally unproblematic during their adult years. Generally speaking, the more serious or persistent the offenders, the earlier in life their criminality will be evident. Thus, Hirschi and Gottfredson assumed that some individual-level phenomenon, akin to a criminal propensity, explained why the "worst" offenders tended to start their criminal careers early and committed crime with greater frequency than others did. In this sense, criminologists needed to know about an individual offender at only one point in time, because his or her propensity was stable throughout life. Consequently, cross-sectional data and designs that capture the characteristics of an individual at a discrete time yielded the same substantive findings as if data had been collected on an individual yearly for 30 years. High-rate offenders always offended more than low-rate offenders and vice versa. It is for this fundamental reason that Hirschi and Gottfredson were critical of longitudinal designs and their exorbitant costs.[29]

Their 1986 essay "The True Value of Lambda Would Appear to Be Zero: An Essay on Career Criminals, Criminal Careers, Selective Incapacitation, Cohort Studies, and Related Topics" raised several concerns about the idea and study of career criminals. These were the following: (a) the idea of a career criminal is more than a century old and has been recurrently studied as criminal justice systems attempt to deal with habitual criminals; (b) such criminals are sufficiently rare that they are not attractive targets of criminal justice policy; (c) given the salience of a prior record, career criminals will tend to be older when it is discovered that they have a lengthy record, therefore they will be incarcerated for their prior conduct when their current conduct illustrates a reduction in crime; and (d) more succinctly, even the offending path of career criminals follows the age-crime curve. Two additional papers continued to assail longitudinal research and the programmatic and funding implications of criminal career research. Here, Gottfredson and Hirschi explicitly revealed the logic that would culminate in their general theory and serve as a foil to the criminal career paradigm:

> The longitudinal study is a consequence of particular theories or orientations toward the causes of crime. Theories that see crime as a consequence of development processes or stages . . . an occupation or state one moves into and out of . . . or the consequences of positive learning by always malleable individuals—all suggest the desirability or necessity of following individuals over time. Other theories see crime as a consequence of relatively stable characteristics of people and the predictable situations and opportunities they experience. These theories do not presume that major changes in criminal activity are associated with entry into or exit from roles, institutions, or organizations. Such theories are therefore adequately tested at any point in the life course, the particular point selected by reference to expected distributions of the important variables.[30]

The responses to Gottfredson and Hirschi's claims were not nearly as vociferous and tended to focus on methodological issues and the general viability of criminal career research. To its defenders, such as Alfred Blumstein, Jacqueline Cohen, and David Farrington, the criminal career approach was not an official theory but merely a strategy for studying various components of an offending career. On this point, they stressed that *career* was meant to describe a longitudinal sequence of behaviors, not an indication of remunerative success. Moreover, adherents of the criminal career paradigm seemed to pay little credence to Gottfredson and Hirschi's sometimes unrelenting cries about the purported misappropriation of federal research dollars.[31]

Although this debate carried on somewhat gratuitously in the pages of the journal *Criminology*, the heart of their disagreement was important and should not be minimized. Gottfredson and Hirschi, as well as other adherents of general or propensity explanations, offer a sweeping and parsimonious assessment of human behavior. Conduct, whether it is good or bad, conventional or criminal, is predicated on the very nature of the actor. Once established, our constitutional essence and behavioral repertoire are not going to change substantively and are nowhere near as susceptible to outside influences as developmental theorists assert. That the worst criminals have the earliest onset, offend at the highest levels, commit more various forms of crime, and desist later is proof positive of their inner pathology. On this point, propensity theorists have the developmental camp in a logical corner.

However, Gottfredson and Hirschi go overboard in selling the age-crime curve and the universality with which offenders discontinue their offending careers. If the age effect were so robust, we would never read of serious criminal violence committed by adults in their 30s, 40s, 50s, and so on. They are correct in noting that selective incapacitation strategies are too late in neutralizing career criminals during their worst, most active periods of offending; however, these offenders have much future criminal behavior to neutralize. Of course, childhood and adolescent factors and delinquencies are important, but adult offenders commit nearly 70% of the crime in the United States, the bulk of it the contribution of career offenders. In this sense, scholars who championed the criminal career paradigm were correct in emphasizing the study of the various parameters of the criminal career. The correlates of onset, continuity, and desistance and the role that social institutions play in shaping these parameters were worthy of criminological inquiry because offenders frequently did change their offending patterns in sometimes unpredictable ways. Consequently, if human behavior were more dynamic than static, multiple points of data collection and observation were needed, especially because longitudinal designs allowed for each person to serve as his or her own control over time.

Theoretical Challenges and Summary Issues

Travis Hirschi and Michael Gottfredson have suggested that "debates about facts are often thinly disguised debates about theory."[32] This clearly characterizes the criminal career paradigm and is directly relevant to the manner in which scholars conduct research. By and large, studies utilizing self-reported data, general population samples, and prospective longitudinal designs were far and away concordant with the developmental perspectives described in Chapter 3. On the other hand, official data, offender samples, and retrospective/cross-sectional designs were aligned with the propensity perspective. Daniel Nagin and Raymond Paternoster also noted this trend in their review of research investigating the state dependence (life circumstances) and population heterogeneity (propensity) concepts. In their words,

> The common ground in studies that show strong state dependence effects is that they used generally "conventional" samples (student samples where there were few arrests) and the outcome variable was based on self-reports. Studies that show strong evidence of population heterogeneity employ more high-risk samples and are based on official data (convictions or arrests).[33]

Thus, a segregation of sorts is currently going on in criminal career research. Samples of "bad apples" found compelling evidence of a criminal propensity and tended to support its theoretical principles, whereas samples of "good apples" showed developmental pathways and validated that perspective. A variety of criminal career researchers have noted the bifurcated relationship between the criminality of the sample and the favored theoretical idea; indeed, some have explicitly acknowledged that the exclusion of pathological offenders from their samples was one potential reason why propensity perspectives have not been empirically supported by their own research.[34]

Traditional probability samples and even prospective birth cohorts are almost entirely devoid of the most serious types of offenders; thus, these data sources are largely unhelpful in testing propensity theories as they relate to career criminals. Consequently, these data sources should be used to evaluate developmental theory only. Samples containing arrestees, prisoners, parolees, death row inmates, and the like should be used to evaluate propensity theories. Not appropriately matching the research questions to the criminality of the research participants infused unnecessary dissent into the research community. Indeed, it is becoming increasingly clear that there are two offender archetypes at play in society: noncareer criminals and career criminals.[35] It is likely that Gottfredson and Hirschi, as well as Wilson and Herrnstein, employed such forceful language in their arguments because they had a clear view of what the individual criminal offender was like and, consequently, which research methods would best describe his or her offending. What was at stake, in their eyes, was the very conceptualization of human nature.

Gottfredson and Hirschi and their self-control theory are often viewed as antithetical to the study of career criminals, based largely on their involvement in the heated exchange during the 1980s.[36] Such a view is wrong. For at least two reasons, self-control and any propensity-based theory should be the theoretical perspective used to guide research of the worst offenders. First, propensity theories directly or indirectly denote a darker, more cynical view of human nature. For example, the overarching assumption of control theories is that humans are naturally prone to deviance unless reined in by others. It is no coincidence that the hopefulness of treatment efforts are explicitly linked to developmental, not propensity, theories. Second, propensity theories, like developmental approaches, point to the profound importance of early-life socialization and early family environments in developing and exacerbating antisocial tendencies. These early-life experiences are a major reason why chronic antisocial behavior is so stable, tenacious, and difficult to reduce, particularly when offenders are older—its foundations were cemented at conception or shortly thereafter. Because of the seeming intractability of problems arising in early family life, propensity theories are not ideologically linked to public policy, such as prevention.

Finally, what was not included in the exchange between propensity theorists and advocates of the criminal career paradigm is noteworthy for its absence. The central challenge levied by propensity theory, and the reason why it is often challenged, is that career criminals are simply bad. Career criminals are bad people who recurrently do bad things to other people. It is the realization that a small cadre of people are profoundly bad that served as the subtext of the earlier arguments. The reasons that longitudinal research yields little fruit and therefore cannot justify its high costs are because the nefariousness of career offenders is evident in early childhood and shows little hope of dissipating. Indeed, aggression is as stable an individual trait as intelligence, and whereas high intelligence contributes to all sorts of positive outcomes, high aggression contributes to an equal share of negative outcomes.[37] Thus, it does not matter when one collects data—career criminals will demonstrate some pronounced form of antisocial behavior at every point of data collection. Their pathology might development from "bad" to "worse" or "worse" to "bad," but this is hardly a substantive reason to believe that anything is really changing. For reasons largely beyond their control but directly attributable to their culpable parents, career criminals have grim life chances. As such, their early experiences of being victimized soon give way to their victimizing others. As part of this cycle, empathy hardens and turns to anger and resentment, and we want the career criminal to be dealt with especially by retributive means.

Conclusion

In a classic article in *American Sociological Review*, criminologists David Rowe and Wayne Osgood correctly noted that genetic explanations of crime were traditionally either ignored or ridiculed by the discipline. Moreover, they indicated that those who dared to suggest that biology played any role in the explanation of human behavior were cast as examples of unenlightened, reprehensible thinking.[38] For a time, sociologists tended to deny the place of other viewpoints. For this reason, it is easy to see why propensity explanations of habitual criminality met with such resistance. Fortunately, this has changed.

Recently, Julien Morizot and Marc Le Blanc conducted a study that followed samples of offenders and nonoffenders over a span of 25 years to assess the developmental track of their personality. They found evidence that was supportive of developmental and propensity theories. In their words,

> The polarization of opposing viewpoints "continuity and change" or "plaster and plasticity" seems inappropriate. Both continuity and change are observable. On the one hand, the magnitude of the rank-order continuity estimates, particularly during adulthood, clearly showed that individual differences in personality tend to be quite stable across time. This supports a central assumption of the trait position. On the other hand, the mean-level continuity

assessment revealed a nontrivial maturational trend toward a better psychological adjustment from adolescence to midlife. This indicates that traits are not developmentally static predispositions.[39]

What this implies is that both theoretical camps have merit when depicting the personality, behaviors, and the very nature of career criminals.

Notes

1. Herrnstein, R. J. (1995). Criminogenic traits. In J. Q. Wilson & J. Petersilia (Eds.), *Crime* (pp. 39-64). San Francisco: ICS Press.

2. For a review, see DeLisi, M. (2003). Conservatism and common sense: The criminological career of James Q. Wilson. *Justice Quarterly, 20,* 661-674.

3. DeLisi, M. (2003). Self-control pathology: The elephant in the living room. *Advances in Criminological Theory, 12,* 21-38.

4. An excellent primer on the history of psychopathy appears in Arrigo, B. A., & Shipley, S. (2001). The confusion over psychopathy (I): Historical considerations. *International Journal of Offender Therapy & Comparative Criminology, 45,* 325-344.

5. Glueck, S., & Glueck, E. T. (1930). *500 criminal careers.* New York: Knopf (p. 157).

6. Glueck, S., & Glueck, E. T. (1943). *Criminal careers in retrospect.* New York: The Commonwealth Fund (pp. 64, 120); Glueck, S., & Glueck, E. T. (1950). *Unraveling juvenile delinquency.* New York: The Commonwealth Fund (pp. 239-240).

7. Levy, D. M. (1942). Psychopathic personality and crime. *Journal of Educational Sociology, 16,* 99-114; Gough, H. (1948). A sociological theory of psychopathy. *American Journal of Sociology, 53,* 359-366; Robins, L., & O'Neal, P. (1958). Mortality, mobility, and crime: Problem children 30 years later. *American Sociological Review, 23,* 162-171; Robins, L. N. (1966). *Deviant children grown up: A sociological and psychiatric study of sociopathic personality.* Baltimore: Williams and Wilkins.

8. Cleckley, H. (1941). *The mask of sanity.* St. Louis, MO: Mosby; Hare, R. D. (1970). *Psychopathy: Theory and research.* New York: Wiley; Hare, R. D. (1991). *The Hare psychopathy checklist–revised.* Toronto, Canada: Multi-Health System; Hare, R. D. (1993). *Without conscience: The disturbing world of the psychopaths among us.* New York: The Guilford Press; Hare, R. D. (1996). Psychopathy: A clinical construct whose time has come. *Criminal Justice & Behavior, 23,* 25-54.

9. Blair, R. J. R. (1997). Moral reasoning and the child with psychopathic tendencies. *Personality and Individual Differences, 22,* 731-739; Blair, R. J. R. (1999). Responsiveness to distress cues in the child with psychopathic tendencies. *Personality and Individual Differences, 27,* 135-145; Forth, A. E. (1995). Psychopathy

in adolescent offenders: Assessment, family background, and violence. *Issues in Criminological & Legal Psychology, 24*, 42-44; Lynam, D. R. (1996). Early identification of chronic offenders: Who is the fledgling psychopath? *Psychological Bulletin, 120*, 209-234; Lynam, D. R. (1997). Pursuing the psychopath: Capturing the fledgling psychopath in a nomological net. *Journal of Abnormal Psychology, 106*, 1-13; Skilling, T. A., Quinsey, V. L., & Craig, W. M. (2001). Evidence of a taxon underlying serious antisocial behavior in boys. *Criminal Justice & Behavior, 28*, 450-470. For important works that explore the problematic nature of childhood psychopathy, see Edens, J. F., Skeem, J. L., Cruise, K. R., & Cauffman, E. (2001). Assessment of "juvenile psychopathy" and its association with violence: A critical review. *Behavioral Sciences & the Law, 19*, 53-80; Johnstone, L., & Cooke, D. J. (2004). Psychopathic-like traits in childhood: Conceptual and measurement concerns. *Behavioral Sciences & the Law, 22*, 103-125.

10.   Gretton, H. M., McBride, M., Hare, R. D., Shaughnessy, R. O., & Kumka, G. (2001). Psychopathy and recidivism in adolescent sex offenders. *Criminal Justice & Behavior, 28*, 427-449; Hare, R. D., McPherson, L. M., & Forth, A. E. (1988). Male psychopaths and their criminal careers. *Journal of Consulting and Clinical Psychology, 56*, 710-714; Harris, G. T., Rice, M. E., & Cormier, C. A. (1991). Psychopathy and violent recidivism. *Law & Human Behavior, 15*, 625-637; Harris, G. T., Skilling, T. A., & Rice, M. E. (2001). The construct of psychopathy. In M. Tonry & N. Morris (Eds.), *Crime and justice: An annual review of research* (pp. 197-264). Chicago: University of Chicago Press; Hemphill, J. F., Templeman, R., Wong, S., & Hare, R. D. (1998). Psychopathy and crime: Recidivism and criminal careers. In D. Cooke, A. Forth, & R. Hare (Eds.), *Psychopathy: Theory, research, and implications for society* (pp. 375-399). Boston: Kluwer Academic Publishers; Simourd, D. J., & Hoge, R. D. (2000). Criminal psychopathy: A risk-and-need perspective. *Criminal Justice & Behavior, 27*, 256-272.

11.   Porter, S., Woodworth, M., Earle, J., Drugge, J., & Boer, D. (2003). Characteristics of sexual homicides committed by psychopathic and nonpsychopathic offenders. *Law & Human Behavior, 27*, 459-470.

12.   To be sure, there are additional scholars and theoretical approaches that examine longitudinal and developmental processes in severe and chronic antisocial behavior. The works described in the current chapter were included because of their emphasis on adult career criminals. Two especially noteworthy scholars are Kenneth Dodge and Michael Rutter. Recent reviews and summaries of their research programs appear in the following: Dodge, K. A. (2001). The science of youth violence prevention: Progressing from developmental epidemiology to efficacy to effectiveness to public policy. *American Journal of Preventive Medicine, 20*, 63-70; Dodge, K. A., Bates, J. E., & Pettit, G. S. (1990). Mechanisms in the cycle of violence. *Science, 250*, 1678-1683; Dodge, K. A., & Pettit, G. S. (2003). A biopsychosocial model of the development of chronic conduct problems in adolescence. *Developmental Psychology, 39*, 349-371; Rutter, M. L. (1999). Psychosocial adversity

and child psychopathology. *British Journal of Psychiatry, 174,* 480-493; Rutter, M. (2002). Nature, nurture, and development: From evangelism through science toward policy and practice. *Child Development, 73,* 1-21; Rutter, M., Giller, H., & Hagell, A. (1998). *Antisocial behavior by young people.* New York: Cambridge University Press.

13. Shipley, S., & Arrigo, B. A. (2001). The confusion over psychopathy (II): Implications for forensic (correctional) practice. *International Journal of Offender Therapy and Comparative Criminology, 45,* 407-420. Another work that makes important distinctions between antisocial personality disorder and psychopathy is the following: Martens, W. H. J. (2000). Antisocial and psychopathic personality disorders: Causes, course, and remission—A review article. *International Journal of Offender Therapy and Comparative Criminology, 44,* 406-430.

14. Walters, G. D., White, T. W., & Denney, D. (1991). The lifestyle criminality screening form: Preliminary data. *Criminal Justice & Behavior, 18,* 406-418.

15. Walters, G. D. (2003). Predicting criminal justice outcomes with the psychopathy checklist and lifestyle criminality screening form: A meta-analytic comparison. *Behavioral Sciences & the Law, 21,* 89-102.

16. Walters, G. D. (1995). The psychological inventory of criminal thinking styles: I. Reliability and preliminary validity. *Criminal Justice & Behavior, 22,* 307-325; Walters, G. D. (1996). The psychological inventory of criminal thinking styles: Part III. Predictive validity. *International Journal of Offender Therapy and Comparative Criminology, 40,* 105-112; Walters, G. D., Trgovac, M., Rychlec, M., Di Fazio, R., & Olson, J. R. (2002). Assessing change with the psychological inventory of criminal thinking styles: A controlled analysis and multisite cross-validation. *Criminal Justice & Behavior, 29,* 308-331.

17. Raine, A., Brennan, P., & Mednick, S. A. (1994). Birth complications combined with early maternal rejection at age 1 year predispose to violent crime at age 18 years. *Archives of General Psychiatry, 51,* 984-988; Raine, A. (2002). Biosocial studies of antisocial and violent behavior in children and adults: A review. *Journal of Abnormal Child Psychology, 30,* 311-326.

18. Raine, A. (1993). *The psychopathology of crime: Criminal behavior as a clinical disorder.* San Diego, CA: Academic Press (p. 320).

19. Harris, G. T., Rice, M. E., & Lalumiere, M. (2001). Criminal violence: The role of psychopathy, neurodevelopmental insults, and antisocial parenting. *Criminal Justice and Behavior, 28,* 402-426.

20. Wilson, J. Q., & Herrnstein, R. J. (1985). *Crime and human nature: The definitive study of the causes of crime.* New York: Simon & Schuster (p. 40).

21. An intriguing article that explored the taboo relationship between biology and crime and the role of political orientation and explanations of crime is Wright, R. A., & Miller, J. M. (1998). Taboo until today? The coverage of biological arguments in criminology textbooks, 1961 to 1970 and 1987 to 1996. *Journal of Criminal Justice, 26,* 1-19. As Wilson and Herrnstein intended, *Crime and Human Nature*

ushered in a paradigm shift whereby explanations of crime that were not exclusively sociological gained currency.

22.   Wilson & Herrnstein (1985), p. 42, see note 20.

23.   In addition to *Crime and Human Nature*, also see Herrnstein, R. J. (1995). Criminogenic traits. In J. Q. Wilson & J. Petersilia (Eds.), *Crime* (pp. 39-64). San Francisco: ICS Press; Wilson, J. Q. (1983). *Thinking about crime* (Rev. ed.). New York: Vintage Books. For a more detailed exposition of the role that political orientation in criminology, particularly as it relates to conservative scholars like James Q. Wilson, see DeLisi, M. (2003). Conservatism and common sense: The criminological career of James Q. Wilson. *Justice Quarterly, 20*, 661-674.

24.   Gottfredson, M. R., & Hirschi, T. (1990). *A general theory of crime*. Stanford, CA: Stanford University Press (p. 85).

25.   Ibid., pp. 90-91.

26.   Akers, R. L. (1991). Self-control as a general theory of crime. *Journal of Quantitative Criminology, 7*, 201-211; Barlow, H. D. (1991). Explaining crime and analogous acts, or the unrestrained will grab at pleasure whenever they can. *Journal of Criminal Law & Criminology, 82*, 229-242; Geis, G. (2000). On the absence of self-control as the basis for a general theory of crime: A critique. *Theoretical Criminology, 4*, 35-54. Gottfredson and Hirschi themselves and other criminologists have defended the logic of self-control theory. For examples, see DeLisi, M. (2003), note 3, and Hirschi, T., & Gottfredson, M. R. (2000). In defense of self-control. *Theoretical Criminology, 4*, 55-69.

27.   DeLisi, M. (2001). It's all in the record: Assessing self-control theory with an offender sample. *Criminal Justice Review, 26*, 1-16; DeLisi, M. (2001). Designed to fail: Self-control and involvement in the criminal justice system. *American Journal of Criminal Justice, 26*, 131-148; Evans, T. D., et al. (1997). The social consequences of self-control: Testing the general theory of crime. *Criminology, 35*, 475-504; Gibbs, J., & Giever, D. (1995). Self-control and its manifestation among university students: An empirical test of Gottfredson and Hirschi's general theory. *Justice Quarterly, 12*, 231-256; Higgins, G. E. (2002). General theory of crime and deviance: A structural equation modeling approach. *Journal of Crime & Justice, 25*, 71-96; Higgins, G. E. (2004). Gender and self-control theory: Are there differences in the measures and the theory's causal model? *Criminal Justice Studies, 17*, 31-53; Junger, M., & Tremblay, R. (1999). Self-control, accidents, and crime. *Criminal Justice & Behavior, 26*, 485-501; Keane, C., Maxim, P., & Teevan, J. (1993). Drinking and driving, self-control, and gender: Testing a general theory of crime. *Journal of Research in Crime and Delinquency, 30*, 30-46; Longshore, D., & Turner, S. (1998). Self-control and criminal opportunity: Cross-sectional test of the general theory of crime. *Criminal Justice & Behavior, 25*, 81-98; Perrone, D., Sullivan, C. J., Pratt, T. C., & Margaryan, S. (2004). Parental efficacy, self-control, and delinquency: A test of a general theory of crime on a nationally representative sample of youth. *International Journal of Offender Therapy and Comparative Criminology, 48*, 298-312; Piquero, A., & Tibbetts, S.

(1996). Specifying the direct and indirect effects of low self-control and situational factors in offenders' decision making: Toward a more complete model of rational offending. *Justice Quarterly, 13,* 481-510; Schreck, C. (1999). Criminal victimization and low self-control: An extension and test of a general theory of crime. *Justice Quarterly, 16,* 633-654.

28. Pratt, T. C., & Cullen, F. T. (2000). The empirical status of Gottfredson and Hirschi's general theory of crime: A meta-analysis. *Criminology, 38,* 931-964 (p. 952).

29. Hirschi, T., & Gottfredson, M. (1983). Age and the explanation of crime. *American Journal of Sociology, 89,* 552-584.

30. Gottfredson, M., & Hirschi, T. (1987). The methodological adequacy of longitudinal research on crime. *Criminology, 25,* 581-614 (p. 608); Gottfredson, M., & Hirschi, T. (1988). Science, public policy, and the career paradigm. *Criminology, 26,* 37-55; Gottfredson, M. R., & Hirschi, T. (1986). The true value of Lambda would appear to be zero: An essay on career criminals, criminal careers, selective incapacitation, cohort studies, and related topics. *Criminology, 24,* 213-234.

31. Blumstein, A., Cohen, J., & Farrington, D. P. (1988). Criminal career research: Its value for criminology. *Criminology, 26,* 1-35; Blumstein, A., Cohen, J., & Farrington, D. P. (1988). Longitudinal and criminal career research: Further clarifications. *Criminology, 26,* 57-74; Tittle, C. R. (1988). Two empirical regularities (maybe) in search of an explanation: Commentary on the age/crime debate. *Criminology, 26,* 75-85.

32. Hirschi, T., & Gottfredson, M. R. (2001). Control theory and the life-course perspective. In A. Piquero & P. Mazerolle (Eds.), *Life-course criminology: Contemporary and classic readings* (pp. 229-241). Belmont, CA: Wadsworth (p. 230).

33. Nagin, D. S., & Paternoster, R. (2000). Population heterogeneity and state dependence: State of evidence and directions for future research. *Journal of Quantitative Criminology, 16,* 117-144 (p. 133).

34. Bartusch, D. J., Lynam, D., Moffitt, T. E., & Silva, P. A. (1997). Is age important? Testing a general versus a developmental theory of antisocial behavior. *Criminology, 35,* 13-48 (p. 41); Paternoster, R., & Brame, R. (1997). Multiple routes to delinquency? A test of developmental and general theories of crime. *Criminology, 35,* 49-84 (p. 76); also see Benda, B. B., & Toombs, N. J. (2002). Two preeminent theoretical models: A proportional hazard rate analysis of recidivism. *Journal of Criminal Justice, 30,* 1-12; Cernkovich, S. A., & Giordano, P. C. (2001). Stability and change in antisocial behavior: The transition from adolescence to early adulthood. *Criminology, 39,* 371-410; Fergusson, D. M., Horwood, L. J., & Nagin, D. S. (2000). Offending trajectories in a New Zealand birth cohort. *Criminology, 38,* 525-552; Pulkkinen, L., Virtanen, T., Klinteberg, B., & Magnusson, D. (2000). Child behavior and adult personality: Comparisons between criminality groups in Finland and Sweden. *Criminal Behavior & Mental Health, 10,* 155-169.

35. For example, see Cohen, L. E., & Vila, B. J. (1996). Self-control and social control: An exposition of the Gottfredson-Hirschi/Sampson-Laub debate. *Studies on Crime & Crime Prevention, 5,* 125-150; Farrington, D. P., & Loeber, R. (2000). Some benefits of dichotomization in psychiatric and criminological research. *Criminal Behavior & Mental Health, 10,* 100-122.

36. See Tracy, P. E., & Kempf-Leonard, K. (1996). *Continuity and discontinuity in criminal careers.* New York: Plenum (pp. v-xiii).

37. Loeber, R., & Hay, D. (1997). Key issues in the development of aggression and violence from childhood to early adulthood. *Annual Review of Psychology, 48,* 371-410; Olweus, D. (1979). Stability of aggressive reaction patterns in males: A review. *Psychological Bulletin, 86,* 852-857.

38. Rowe, D. C., & Osgood, D. W. (1984). Heredity and sociological theories of delinquency: A reconsideration. *American Sociological Review, 49,* 526-540. Also see Osgood, D. W., & Rowe, D. C. (1994). Bridging criminal careers, theory, and policy through latent variable models of individual offending. *Criminology, 32,* 517-554; Rowe, D. C., Osgood, D. W., & Nicewander, W. A. (1990). A latent trait approach to unifying criminal careers. *Criminology, 28,* 237-270.

39. Morizot, J., & Le Blanc, M. (2003). Continuity and change in personality traits from adolescence to midlife: A 25-year longitudinal study comparing representative and adjudicated men. *Journal of Personality, 71,* 705-756 (p. 750).

5

The Politics of Career Criminals

Box 5.1 (Continued)

Contact Officer: Sgt. William Halmry, 1405

Agency: Calgary PD

Charge 1: Operating motor vehicle while intoxicated (45-18-2005)
Charge 2: Operating while intoxicated/exceed .150% (45-18-2011)
Charge 3: Operating motor vehicle w/restrained license (45-18-1079)

Synopsis

Defendant (John Michael Jamison, 1959/10/14, hereafter referred to as def) was observed driving along the right shoulder of Highway 210 at 2234 on November 12, 2003, in the city of Calgary, province of Alberta, Canada. Upon contact, arresting officer noticed a strong odor that, based on his training and experience, is consistent with the odor of alcoholic beverages. In plain sight were 11 empty bottles of Heineken beer strewn about the interior of the vehicle, a 2000 Toyota Camry. Def manifested visible indications of alcohol intoxication: slurred speech, flushed complexion, watery eyes, and lumbering motor skills. Def instantly advised the officer that he was extremely intoxicated and expressed a desire to be arrested. Immediately, def was advised of his legal rights and protections against discussing his conduct with the officer, which def eagerly waived. Def politely declined roadside sobriety tests. Def submitted to a portable breath test (PBT), which yielded a blood alcohol content (BAC) of 0.227%. Def was transported to local corrections, where he was administered another PBT that yielded a BAC of .251%. PBT results, emptied beer bottles, and def's acknowledgment of driving while intoxicated were entered as the state's evidence.

Social History

Def was widowed on October 1, 2003. Def's spouse died from natural causes related to brain cancer. Def had been continuously married for 21 years to the deceased. Def has no biological or adoptive children and no dependents.

Def has lived in Calgary for 17 years, is a homeowner, and has resided in same domicile for 11 years. Def is employed with Financial Systems as a certified public accountant. Def has been continuously employed with Financial Systems since 1981. Def has B.S. degree with honors in accounting from the University of Toronto, where he graduated in May 1981.

Substance Abuse

Def reports no current or past involvement in use of illegal narcotics. Def reports never using marijuana, cocaine, opiates, amphetamines, or any schedule I or II controlled substance. Def reports taking Tylenol w/codeine two times during adulthood as pain medication prescribed after podiatric surgery (ingrown toenails). Pharmaceutical check confirms two prescriptions for Tylenol-3; no additional medications.

Def reports increased drinking since spouse's death. Def reports drinking approximately 75 beers per week for the past 4 weeks. Def reports profound sadness at wife's passing and that alcohol helps to control his feelings. Def reports no additional clinical signs of depression.

Criminal History

Def reports no prior juvenile or adult criminal history; none found via Interpol, local, province, and national records, or American NCIC. Driver's history revealed no prior citations.

Def reports police contact 10 days ago in which def appeared to be intoxicated in public. Def was observed walking from local alcohol establishment to his home. Officer conducted welfare and warrants check and followed def to his residence. Def reports/records confirm no citation was issued.

Assessment

Def poses little to no risk to community for flight, danger, or recidivism. Scores on Risk Assessment Inventory Instrument were 0, 1, and 0, respectively. Def has outstanding community ties but little

(Continued)

Box 5.1 (Continued)

social support. Def is cooperative, remorseful, and embarrassed about his arrest. Def seems amenable to treatment.

Recommendation

Sentence: Deferred prosecution
Term: 6 months
    Conditions: 40 hours counseling w/treatment staff re: alcohol use and dealing w/loss of spouse.

SOURCE: Calgary Police Department, Bureau of Pretrial Services and Bail, Pre-Sentence Investigation.

NOTE: This is a fictional profile; any similarity to an offender, living or dead, is purely coincidence.

Box 5.2   Ohio Department of Rehabilitation and Correction Inmate Dossier

************************Not for public dissemination*******************

Inmate Name: Jackson Michael Copeland

Aliases

Jack Copeland	Jim Coplin
Jackie Copeland	James Michaels
Jackie Cope	Steve D'Ontario
Johnny Copeland	Joseph Branch
Mike Copeland	Rich Foster
Johnny Mike	Richard Foster
Leroy Johnson	Dick Foster
Lou Johnson	Dick Rogers
Jim Copin	Dick Copeland

Physical

Race: W
Sex: M
Height: 604

Weight: 240
Hair/Eyes: BRO/BLU
Skin: Drk

Date(s) of Birth

January 1, 1940 (22 variations of DOB)

Place(s) of Birth

Akron, Ohio

Identifiers

SC L Arm/SC R Arm/SC Face/SC R Leg/GSW L Leg/GSW R Chest/GSW L Arm/SC Chest/SC Abdomen/TAT R Forearm/TAT L Forearm/TAT L Arm (Multiple)/TAT R Arm (Multiple)/TAT R Chest/TAT L Hand/TAT R Hand

Commitment Information

Inmate Copeland awaits execution upon 3 convictions for aggravated murder and ancillary crimes during crime spree committed while Inmate Copeland was on escape status from Mansfield Reformatory.

Profile Classifications

Public Risk: 10
Violence: 10
Escape: 10
Institutional Risk: 10
Assaultive: 10
Suicide: 1
STG: 1
Education: N/A Condemned
Vocational: N/A Condemned
Treatment: N/A Condemned
Visitation: None

(Continued)

Box 5.2 (Continued)

Disciplinary Record

Disobeying order: 31 cts.
Assault w/weapon: 2 cts.
Fighting: 3 cts.
Verbal abuse officer: 14 cts.
Possess weapon: 3 cts.
Disrespect staff: 11 cts.
Throw bodily fluids: 11 cts.
Malingering: 3 cts.
Failure to clear room: 4 cts.

Juvenile Social Profile

Official records destroyed. Based on prior prison dossiers, Inmate Copeland became ward of the State of Ohio at age 7 upon death of biological mother, who was murdered by intimate acquaintance. Biological father's whereabouts are unknown. Inmate Copeland was first adjudicated in 1949 (age 9) for housebreaking (burglary), arson, and brandishing a deadly weapon. Inmate Copeland was committed to State Training School for Boys for 3 years. Inmate Copeland was released to his maternal grandmother, who became his legal guardian. Inmate Copeland was adjudicated in 1953 (age 13) for arson, robbery w/force, gross sexual imposition on minor, and possession of firearm, and returned to State Training School for Boys for 3 years. During incarceration, Inmate Copeland was adjudicated for multiple counts of sodomizing other inmates and attempted murder of another inmate. In 1956, Inmate Copeland was transferred to the Ohio State Reformatory, where he terminated his sentence in 1958. Prison psychiatric staff assessed Inmate Copeland and determined that he manifested acute antisocial personality disorder (psychopathy).

Arrest History

1—Arrested or received 1958/01/30

Agency: Erie PA Police Department
Charge 1: Joyriding
Charge 2: Drunk Driving

Charge 3: Unauth Use Vehicle
Charge 4: Ill Poss Firearm
Charge 5: Corrupt Minor
Court: Prosecutor Rejected Filing of Charges

2—Arrested or received 1958/02/02

Agency: Albany NY Police Department
Charge 1: Joyriding
Charge 2: Drunk Driving
Charge 3: Unauth Use Vehicle
Charge 4: Ill Poss Firearm
Charge 5: Corrupt Minor
Charge 6: Enable Runaway
Charge 7: Viol Dyer Act
Charge 8: Viol Mann Act
Court: Charges 1-8 Guilty Plea
Sentence: NY DOC, Indeterminate to 4 Yrs
Federal sentence to be served concur with state
charges order of United States Attorney

3—Arrested or received 1958/03/24

Agency: Auburn Penitentiary
Sentence: Indeterminate to 4 Yrs

4—Arrested or received 1961/11/01

Agency: Onondaga County (NY) Sheriff's Department
Charge 1: Rob w/Firearm
Charge 2: Rob w/Firearm
Charge 3: Aggrav Menacing
Charge 4: Murder w/Malice
Court: No Disposition

5—Arrested or received 1962/04/26

Agency: Syracuse NY Police Department
Charge 1: DUI
Charge 2: Unauth Use Vehicle

(Continued)

Box 5.2 (Continued)

Charge 3: No Operator Insurance
Charge 4: Drive w/o Valid DL
Court: Charges 1-4 Dismissed

6—Arrested or received 1962/05/30

Agency: Rochester NY Police Department
Charge 1: Rob w/Firearm
Charge 2: Rob w/Firearm
Charge 3: Aggrav Menacing
Charge 4: Aslt w/Intent to Rape
Charge 5: Aslt w/Intent to Kill
Court: Guilty at Trial on Charges 1-3; Charges 4-5 Dismissed
Sentence: 8 Yrs NY DOC

7—Arrested or received 1962/08/14

Agency: Attica Prison
Sentence: 8 Yrs

8—Arrested or received 1965/09/15

Agency: New York Dept. Parole and Probation
Charge 1: Release Conditional Parole 2 Yrs

9—Arrested or received 1965/12/18

Agency: Poughkeepsie NY Police Department
Charge 1: DUI
Charge 2: Domestic Battery
Charge 3: Aslt
Charge 4: Child Abuse/Willful Cruelty
Charge 5: Resist Arrest
Charge 6: Obstruct Police
Court: Held
Disposition: Parole Detainer
Sentence: 173 D Jail, Parole Reinstated

10—Arrested or received 1967/03/10

Agency: Summit County OH Sheriff's Department
Charge 1: Abduction
Charge 2: Rape
Charge 3: Lewd Acts on Minor
Charge 4: Resist Arrest
Charge 5: Obstruct Police
Charge 6: Aslt on Police Off
Charge 7: Ex-felon Possess Weapon
Charge 8: Attempt to Disarm Officer
Court:
Charge 1: Guilty Plea
Charge 2: Guilty Plea
Charge 3: Dismissed
Charge 4: Dismissed
Charge 5: Dismissed
Charge 6: Guilty Plea, Simple Aslt
Charge 7: Guilty Plea
Charge 8: Guilty Plea
Sentence: Ind-40 Yrs Ohio DOC

11—Arrested or received 1968/01/02

Agency: Mansfield Reformatory
Sentence: Ind-40 Yrs

12—Arrested or received 1977/06/05

Agency: Ohio Board of Parole
Sentence: 5 Yrs Supervised Release; Request to Relocate to Los Angeles
Approved (CADOC)

13—Arrested or received 1978/11/11

Agency: Los Angeles Police Department
Charge 1: Poss Controlled Substance
Charge 2: Poss Inject Device
Charge 3: Poss Drg Paraph

(Continued)

Box 5.2 (Continued)

Charge 4: Solict Prost
Court: Charges Dismissed

14—Arrested or received 1979/01/12

Agency: Los Angeles County Sheriff's Department
Charge 1: Under Influence Controlled Substance
Charge 2: Vagrancy
Charge 3: Commercial Burglary
Charge 4: Solict Prost
Charge 5: Failure to Appeal
Court: Held
Disposition: Guilty Plea
Sentence: 21 D Jail

15—Arrested or received 1979/03/10

Agency: San Francisco Police Department
Charge 1: Under Influence Controlled Substance
Charge 2: Commercial Burglary
Charge 3: Poss Burg Tools
Charge 4: Ill Poss Firearm
Charge 5: Poss Drg Paraph
Charge 6: Furnish Dwelling for Drug Sales
Charge 7: Poss LT 1 oz MJ
Court: Prosecution Rejected Filing of Charges

16—Arrested or received 1979/05/02

Agency: Marin County Sheriff's Department
Charge 1: Under Influence Controlled Substance
Charge 2: Burglary 2
Charge 3: Burglary 2
Charge 4: Ill Poss Firearm
Charge 5: Robbery by Force
Charge 6: Resist Arrest
Court: Charges 1-4 Dismissed
Charge 5: Guilty Plea Fel

Charge 6: Guilty Plea Fel
Sentence: 3 Yrs State Prison

17—Arrested or received 1979/05/04

Agency: California Board of Parole
Disposition: Violation
Sentence: 3 Yrs Prison Concurrent

18—Arrested or received 1982/07/01

Agency: Cuyahoga County OH Sheriff's Department
Charge 1: DWI
Court: Guilty Plea
Sentence: 45 D Jail

19—Arrested or received 1982/08/26

Agency: Lorain County Sheriff's Department
Charge 1: Public Intox
Charge 2: Disord Condt
Charge 3: Public Fighting
Charge 4: Vagrancy
Charge 5: Solict Prost
Court: Dismissed

20—Arrested or received 1982/10/30

Agency: West Virginia State Patrol
Charge 1: DWI
Charge 2: Resist Arr
Charge 3: No Operator Insurance
Charge 4: Driving w/o Valid License
Court: Guilt Plea to All Charges
Sentence: 20 D Jail, $

21—Arrested or received 1983/01/01

Agency: Cincinnati OH Police Department
Charge 1: Brawling

(Continued)

Box 5.2 (Continued)

Charge 2: Aslt w/Deadly Weapon
Charge 3: Aslt w/No Intent to Kill
Charge 4: Public Intoxication
Charge 5: Brandishing
Charge 6: Under Influence Controlled Subs
Charge 7: Resist Arr
Charge 8: Obstruct Police
Charge 9: Obstruct Ops
Charge 10: Habitual Criminal Offender
Court:
Charge 1: Guilty Plea
Charge 2: Guilty Plea
Charge 3: Dismissed
Charge 4: Guilty Plea
Charge 5: Dismissed
Charge 6: Dismissed
Charge 7: Dismissed
Charge 8: Dismissed
Charge 9: Dismissed
Charge 10: Dismissed
Sentence: 720 D Hamilton County Jail

22—Arrested or received 1986/03/15

Agency: Rochester NY Police Department
Charge 1: Domestic Violence
Charge 2: Aslt 3
Charge 3: Aslt 3
Charge 4: Child Abuse 2
Charge 5: Resist Arrest
Charge 6: Obstruct Police
Court: No Disposition

23—Arrested or received 1993/10/10

Agency: Akron Police Department
Charge 1: Domestic Violence

Charge 2: Poss Schedule II (Cocaine)
Charge 3: Poss Drug Paraph
Charge 4: Resist Arrest
Charge 5: Obstruct Police
Charge 6: Aslt on Police Off
Charge 7: Ex-felon Possess Weap
Charge 8: Agg Robbery
Charge 9: Agg Robbery
Charge 10: Habitual Criminal Offender
Court:
Charge 1-7: Dismissed
Charge 8: Guilty Plea
Charge 9: Guilty Plea
Charge 10: Dismissed
Sentence: 20 Yrs Prison

24—Arrested or received 1993/12/12

Agency: Mansfield Reformatory
Sentence: 20 Yrs

25—Arrested or received 2003/11/05

Agency: Akron Police Department and Summit County District
   Attorney
Charge 1: Agg Murder
Charge 2: Agg Robbery
Charge 3: Agg Murder
Charge 4: Agg Robbery
Charge 5: Agg Murder
Charge 6: Agg Robbery
Charge 7: Murder
Charge 8: Agg Robbery
Charge 9: Escape Correctional Facility
Charge 10: Escape With Force
Charge 11: Auto Theft
Charge 12: Agg Aslt

(Continued)

Box 5.2 (Continued)

Charge 13: Kidnap
Charge 14: Burg Dwelling
Charge 15: Rape
Charge 16: Agg Robbery
Charge 17: Burg Dwelling
Charge 18: Burg Dwelling
Charge 19: Rape
Charge 20: GSI Minor
Charge 21: Rape
Charge 22: Kidnap w/Aggravation
Charge 23: Kidnap w/Aggravation
Charge 24: Att Homicide
Charge 25: Att Homicide Law Enforcement Officer
Charge 26: Felon Posses Firearm
Charge 27: Felon Posses Firearm
Charge 28: Felon Posses Firearm
Charge 29: Felon Posses Firearm
Charge 30: Felon Posses Firearm
Charge 31: Felon Posses Firearm
Charge 32: Felon Posses Firearm
Charge 33: Felon Posses Firearm
Court:
Charges 1-26: Guilty at trial
Charges 27-33: Dismissed
Sentence:

Charge 1: Death
Charge 2: Life
Charge 3: Death
Charge 4: Life
Charge 5: Death
Charge 6: Life
Charge 7: Life
Charge 8: Life
Charge 9: Life
Charge 10: Life
Charge 11: 25 Yrs

Charge 12: 25 Yrs
Charge 13: Life
Charge 14: Life
Charge 15: Life
Charge 16: 50 Yrs
Charge 17: 40 Yrs
Charge 18: 40 Yrs
Charge 19: Life
Charge 20: 50 Yrs
Charge 21: Life
Charge 22: Life
Charge 23: Life
Charge 24: 75 Yrs
Charge 25: 75 Yrs
Charge 26: 5 Yrs

26—Arrested or received 1993/11/12

Agency: Mansfield Reformatory
Sentence: Death (X3) Consecutive + 14 Life w/o Parole + 385 Yrs Ohio DRC

SOURCE: National Crime Information Center FBI Identification Record, Interpol, Ohio Bureau of Investigation, Ohio DRC Diagnostic and Classification Unit, inmate self-reports with Dr. Nelson Bentley, Ph.D.

NOTE: This is a fictional profile; any similarity to an inmate, living or dead, is purely coincidence.

Introduction

The vignettes from previous chapters and the offender profiles shown in Boxes 5.1 and 5.2 illustrate two ideal types of offenders. On one hand is the fairly nonserious offender, whose trouble with the law is linked to life circumstances relating to social institutions such as family or work. Chronic offending from this perspective unfolds developmentally. On the other hand is the serious, violent offender, whose repeated violations of the law are a way of life. The extremity of his conduct lends credence to the idea that habitual antisocial behavior is the manifestation of some pathology or criminal propensity.

It is important to recognize that the theoretical perspective that one believes best represents the evidence is not wholly removed from one's ideological worldview. Whether one believes that serious criminals are changeable speaks to ideological assessments of the character and nature of human beings and their behavior. For some, the term *career criminal* is a label that will serve to further stigmatize and exacerbate the risk factors that chronic offenders experience. For others, this moniker is the mark of Cain.

This chapter explores three of the more controversial issues related to career criminals. The first and most important of these issues is the ethical concerns among criminologists about the scientific inability to accurately predict chronic offending. Although criminologists have confidently identified the small group of inveterate criminals, prospectively identifying them has proven more difficult. As a result, scholars are equivocal, judicious, and rightly concerned that mistakenly punishing offenders purported to be career criminals carries with it intolerable human and fiscal costs. The dilemmas of prediction and singularly identifying individual offenders are examined herein at length.

The remaining two issues, news media coverage and academic politics, are less central to criminology but nevertheless figure into the collective understanding of career criminals. However, like the ethical problem with prediction, they serve to weaken our resolve to appropriately respond to the challenges posed by career criminals. News media outlets devote considerable resources toward covering crime but are largely unhelpful in elucidating the career criminal problem. For example, the extensive coverage of horrendous crimes often fails to make the explicit connection that these crimes are disproportionately the work of chronic offenders. This is important because the public indignation that crime news generates is often misplaced toward criminal offenders generally. This can contribute to a public demand to get tough on crime generally instead of the more cost-effective and efficient focus on career criminals. Additionally, news media accounts inconsistently present habitual criminals as sympathetic figures who are victims of social disadvantage, strident criminals who take advantage of loopholes in the lenient criminal justice system, and victims of a needlessly harsh criminal justice system. These competing images create diffuse skepticism about career criminals and the appropriateness of criminal justice policies to control them.

Finally, a peripheral but lingering idea in criminology is the belief that career criminals are social constructions that serve as fodder to promote conservative, crime-control interests. The social constructionist perspective and its attendant political ramifications stand in opposition to the empirical or positivist stance that career criminals are genuine threats to public safety. The constructionist view is critiqued here. While this discussion is critical, it is important to recognize that, at the very least, the social constructionist viewpoint illustrates a theoretical, and perhaps ideological, unwillingness to reconcile empirical data with one's belief system. Although located to the left of mainstream developmental theories, the constructionist arguments demonstrate just how politically loaded a topic such as career criminals is.

The Ethical Quandaries of Prediction

At a variety of points in the criminal justice system, practitioners employ prediction to guide their decision making when processing criminal offenders. Traditionally, prediction was a clinical assessment based on the individual's gut feeling that was itself rooted in experiential knowledge. There are many examples of how this manifests. Police officers weigh a prediction of the likelihood that a defendant will appear in court when issuing a summons or making an arrest. Pretrial service personnel similarly predict the risks of flight, recidivism, and danger that an individual poses when ascertaining bond. Probation and parole officers gauge their supervision of clients based on intuitive predictions of how risky their clients are. In all of these contexts, the evidence that professionals utilize when making predictions of future conduct is the prior conduct of the same individuals. It is a psychological truism that the best predictor of future behavior is past behavior.[1]

Despite this axiom, many criminal offenders behave in unpredictable ways, and forecasting their future conduct has proven difficult. This has been particularly frustrating to criminologists and policy makers who seek to identify the small group of career criminals. Prediction has evolved from clinical assessments to the use of actuarial instruments composed of criteria that empirically relate to criminal offending. A controversial example of the actuarial approach is the scale developed by RAND researcher Peter Greenwood with assistance from Allan Abrahamse. Based on data derived from self-reported criminal records of 2,190 male jail and prison inmates in California, Michigan, and Texas, the Greenwood Scale contained seven items thought to predict chronic offending. The items were distilled from the offense backgrounds and social characteristics of the most recidivistic prisoners and are the following: prior incarceration for the same type of offense, incarceration for more than half of the preceding 2 years, conviction prior to age 16, juvenile incarceration, recent narcotic use, adolescent narcotic use, and employment for less than half of the preceding 2 years. Offenders were scored (0 = no, 1 = yes) for each characteristic. Those with cumulative scores of 0 or 1 were considered low-rate, those who scored 2 or 3 were medium-rate, and those who scored 4 or higher were high-rate criminals.

Overall, Greenwood and Abrahamse estimated that 27% of offenders were low-rate, 44% were medium-rate, and 29% were high-rate. Incarcerating only the latter group would reduce the robbery rate by 15% while reducing the total robbery incarceration rate by 5%. A similar 15% reduction in burglary would require a 7% increase in the burglar inmate population. Overall, the scale correctly predicted just 51% of offenders. After its publication, scholars found a variety of shortcomings with the Greenwood Scale and its purported ability to prospectively identify chronic offenders and reduce the prison population. For example, the scale had a false positive rate in excess of 50%. This meant that half of the offenders predicted to be high-rate actually were not. Thus, incarcerating them on the basis of their predicted risk would not only produce unnecessary prison costs but also, and more important, imprison those who were not career criminals. Moreover, the scale had a false negative rate of about 16%, which meant that nearly one in five career criminals was missed. In a later work, Greenwood himself largely concurred with his critics about the difficulty in predicting chronic offenders.[2]

In the intervening years, other criminologists have attempted to refine the Greenwood Scale to arrive at a more accurate prediction instrument. Although they were applied to new and diverse samples of offenders and contained refined scale items, prediction instruments continued to yield false negative rates in excess of 50% and be largely ineffective at identifying career offenders.[3] In fact, prediction scales appeared to be more equipped at predicting low-rate offenders. For example, Hennessey Hayes and Michael Geerken ingeniously noted that although prediction instruments were ineffective at identifying the high-rate offenders, they were quite accurate at identifying low-rate offenders. Indeed, their instruments and prior ones correctly predicted 60% to 84% of low-rate offenders. As a result, Hayes and Geerken suggested that policy makers should focus on the majority of offenders who are not career criminals and whom prediction instruments can identify. Moreover, they proposed that noncareer offenders could be selected for early release from prison since their low propensity for recidivism could confidently be assessed. Another recent scaling effort also demonstrated that while identifying career criminals is difficult, identifying benign offenders is not. Recently, Matt DeLisi developed a theoretically informed scale to identify the life-course persistent offender conceptualized by Terrie Moffitt. The scale was amazingly accurate in predicting outcomes for nonchronic offenders. For example, when identifying low-rate offenders for violent arrests, property arrests, felony convictions, and prison sentences, the current identifications were 94%, 88%, 93%, and 95%, respectively. Like prior efforts, the scale identified high-rate offenders at rates no better than chance.[4]

Numerous scholars have levied critiques, at times impassioned, against prediction instruments because of their inaccuracy and the attendant ethical dilemmas. Mark Moore succinctly summarized these critiques:

> There are problems with the idea of relying on predictive tests. To retributivists, it seems wrong to impose criminal liabilities on the basis of predictions of further criminal acts. To many others, it seems wrong to impose liabilities on people who are falsely predicted to commit crimes in the future. Still others worry about the characteristics that will be used in the predictive tests, thinking that it would be wrong to use characteristics that were not under the control of the offenders and were not themselves criminal in nature. And there are always the questions of exactly at what point in the criminal justice process the tests would be applied and what consequences the use of the tests would have for criminal offenders.[5]

Despite the genuine concerns of scholars and the empirical inadequacy of many of their prediction instruments, prediction has and will continue to be practiced in criminal justice vis-à-vis career criminals. Fortunately, one area where prediction has fared better is the risk prediction instrument used by federal parole. For more than 30 years, the U.S. Parole Commission's Salient Factor Score has proven to be an effective actuarial device in predicting career criminality among federal offenders. The Salient Factor Score contains measures such as prior adjudications and convictions, prior commitments of more than 30 days, active criminal justice status, age, and heroin addiction. It is reverse-coded; thus, offenders who scored 0 to 3 are assessed as poor risks, 4 to 5 are fair risks, 6 to 7 are good risks, and 8 to 10 are very good risks. Over the years, the Salient Factor Score has been streamlined and refined to encompass only criminal history–relevant items and replicated on multiple validation samples.[6]

In my opinion, the inability to prospectively identify career criminals via prediction instruments and the ethical questions that this failure raises have been extremely damaging. Many criminologists are rightfully concerned about attempts by policy makers and the criminal justice system to selectively focus on individual offenders in a forecasting context. By and large, we have been unable to do so, and most prediction instruments work only as well as if one had flipped a coin to assess dangerousness or likelihood of recidivism. Obviously, this is unacceptable. Not only does this serve as an impetus for future researchers to develop better actuarial devices, but it also serves as a cautionary tale for the academic community to treat with apprehension claims that career criminals can be identified in advance.

Media Portrayals of Career Criminals

To be sure, the mass media coverage of crime, criminals, and the criminal justice system is extensive. Newspapers from the smallest village to the largest metropolis provide daily stories of criminal acts that occur in the community. A regular feature of the American newspaper is the police blotter, a daily or weekly listing of community residents and other persons who have been arrested by local authorities. On television, crime-related stories are often the lead story on local news programs, and television movies and scores of programs are entirely devoted to criminal justice issues. The number of Internet sites devoted to crime is innumerable. In short, crime is integral to the news media, especially in the United States.

As mentioned earlier, when dealing explicitly with career criminals, the media transmit inconsistent and often conflicting messages. Media coverage of career criminals is organized into three camps: coverage of crime events that often fails to make the explicit point that the preponderance of crimes are committed by career offenders; coverage that is often sympathetic to career criminals because of adversities that the defendants themselves have endured; and coverage that alternately portrays the criminal justice system and crime-control policies as absurd, needlessly punitive, ineffective, and unfair to career criminals.

The Criminological Significance of Career Criminals

Frequently, atrocious criminal events—the ones that inspire the most outrage and fear among community residents—are the handiwork of chronic offenders. Across the nation, there are regrettably many incidents demonstrating this point.

In Missouri, a woman was kidnapped, brutalized, and raped for several hours before she was able to escape her captor. Ultimately, the defendant in the case pleaded guilty to seven counts of sodomy in exchange for the dismissal of numerous other felony charges. It was later discovered that the defendant had been imprisoned for 20 of the previous 21 years for prior convictions for murder, assault, robbery, burglary, and assorted other offenses. While on parole in 1990, the defendant committed a similar incident where he kidnapped and repeatedly sodomized a young woman—and this case resulted in an acquittal!

In Illinois, residents of the Chicago Cabrini-Green housing projects were shocked by the brutal attack of a young girl who was raped and beaten to such a degree that she was left blind, mute, and crippled. The 26-year-old defendant in this case was sentenced to 120 years in prison. Records maintained by the Illinois Department of Corrections indicated that the defendant had been imprisoned at age 18 for convictions for armed robbery and attempted aggravated criminal sexual assault.

In Connecticut, a 27-year-old man was charged in the stabbing deaths of his aunt and her two children before leading the police to the skeletal remains of a woman who had been missing. Court records indicated that the man had 23 prior convictions, including 9 felony convictions in the past 10 years.

In California, an armed man abducted two teenage girls from a youth hangout and bound their male companions with duct tape. After raping both girls, the perpetrator drove for 100 miles to an isolated area where, according to the victims, he announced that he was going to murder both women and bury them. Miraculously, the police caught up to them seemingly moments before the perpetrator was going to commit the double homicide. Police shot the abductor to death. As savage as this scenario was, it became increasingly clear that it was only the latest exploit of this violent career criminal. At the time of his death, the man was wanted in California on five counts of rape, the alleged victim being his own step-daughter, and in Nevada for carjacking. For nearly two decades, he had accumulated several arrests and convictions in several states, including prison terms for burglary, methamphetamine possession, and grand theft.

In Pennsylvania, a 7-year-old girl gnawed her way through duct tape bindings and broke a window after being abducted and left in a basement for 24 hours. The suspects in the case allegedly abducted the girl and threatened to kill her unless their sizable ransom was paid. As the case unfolded, it was learned that both suspects had lengthy criminal records, including multiple arrests for drug violations and crimes of violence. It was later learned that the pair had abducted the girl because they believed her family had recently received a sizeable insurance settlement.

In Oklahoma, two convicts escaped from the Oklahoma State Penitentiary. One defendant was serving a life sentence for the murder and rape of an 81-year-old woman, an act committed when the perpetrator was just 17 years old. After capture, the defendant was convicted of two escape-related charges and, according to prison records, first-degree manslaughter after he had been incarcerated for 6 years. The prison record for the other escapee was even more prolific. As a juvenile, he was convicted and incarcerated for four counts of kidnapping, four counts of burglary, and three counts of theft. He previously escaped from prison while serving sentences for these crimes before receiving a 20-year sentence for kidnapping, assault on a police officer, escape, and conspiracy charges. Thus, the instant offense was his third escape from prison in less than a decade.

In Nevada, a 33-year-old man was sentenced to death for murder and armed robbery, a case in which he used a 15-year-old female runaway to lure the victim to a motel with a ruse of sex. During the murder trial, a former victim of the defendant testified that he raped her at knifepoint in Illinois. Records also show that the defendant had served prison time in Ohio for burglary and parole violations.

In Ohio, two men killed a promising high school football star for what appeared to be a robbery. One man was convicted of 15 criminal counts, including murder, attempted murder, and assault, and received a 46-year-to-life sentence. Records indicate that the defendant had already been committed to state prison on three separate occasions for drug trafficking, weapons charges, escape, and failure to comply with court orders. The other accused, who is awaiting a retrial, had four prior prison stints for crimes such as property, drug, weapons, and escape charges. Also in Akron, Ohio, a man was sentenced to life in prison without parole and classified as a violent sexual predator for the kidnapping and rape of a 9-year-old girl. Ohio prison records indicate that the same man was convicted of corrupting a minor and escape in 1992 (1-year sentence), gross sexual imposition in 1992 (3-year sentence), and rape in 1998 (4-year sentence).[7]

The recurrent theme is that persons who are no strangers to the criminal justice system often account for serious violent crimes that constitute the news. Unfortunately, the significance of this is not often explored. By not stressing the explicit link between career criminals and the incidence of crime, the news media lose an opportunity to inform the public. Instead, news consumers are left with the idea, which is sometimes correct, that the criminal justice system accords considerable leniency to criminal offenders, even high-rate ones. This creates public indignation directed against criminals writ large and calls for tougher criminal justice, a situation that policy makers are often willing to oblige. Thus, public outrage over crime tends to be general and unfocused, not specific and concentrated on the small cadre of career criminals. In the place of cries to stop the "violent few" is general rancor. Even offenders buy into this. For example, a frequent offender who was imprisoned for robbery after being paroled early for a prior robbery conviction has launched a $1.6 million suit against prison and parole officials. The offender asserts that the *state* was responsible for his crimes because it knew full well that career offenders like himself are incorrigible and recidivate upon release.[8]

The Sympathetic Life of Career Criminals

The media's tendency to miss the criminological import of crime events committed by chronic offenders is unfortunate but somewhat innocuous. Portraying them as victims of social circumstances rather than their own pathologies is more problematic. Because many career offenders were themselves the victims of considerable cruelty and disadvantage during their childhood, it is somewhat easy to empathize with them.[9] However, does empathy compete with our desire to morally condemn and punish repeat offenders? The following news accounts address the tension between compassion and a desire to punish.

In Florida, a 67-year-old woman was sentenced to 4 years in prison for five felonies related to masterminding a multicity pickpocket enterprise. The frail woman—who suffers from kidney failure and arthritis, and is wheelchair-bound—clearly presented herself as a sympathetic defendant. Florida prison records indicated that the woman had been imprisoned twice previously, both for grand theft, and served two probation sentences for cocaine possession and grand theft. Between the ages of 46 and 67, the defendant amassed nine felony convictions.

An increasingly contentious debate centers on the appropriateness of executing defendants who are either mentally ill or mentally retarded. Two recent cases, both occurring in Texas, are illustrative. The U.S. Supreme Court recently decided that the execution of the mentally retarded constituted a violation of the 8th Amendment's proscription against cruel and unusual punishment. The case involved a man with an IQ of about 60 who was convicted of raping, stomping, and mortally stabbing a woman in 1979. Often relegated to the back paragraphs in articles covering this case was the fact that the defendant was on parole after serving less than 2 years of a 5-year sentence for a previous rape conviction. Another Texas inmate with diagnosed paranoid schizophrenia was executed in 2003 for killing a woman who resisted his attempts to rape her. Arrest records indicated that the defendant told authorities that he killed the woman simply because he *wanted* to be returned to prison. Texas prison records indicated multiple prior stints in prison for crimes such as aggravated robbery with a deadly weapon, burglary, arson, and assorted parole violations.

In California, a defendant was executed for the murder of an 81-year-old woman who was shot in the face after the defendant burglarized her home. The man was only the 10th person to be executed in California since capital punishment was reinstated in 1978. As the execution approached, defenders suggested that the defendant should be spared because of his brutal childhood at the hands of an abusive father and mentally ill mother. Other apparently redeeming features of the defendant were that he had suffered from ineffective defense counsel and, while on death row, learned Latin and had begun to write poems about repentance. The defendant's prison dossier tells a different story. The defendant was an escapee from Utah State Prison, where he was serving time for multiple convictions for aggravated burglary. While imprisoned, he murdered another inmate and assaulted several other inmates and staff. He admitted to killing at least six people in Nevada but was never charged.

In Florida, a man died while on death row—just before the Innocence Project used forensic evidence to prove that he was actually innocent of the charges for which he was condemned. (The vital role of the Innocence Project is discussed in Chapter 6.) For good reason, the miscarriage of justice received a great deal of condemnatory press coverage. Unfortunately, the outrage that should have been directed against the error-prone criminal justice system was redirected by attempting to lionize the defendant by lamenting his lifetime of disadvantage. Moreover, the defendant, who was actually innocent of the murder charges that wrongfully resulted in his placement on death row, had previously been convicted of two separate killings, one when he was just 13 years old and the other when he was 18 years old. Of course, miscarriages of justice are intolerable;

however, it was questionable to suggest that this person was an innocent angel unscrupulously plucked from the streets. Indeed, he had two prior murders underneath his belt, circumstances that undoubtedly contributed to his wrongful arrest and ultimate prosecution.

In sum, a variety of sociological hardships have been invoked to cast collective pity on the lives, circumstances, and behaviors of career criminals. At times, these hardships have been presented as extenuating circumstances or justifications for habitual criminal behavior. This deflects needed attention from the habitual criminal conduct and can have calamitous consequences. A famous example is the case of Jack Henry Abbott. Abbott became famous for his book *In the Belly of the Beast,* which consisted of letters he had written to author Norman Mailer while serving time in New York for bank robbery and the fatal stabbing of another inmate. Abbott's writings were attractive to the intelligentsia of that era, especially Mailer, who lobbied for Abbott's parole. Abbott was indeed paroled in 1981 but he was at large for a mere 6 weeks before stabbing a man to death outside of a restaurant. He was subsequently prosecuted and sent back to prison, where he died of suicide in 2002.[10]

The Mercurial Criminal Justice System

The news media provide numerous examples of events supporting the view that the criminal justice system inappropriately responds to career criminals. In one view, the leniency of the criminal justice system and the unwillingness of its operatives to take the criminality of the worst offenders seriously contribute to additional crime. From another perspective, the criminal justice system is portrayed as a bully—the mean-spirited Goliath who sets chronic offenders up for failure or inflicts needlessly cruel policies on them. The following contains examples from each perspective.

A case that received nationwide publicity was the December 2000 escape of seven violent career criminals from a maximum-security prison in Texas. While in flight from prison, the men committed additional felonies culminating in the murder of an Irving, Texas, police officer during the robbery of a sporting goods store. Ultimately, the seven were captured. One defendant committed suicide, three were sentenced to death, and three were sentenced to lesser prison terms. Prior to the escape, the inmate leader was serving multiple life sentences upon convictions for 13 counts of aggravated kidnapping with a deadly weapon, 4 counts of aggravated robbery with a deadly weapon, and burglary. Prior to their escape, the other two condemned offenders were serving time for capital murder with a deadly weapon and aggravated robbery with a deadly weapon (with two previous commitments for the same offenses), respectively. In fact, the latter offender had the temerity to blame the killing of the police officer on the victim, suggesting that had the officer been better trained, he could have avoided being ambushed and executed by the escaped convicts.

Citizens have begun to mobilize in Massachusetts out of frustration over the lack of veracity that judges have in dealing with habitual offenders. For example, an offender who had amassed more than 100 arrest charges during a 27-year offending career was recently released on a personal recognizance bond after an arrest for shoplifting, drug possession, and four active warrants. His record contained 9 arrests for assault with a dangerous weapon in addition to an assortment of property, drug, and public-order crimes. In California, the case of an ex-convict charged with murdering an undercover police officer is illustrative of the potential risks of not appropriately and competently dealing with chronic offenders. The defendant should have been incapacitated by the state's three-strikes statute; however, prosecutors mistakenly concluded that his six armed robbery convictions constituted a single firearm possession case, not six separate violent felonies. As a result, he had been sentenced to 32 months in prison instead of 25 years to life.

Prior to leaving office in the midst of a corruption scandal, Governor George Ryan pardoned four death row inmates and commuted the sentences of all condemned offenders to life imprisonment in Illinois. The unprecedented move occurred because of allegations from some death row inmates who claimed that Chicago police officers beat them into confessing to capital offenses. The move received praise from civil libertarian groups yet evoked outrage from criminal justice and victim's rights organizations. Interestingly, one of the pardoned inmates remained behind bars for additional convictions that presumably were not the outcome of police corruption. According to records maintained by the Illinois Department of Corrections, the individual (whose death sentence for murder and 15-year sentence for armed robbery were overturned pardoned) remains behind bars upon convictions for home invasion, rape, armed robbery, deviant sexual assault, aggravated kidnapping with no ransom, and kidnapping with secret confinement. The offender is expected to be paroled in November 2023 when he is 61 years old.

Not dealing with serious criminals in the harshest manner possible is not limited to the United States. In Canada, a career criminal who was on day parole while serving a life sentence for armed robbery committed seven drug-related homicides. The offender, whose official record dated to 1974, had compiled a record containing 36 prior convictions including 2 attempted murders, 2 escapes from prison, and multiple armed robberies. Another Canadian offender, serving a 5-year sentence for kidnapping and aggravated assault in which the victim needed reconstructive surgery, continued to plague correctional staff with his misconduct behind bars. Twice, the defendant was diagnosed as a prototypical psychopath. In Vancouver, a serial burglar with more than 100 burglary arrests or convictions on his 13-year criminal record received a mere 5- to 8-month sentence after burglarizing a home and stealing nearly $6,000 worth of property. Finally, another Vancouver case involved a career criminal who received unexpected leniency from the judge. The 47-year-old offender with 33 property-related convictions on his record received a 2-year probation sentence for credit card fraud and theft. The reasoning for the light sentence was that incarceration was ineffective in reducing this offender's criminal behavior; thus, it should not be used further. Ironically, the presiding judge in the case was the individual who offered this rationale while imposing the meager sentence.[11]

In other circumstances, the news media document scenarios whereby career criminals are punished in seemingly draconian ways. In this view, the response of the criminal justice system to career criminals is framed as gratuitous, costly, and ineffective. A recent case that speaks to this is the recent life sentence administered to an Oklahoma offender who spat at and bit officers as they responded to a domestic violence incident. The news report portrayed the application of a life sentence as unjustified given the defendant's "history of drug and alcohol abuse" and "limited education." Imprisoning an offender for life for spitting on any officer also sends the message that the criminal justice system will respond with ferocity if one of its own operatives is victimized. The article did acknowledge that the defendant had prior felony convictions that qualified him for the life sentence. Fortunately, Oklahoma is a state with excellent online access to the records of its prisoner population. Based on the name and age parameters given in the news article, one can quickly obtain the prison profile of this offender. Prior felony convictions were unearthed: two prior convictions for first-degree rape, two convictions for burglary, and one conviction for unauthorized use of a vehicle. The message of incapacitating an offender with "prior felony convictions" is a different one than the message that would have been sent by stating that two of these were for rape. Indeed, the apparent severity of the life sentence becomes contextually different for an offender with such a violent criminal past.

A recent California case involved the application of a third strike against an offender convicted of stealing $11 worth of wine, lip balm, and breath freshener—an oversight that defense counsel asserted was the result of a brain injury that causes forgetfulness. The article also stated that the defendant had 17 prior felonies on his record, including the home invasion–robbery–rape of a woman and her 15-year-old daughter, the attempted murder of a police dispatcher, and a half-dozen armed robberies. Interestingly, the punishment for the $11 theft was included in the "weird news" section of the local newspaper.

The lawful application of statutes designed to target and neutralize the worst criminal offenders has been portrayed as inappropriate and, at times, constitutionally dubious. This can create concerns that serve to undermine the retributive rationale that drives the enactment of these laws in the first place. Consequently, the following questions remain unanswered: Why are so many offenders who have been previously convicted of serious, predatory violence serving a fraction of their lengthy prison terms? How is it that an offender can, over a period of decades, amass dozens and even hundreds of arrests, convictions, and sentences? and Why, as communities attempt to cope with heinous crimes committed by career offenders, were these individuals freed in the first place? Because the news media transmit such inconsistent images of career criminals, casting them in varied roles ranging from monster to victim, we are uncertain about them. Thus, we cannot be convinced that an $11 theft resulting in a life sentence is absurd, because it could be more or less outrageous than the continued recidivism of chronic offenders and the unwillingness of the criminal justice system to mete out punishment. For instance, in Colorado, an offender with 177 arrests was portrayed as the victimized pawn of a purported ploy by the local criminal justice system to induce voters to pass a jail expansion issue.[12]

Academics and Career Criminals

Travis Hirschi and the late Michael Hindelang, two of the most influential criminologists, once had this to say about their peers:

Few groups in American society have been defended more diligently by sociologists against allegations of difference than ordinary delinquents. From the beginning, the thrust of sociological theory has been to deny the relevance of individual differences to an explanation of delinquency, and the thrust of sociological criticism has been to discount research findings apparently to the contrary.[13]

To be sure, the overwhelming majority of criminologists (regardless of their political orientation) fully recognize the existence of career criminals and the nefariousness of their conduct. Unfortunately, not all criminologists do. Over the years, some have mounted a veritable campaign against the career criminal and the policies designed to neutralize him. In part, their uneasiness about the worst offenders stems from predominantly liberal political leanings that are fundamentally oriented against the idea of preternaturally antisocial people. Evidence of this is provided here.

There is no doubt that criminologists, as academics, are significantly more liberal in their political philosophy than the general population.[14] For example, Anthony Walsh and Lee Ellis polled members of the American Society of Criminology to assess their self-reported political orientation and preferred theoretical explanation for criminal behavior. They found that more than half (50.3%) of the criminologists identified as liberal and another 8.2% identified as radical or extreme left. Nearly 26% of criminologists reported that they were moderates, and only 15.6% self-identified as conservative. Significant differences existed across the groups in terms of their preferred theoretical perspective, leading Walsh and Ellis to suggest that political perspectives, whether they are linked to empirical evidence, are a significant component of criminological theorizing. Indeed, the American Society of Criminology has taken an organizational stand against capital punishment. It is difficult to imagine such a stand occurring among crime control–minded conservatives.

Two voices from diametric political angles have written about the liberal orthodoxy among criminologists. According to David Garland,

For the educated middle classes, a "civilized" attitude towards crime-stressing social circumstances rather than individual responsibility . . . has been a sign of cultural distinction making off urbane, educated, cultured opinion from the more vulgar, more reactionary views. To adopt a correctionalist, non-punitive attitude was, at once, to disdain the vulgarities of the under-educated, to express compassion for the poor masses, and *to further their professional interest* [italics added].[15]

Social critic and scholar Thomas Sowell similarly commented on the professional orientation of criminologists:

> In this formulation [political correctness]—common among the intelli-gentsia—people are in jail because they cannot function in this society. It is not that they do not choose to function, but to prey on others instead . . . usu-ally neither evidence nor logic is asked or given for such blanket indictments of "society" or for a non-judgmental view of criminals. It is simply part of the zeitgeist and a shortcut to distinction-cheap-glory to take a stand against "society."[16]

Like those in other areas of work, criminologists develop a professional identity and political persona that are commensurate with the norms of their profession. Against the backdrop of a liberal academic community, it should be expected that some scholars were hesitant to acknowledge the existence of a small cadre of career criminals. Furthermore, considerable resistance should be expected against public policies designed to stop career criminals (recall the discussion at the beginning of this chapter). Unfortunately, academic dissension can carry heavy costs, namely equiv-ocating the willingness to address serious repeat criminals. One of the techniques that academicians use that bears on these costs is social con-structionism, the worldview that the objective and empirical are in fact subjective and manufactured.

Constructing the Career Criminal

As early as the 1930s, some within criminology demonstrated an unusual solicitude for criminal offenders and an equally visceral distaste for offi-cial social control. For example, Frank Tannenbaum described the process of sanctioning the criminal offender as the dramatization of evil.[17] The progenitor of the social constructionist school in criminology may very well be one of the discipline's most hallowed figures, Edwin Sutherland. In two articles published in 1950, Sutherland voiced his concern about the creation and diffusion of laws aimed at offenders who engaged in sexu-ally predatory offenses.[18] According to Sutherland, isolated incidents of serious crimes committed by sexual psychopaths received nationwide media coverage and were blown out of proportion to the extent that such events were isolated, rare events in the overall picture of crime. As the news of the bad acts of sexual psychopaths spread, community residents became increasingly panicked and clamored for the system to protect them. In haste, policy makers enacted legislation that was driven by this expressive indignation toward violent sexual predators.[19]

Sutherland's work is characteristic of the social constructionist approach used in studying the worst type of offenders, such as career criminals or sexual psychopaths. First, legislation that results from politically mobilized citizens who are outraged by crime is often disparaged as resulting from "moral panic." The motivation for decrying indignation against serious criminals is perhaps a good one. Incidents of atrocious violence, committed by career criminals or otherwise, are rare compared to the prevalence of mundane crimes such as burglary, larceny, auto theft, drug violations, simple assault, and the like. In this sense, constructionists are correct in noting that the dangers posed, in probability terms, by serious violent criminals are relatively rare. To illustrate this point, scholars cleverly show that the dangers posed by ordinary household events exceed the likelihood that one will be abducted, raped, and killed by a psychopath. Thus, when considering all of the crimes that occur across the larger criminological landscape, panic does appear unwarranted and probably should not drive policy.[20]

A more troubling aspect of this approach centers on the skepticism surrounding serious violent criminals who engage in behaviors like murder, rape, and abduction. It is as if scholars with this worldview deny the very existence of offenders whom more than a century of researchers have identified. For example, Jonathan Simon reviewed the history of the career criminal offender as it relates to criminology and suggested that hard-core recidivists were born from a relationship between government and criminology. In this view, criminologists are weary of the very notion of the career criminal but invoke this "bogeyman" out of a social duty to assuage public fears.[21] Some have taken this logic even further by imputing diabolical motives among those who stress crime-control measures. For example, Elliott Currie likened the conservative, tough-on-crime movement of the latter 20th century to social Darwinism with his insinuation that the belief that violent or wicked people exist is analogous to believing or advocating a Darwinian social engineering program.[22]

Alida Merlo and Peter Benekos suggested that the presentation of atrocious crimes creates the misguided belief that most crimes are random and heinous. However, they expressed concern that the publicity surrounding the exploits of career offenders galvanizes the collective fear of crime and facilitates the easy passage of "quick-fix" policies. The examples that they provided include Megan's Law, originally a New Jersey law that requires states to notify communities when sex offenders move into their neighborhood; and two New York laws—Jenna's Law, which is a measure to end parole for all violent felons, and Joan's Law, which imposes a life imprisonment without parole sentence for murder-rapes when the victim is younger than 14.[23] Merlo and Benekos are correct in the sense that retributive policy, in the absence of front-end prevention policies, will not meaningfully fix the crime problem. However, it is an important first step.

Even criminal career researchers are occasionally guilty of mollifying the certainty about career criminals. For example, scholars from the Columbus, Ohio, Dangerous Offender Project suggested that "the violent-monster theme occurs frequently in popular and criminal literature . . . although such persons do exist, they do not appear in our samples in sufficient numbers to perpetuate the myth as a serious problem." On the basis of quantitative analyses of official records, Alfred Blumstein and Soumyo Moitra concluded that "the long-record 'career criminal' is as likely as the shorter-record persister to have made the current arrest his last. In that event, locking up the 'career criminal' averts no more crimes than locking up any other persister."[24] Statements such as these are unfortunate because they contradict the very rationale for studying career criminals. The very reason that career criminals are fodder for research and policy is that so few offenders commit so much of the crime. The very language used by constructionists (e.g. "moral panic") suggests that punitive responses to violent crime or violent criminals are knee-jerk reactions of moralistic people who unfairly stand in judgment of others. It is unclear how outrage against predatory behavior is viewed as moralistic. For example, Sutherland stated, "'Molestation' is a weasel word and can refer to anything from rape to whistling at a girl."[25] What is a "weasel" word? Did Sutherland imply that molestation is inexact and should not be used? It would seem that a term such as *molestation* is in the same family as sexual battery, rape, and the like. Indeed, there exists cross-cultural consensus about the wrongfulness of crimes that Sutherland described.[26] By suggesting that moralists are imposing their viewpoints on others is tantamount to suggesting that predatory criminals and violent crimes are accepted by some segments of our society. This is not the case.

Part and parcel of this approach is the portrayal of the criminal justice system, not violent repeat offenders, as the real threat to public safety.[27] Again, Sutherland was prescient in this regard, once stating that laws enacted to proscribe the violence committed by sexual psychopaths may be more injurious to society than the violence committed by predatory criminals. In conflict theory terms, David Greenberg stated that it is psychologically easier, I suggest, to overcome normative reservations about incarcerating on the basis of predicted future acts rather than past conduct, when one believes that those to be incarcerated are a different, criminal breed, not like the rest of us. If candidates for incarceration are members of a feared or despised minority group, as is often the case in American courts today, such beliefs are especially easy to accept.[28]

Similarly, in their review of the National Academy of Sciences report on criminal careers and career criminals, Sheldon Messinger and Richard Berk claimed that the methods of crime control being devised to contain and incapacitate career criminals were more fearsome and dangerous than the offenders themselves. In other words, just as criminology was making the study of career criminals one of the discipline's central areas of inquiry, a minority of voices began to assail the very concept of the career offender and the presumably draconian policies designed to remove them from circulation.

As discussed at the onset of this chapter, the main source of this discontent centered on the ethical and logistical problems in identifying or predicting career criminals. However, some took this concern further because of their discomfort with the state deciding who was dangerous. What criteria would be used? Given what is known about the significance of early onset of problem behaviors, would society be served well by incarcerating for life any person who is arrested before the age of 10? Similarly, should delinquent youth who are contacted by the police for violent crimes be removed from circulation? Does an early involvement in violence portend a life of crime? The Philadelphia birth cohort studies found that minorities were significantly more likely than whites to be habitual offenders. Thus, should the criminal justice system focus its energies toward nonwhite offenders? These were some of the questions on the minds of criminologists who debated, often vociferously, the slippery slope of the career paradigm and its policies such as selective incapacitation.

Conclusion

Career criminals have proven to be controversial figures among scholars, policy makers, media outlets, and the general public. Theoretical explanations for habitual criminality, the presentation of chronic offenders in the news media, and viewpoints about the appropriateness of the state in controlling them differ. For some, career criminals are somewhat sympathetic figures who are exploited by a largely sensationalistic news media and susceptible to anticrime public sentiment. For others, career criminals are accorded too many opportunities to slip through the cracks of a disorganized and lenient criminal justice system. Evidence for each perspective is provided in bulk by numerous media outlets. Regrettably, this creates an unclear picture of whether the criminal justice system is overly lenient and soft on crime, excessively harsh and damaging to society, or somewhere in between. Similarly, inconsistent messages are transmitted regarding whether the career criminal is real or imagined, a volitional actor or an acted-upon victim.

Although career criminal research is a dominant research area, dissenting voices within the discipline have heaped counterproductive political issues upon the study of high-rate offenders. In some ways, this work continues the tradition of academic solicitude toward criminals that previous scholars have written about. It is critical to remember that the halfhearted acknowledgment that career criminals do in fact exist but that their numbers are relatively low and therefore do not warrant the hype, press clippings, or research devoted to them misses the point entirely. Career criminals are, ipso facto, rare in number, extreme in behavior, and bad in totality. They are not conjured images of bad apples to play upon the base impulses of the general public.

Finally, a more common and central concern among criminologists is the poor record of prediction instruments in identifying career criminals for punishment purposes. This failure creates serious ethical and logistical problems and contributes to the inability of the criminal justice system to effectively control high-rate offenders.

Notes

1. Gottfredson, S. D., & Gottfredson, D. M. (1986). Accuracy of prediction models. In A. Blumstein, J. Cohen, J. A. Roth, & C. A. Visher (Eds.), *Criminal careers and "career criminals"* (Vol. 2, pp. 212-290). Washington, DC: National Academy Press (p. 239).

2. Cohen, J. (1983). Incapacitation as a strategy for crime control: Possibilities and pitfalls. In M. Tonry & N. Morris (Eds.), *Crime and justice: An annual review of research* (Vol. 5, pp. 1-84). Chicago: University of Chicago Press; Visher, C. A. (1986). The RAND inmate survey: A reanalysis. In A. Blumstein, J. Cohen, J. A. Roth, & C. A. Visher (Eds.), *Criminal careers and "career criminals"* (Vol. 2, pp. 161-211). Washington, DC: National Academy Press; von Hirsch, A. (1985). *Past or*

future crimes: Deservedness and dangerousness in the sentencing of criminals. New Brunswick, NJ: Rutgers University Press; Greenwood, P. W., & Turner, S. (1987). *Selective incapacitation revisited: Why the high-rate offenders are hard to predict.* Santa Monica, CA: RAND Corporation.

3. Auerhahn, K. (1999). Selective incapacitation and the problem of prediction. *Criminology, 37,* 703-734; Decker, S., & Salert, B. (1986). Predicting the career criminal: An empirical test of the Greenwood scale. *Journal of Criminal Law and Criminology, 77,* 215-236; Miranne, A. C., & Geerken, M. R. (1991). The New Orleans inmate survey: A test of Greenwood's predictive scale. *Criminology, 29,* 497-516.

4. Hayes, H. D., & Geerken, M. R. (1997). The idea of selective release. *Justice Quarterly, 14,* 353-370; DeLisi, M. (2001). Scaling archetypal criminals. *American Journal of Criminal Justice, 26,* 77-92.

5. Moore, M. H. (1986). Purblind justice: Normative issues in the use of prediction in the criminal justice system. In A. Blumstein, J. Cohen, J. A. Roth, & C. A. Visher (Eds.), *Criminal careers and "career criminals"* (Vol. 2, pp. 314-355). Washington, DC: National Academy Press (p. 351). Other summaries or reviews on the topic appear in Gottfredson, S. D., & Gottfredson, D. M. (1986). Accuracy of prediction models. In A. Blumstein, J. Cohen, J. A. Roth, & C. A. Visher (Eds.), *Criminal careers and "career criminals"* (Vol. 2, pp. 212-290). Washington, DC: National Academy Press; Mathiesen, T. (1998). Selective incapacitation revisited. *Law and Human Behavior, 22,* 455-469; Monahan, J. (1996). Violence prediction: The past twenty and the next twenty years. *Criminal Justice and Behavior, 23,* 107-120; Moore, M. H., Estrich, S. R., McGillis, D., & Spelman, W. (1984). *Dangerous offenders: The elusive target of justice.* Cambridge, MA: Harvard University Press; Silver, E., & Miller, L. (2002). A cautionary note on the use of actuarial risk assessment tools for social control. *Crime & Delinquency, 48,* 138-161; Webster, C. D., Hucker, S. J., & Bloom, H. (2002). Transcending the actuarial versus clinical polemic in assessing risk for violence. *Criminal Justice and Behavior, 29,* 659-665.

6. Hoffman, P. B. (1994). Twenty years of operational use of a risk prediction instrument: The United States Parole Commission's Salient Factor Score. *Journal of Criminal Justice, 22,* 477-494; Hoffman, P. B., & Beck, J. L. (1985). Recidivism among released federal prisoners: Salient Factor Score and five-year follow-up. *Criminal Justice and Behavior, 12,* 501-507; Janus, M. G. (1985). Selective incapacitation: Have we tried it? Does it work? *Journal of Criminal Justice, 13,* 117-130. To be sure, there are other actuarial instruments that have proven effective in predicting violence (although perhaps not necessarily career criminality), and not all criminologists are so skeptical about the prospects of prediction. For examples, see Brantley, A. C., & Ochberg, F. M. (2003). Lethal predators and future dangerousness. *FBI Law Enforcement Bulletin, 72,* 16-22; Monahan, J., et al. (2000). Developing a clinically useful actuarial tool for assessing violence risk. *British Journal of Psychiatry, 174,* 312-319; Stevens, D. J. (2000). Identifying criminal predators, sentences, and criminal classifications. *Journal of Police and Criminal Psychology, 15,* 50-71.

7.   The references for these events appear in the following order: Batz, J. (2002). Fail safe. Retrieved October 9, 2002, from http://www.riverfronttimes.com/issues/2002-10-02/feature.html/print.html; Associated Press. (2002). Officials approve settlement to "Girl X" who was beaten, raped in public housing. Retrieved April 18, 2002, from http://www.courttv.com/news/2002/0417/rapesettlement_ap.html; Associated Press. (2002). Man charged in stabbing death of his aunt and two children. Retrieved January 2, 2001, from http://www.courttv.com/news/2000/1229/stabbing_ap.html; Johnson, A., Brunker, M., Lewis, G., The Associated Press, & Reuters. (2002). Teen girls rescued; kidnapper killed. Retrieved August 2, 2002, from http://www.msnbc.com/news/788577.asp; Fazlollah, M., Achrati, N., & Soteropoulos, J. (2002). Suspected kidnappers, family have web of ties. Retrieved July 25, 2002, from http://www.philly.com/mld/philly/news/local/3731617.htm; Associated Press. (2001). Two escape from Oklahoma prison. Retrieved January 16, 2001, from http://www.msnbc.com/news/516690.asp?0nm=-239; Puit, G. (2003). Jury sentences career criminal to death. Las Vegas Review-Journal, p. 1B. Retrieved October 2, 2003, from http://www/lexis-lexis.com/universe/document?_m=110dc2e4064430e32f77b975c0718df3; Gross, A. (2003). Man convicted in murder at car wash gets 46 years to life. Retrieved March 14, 2003, from http://www.ohio.com/mld/beaconjournal/news/loca/states/ohio/counties/summit_county/5; Chancellor, C. (2003). Rapist gets life term. Retrieved January 14, 2003, from http://www.philly.com/mld/beaconjournal/4942006.htm?template=contentModules/printstory

8.   The American Enterprise. (2002, April-May). 13 (3), 9. Retrieved March 13, 2003, from http://web5.infotrac-college.com/wadsworth/session/595/683/33158061/27!xrn_7_0_A845

9.   Elkins, I. J., Iacono, W. G., Doyle, A. E., & McGue, M. (1997). Characteristics associated with the persistence of antisocial behavior: Results from recent longitudinal research. Aggression and Violent Behavior, 2, 101-124; Thornberry, T. P., Ireland, T. O., & Smith, C. A. (2001). The importance of timing: The varying impact of childhood and adolescent maltreatment on multiple problem outcomes. Development and Psychopathology, 13, 957-979.

10.   The references for these events appear in the following order: Associated Press. (2002). "Mother of all pickpockets" sentenced. Retrieved June 3, 2002, from http://www.courttv.com/people/scm/scm_053002.html; Biskupic, J. (2001). Retarded killer's appeal goes before high court. Retrieved March 26, 2001, from http://www.usatoday.com/news/court/2001-03-25-retardedkiller.htm; Associated Press. (2003). Mentally ill inmate facing death this week loses clemency bid. Retrieved March 26, 2003, from http://www.cnn.com/2003/LAW/03/25/texas.execution.ap/index.html; Associated Press. (2002). California executes former escaped convict for 1980 killing of 81-year-old woman. Retrieved January 29, 2002, from http://www.courttv.com/news/2002/0129/execution_ap.html; Walsh, F. (2003). Frank Lee Smith's long hard life. Retrieved October 1, 2003, from http://www.pbs.org/wgbh/pages/frontline/shows/smith/etc/longhard.html;

Reuters. (2000). Panhandler convicted of brick assault. Retrieved November 30, 2000, from http://www.msnbc.com/news/496504.asp; Ripley, A. (2003, February 10). The struggle to stay outside the gates: A year has passed since *TIME* profiled ex-con Jean Sanders. A very hard year. *TIME, 161* (6), 8; Associated Press. (2002). Prison author Jack Henry Abbott commits suicide. Retrieved February 11, 2002, from http://www.foxnews.com/story/0,2933,45212,00.html.

11.   The references for these events appear in the following order: Associated Press & Reuters. (2001). Texas jail-break leader on trial for murder. Retrieved August 14, 2001, from http://msnbc.com/news/613205.asp?0dm=L218N; Ryan, H. (2002). Newbury blames victim for "tragedy." Retrieved January 18, 2002, from http://www.courttv.com/trials/texas7/011702_ctv.html; Scott, A. R. (2003). A career criminal with over 100 charges still walking the streets. Retrieved March 24, 2003, from http://massjudgesaccountability.us/outrages/outrage5.html; Pfeife, S. (2003). Prosecutor's mistake let murder suspect leave prison early. Retrieved March 13, 2003, from http://web5.infotrac-college.com/wadsworth/session/595/683/33158061/20!xrn; Associated Press. (2003). Illinois Gov. George Ryan pardons four death row inmates. Retrieved January 11, 2003, from http://www.courttv.com/news/death_penalty/011003_pardons_ap.html; Sun Media Corp. (2002, August 8). B. C. man charged in murders; drug link touted in 7 slayings in the mid-1990s. *Edmonton Sun*, p. 9; Lisle, L. (2003, February 15). A lock on trouble: Career criminal condo continues to manipulate from behind bars. *The Ottawa Sun*, p. 24; Falcon, M. (2002, November 15). Crown goes easy on career criminal. *The Vancouver Province*, , p. A30; D'Angelo, A. (1998). Career criminal avoids jail: Judge says jail ineffective, tries probation. Retrieved March 24, 2003, from http://www.nsnews.com/issues98/w090798/09049805.html.

12.   The references for these events appear in the following order: Associated Press. (2003). Defense attorney vows to appeal life sentence for spitter. Retrieved July 7, 2003, from http://web.lexis-nexis.com/universe/document?_m=5b0e2edd 1ef132bb; Associated Press. (2003). Strike 3! $11 theft gets career criminal 25 years to life in California prison. Retrieved March 24, 2003, from http://cnews.canoe.ca/CNEWS/WeirdNews/2002/11/15/4555-ap.html; Holland, G. (2002). Justices to debate 3-strikes law. Retrieved November 5, 2002, from http://wire.ap.org/Apnews/center_package.html; Manson, P. (2003, September 5). 3 drug convictions portend life sentence, judge says. *Chicago Daily Law Bulletin*, p. 1; Riccardi, N. (2003, May 27). Prosecutors seek fewer 3rd strikes. *Los Angeles Times*, p. B2; Hebert, A. (2003). Woman says inmate set up to fail. Retrieved September 24, 2003, from http://www.dailycamera.com/bdc/county_news/article/0,1713,BDC_2423_ 2265897,00.html.

13.   Hirschi, T., & Hindelang, M. J. (1977). Intelligence and delinquency: A revisionist review. *American Sociological Review, 42,* 571-587 (p. 571).

14.   For examples, see Lipset, S. M., & Ladd, E. C. (1972). The politics of American sociologists. *American Journal of Sociology, 78,* 67-104; Lipset, S. M. (1982). The academic mind at the top: The political behavior and values of faculty elites.

Public Opinion Quarterly, 46, 143-168; Sowell, T. (1992). *Inside American education: The decline, the deception, the dogmas.* New York: Simon & Schuster; Walsh, A., & Ellis, L. (1999). Political ideology and American criminologists' explanations for criminal behavior. *The Criminologist, 24,* 13-27; Wilson, J. Q. (1983). *Thinking about crime* (Rev. ed.). New York: Vintage. An excellent and honest look at the politics of criminologists and the ways that they influence policy is Cullen, F. T., & Gilbert, K. E. (1982). *Reaffirming rehabilitation.* Cincinnati, OH: Anderson Publishing Company.

15.   Garland, D. (2000). The culture of high crime societies: Some preconditions of recent "law and order" policies. *British Journal of Criminology, 40,* 347-375 (pp. 356-357).

16.   Sowell, T. (1999). *The quest for cosmic justice.* New York: The Free Press (pp. 149-150).

17.   Tannenbaum, F. (1938). *Crime and the community.* New York: Ginn.

18.   Sutherland, E. (1950a). The diffusion of sexual psychopath laws. *American Journal of Sociology, 56,* 142-148; Sutherland, E. (1950b). The sexual psychopath laws. *Journal of Criminal Law and Criminology, 40,* 534-554.

19.   For variations on this theme, see Feeley, M. M., & Kamin, S. (1996). The effect of "three strikes and you're out" on the courts: Looking back to see the future. In D. Shichor & D. K. Sechrest (Eds.), *Three strikes and you're out: Vengeance as public policy* (pp. 135-154). Thousand Oaks, CA: Sage; Kramer, R. C. (1982). From "habitual offenders" to "career criminals": The historical construction and development of criminal categories. *Law & Human Behavior, 6,* 273-293; Surette, R. (1996). News from nowhere, policy to follow: Media and the social construction of "three strikes and you're out." In D. Shichor & D. K. Sechrest (Eds.), *Three strikes and you're out: Vengeance as public policy* (pp. 177-202). Thousand Oaks, CA: Sage. Surette's article is noteworthy because it presents empirical data to support its argument.

20.   To be sure, conservative criminologists can share in the blame of using political rhetoric and moral panics to influence policy. A case in point is Professor John DiIulio and his use of the "superpredator." According to DiIulio (see Bennett, W. J., DiIulio, J. J., Jr., & Walters, J. P. [1996]. *Body count: Moral poverty. . . and how to win America's war against crime and drugs.* New York: Simon & Schuster), the moral poverty that characterized the inner cities would help create a quasi-feral juvenile offender more vicious than any criminal ever seen. The prediction was made in the 1990s, a decade that saw unprecedented reductions in violent crime. Thus, the arrival of waves of young, superpredatory career criminals did not appear as DiIulio envisioned. DiIulio's thesis was derided by mainstream criminology. For other research investigating the role of politics, media construction, and crime, see Benekos, P. J., & Merlo, A. V. (1995). Three strikes and you're out! The political sentencing game. *Federal Probation, 59,* 3-9; Welch, M., Fenwick, M., & Roberts, M. (1997). Primary definitions of crime and moral panic: A content analysis of experts'

quotes in feature newspaper articles on crime. *Journal of Research in Crime and Delinquency, 34,* 474-494; Welch, M., & Roberts, M. (1998). State managers, intellectuals, and the media: A content analysis of ideology in experts' quotes in feature newspaper articles on crime. *Justice Quarterly, 15,* 219-242.

21. Simon, J. (1996). Criminology and the recidivist. In D. Shichor & D. K. Sechrest (Eds.), *Three strikes and you're out: Vengeance as public policy* (pp. 24-50). Thousand Oaks, CA: Sage; Pratt, J., & Dickson, M. (1997). Dangerous, inadequate, invisible, out: Episodes in the criminological career of habitual criminals. *Theoretical Criminology, 1,* 363-384.

22. Currie, E. (2004). Crime, justice, and the social environment. In B. W. Hancock & P. M. Sharp (Eds.), *Public policy, crime, and criminal justice* (3rd ed., pp. 52-69). Upper Saddle River, NJ: Prentice Hall.

23. Merlo, A. V., & Benekos, P. J. (2004). Dynamics of criminal justice. In B. W. Hancock & P. M. Sharp (Eds.), *Public policy, crime, and criminal justice* (3rd ed., pp. 153-175). Upper Saddle River, NJ: Prentice Hall.

24. Miller, S. J., Dinitz, S., & Conrad, J. P. (1982). Careers of the violent: The dangerous offender and criminal justice. Lexington, MA: Lexington Books (p. 87); Blumstein, A., & Moitra, S. (1980). The identification of career criminals from chronic offenders in a cohort. *Law and Policy Quarterly, 2,* 321-334 (p. 329).

25. Sutherland, F. (1950a, p. 143); see note 18.

26. DeLisi, M. (2001). Extreme career criminals. *American Journal of Criminal Justice, 25,* 239-252; Rossi, P. H., Waite, E., Bose, C. E., & Berk, R. E. (1974). The seriousness of crimes: Normative structure and individual differences. *American Sociological Review, 39,* 224-237; Wilson, J. Q. (1997). *The moral sense.* New York: The Free Press.

27. A cottage industry of works exist that generally claim that the criminal justice system and thus the state itself are potentially the greatest threats to public safety and should be the object of our collective fear and the subject of policy reform. Although these works are diverse in their particular subject matter, they are sufficiently similar in their use of a critical perspective that fundamentally questions the righteousness and legitimacy of the criminal justice system and its effects on American society. Rather than being outraged by the behaviors of chronic offenders, these works demonstrate enmity toward the system. A quotation that captures the tenor of this scholarship was written by Harry Allen: "To paraphrase Winston Churchill, the standard of human decency in a society is reflected in the way it handles its offenders. If this is so, future historians will judge contemporary American society as located securely in the province of hell." For examples, see Allen, H. E. (1995). The American dream and crime in the 21st century: Presidential address to the Academy of Criminal Justice Sciences. *Justice Quarterly, 12,* 427-446 (p. 437); Chilton, R. (2001). Viable policy: The impact of federal funding and the need for independent research agendas—The American Society of Criminology 2000 Presidential Address. *Criminology, 39,* 1-8; Christie, N. (1993). *Crime control as*

industry: Toward gulags western style. New York: Routledge; Cullen, F. T., & Wozniak, J. (1982). Fighting the appeal of repression. *Crime and Social Justice, 18,* 23-33; Feeley, M. M., & Simon, J. (1992). The new penology: Notes on the emerging strategy of corrections and its implications. *Criminology, 30,* 449-474; Glaser, D. (1978). The counterproductivity of conservative thinking about crime. *Criminology, 16,* 209-225; Miller, J. G. (1996). *Search and destroy: African-American males in the criminal justice system.* Cambridge, UK: Cambridge University Press; Schwartz, M. D. (2001). One critical criminologist's view of the future and value of ASC. *The Criminologist, 26,* 1-5; Skolnick, J. H. (1995). What not to do about crime: The American Society of Criminology 1994 Presidential Address. *Criminology, 33,* 1-15; Tonry, M. (1995). *Malign neglect: Race, crime, and punishment in America.* New York: Oxford University Press; Wellford, C. F. (1997). 1996 Presidential Address: Controlling crime and achieving justice. *Criminology, 35,* 1-12.

28.   Greenberg, D. F. (1991). Modeling criminal careers. *Criminology, 29,* 17-46 (pp. 39-40).

6

The Criminal Justice System and Career Criminals

Box 6.1　　　SHOCAP Warrant for Fictional Serious Juvenile Offender

Seminole County Sheriff's Office

Career Criminals/Warrants Unit

Wanted:	**Deondrick Lamar Dickerson**
DOB:	June 8 1988
AKA:	Deon, D-Lam, Dickz,
Race:	Black
Sex:	Male
Height:	508
Weight:	150
Hair:	Black
Eyes:	Brown
Address:	450, 50th Street West Palm Beach, FL

(Continued)

Box 6.1 (Continued)

Advisory

The above-mentioned person is wanted on four (4) counts of home invasion and four (4) counts of attempted murder.

Warrant 03CR3002 $500,000 Cash Bond Only

Dickerson is also wanted for questioning as a material witness in three (3) drive-by shootings in the West Palm Beach area.

Dickerson is a single-state offender with prior police contacts in Florida dating to July 1998. Dickerson has prior arrests for strong arm robbery, armed robbery, escape, carrying concealed weapon, possession of illegal weapon, contempt of court, failure to appear, failure to comply, bail jumping, auto theft, homicide, firing weapon into occupied dwelling, burglary, burglary with intent to assault or rob, stalking, menacing, carjacking, truancy, contributing to the delinquency of a minor, aggravated assault with great bodily injury, resisting arrest, obstructing police, and numerous probation and supervised release violations.

Dickerson has repeatedly violated conditions of probation and juvenile aftercare and has been committed three (3) times to juvenile corrections.

Dickerson is known to possess and carry firearms and is highly combative with law enforcement personnel. Be advised when making contact. Dickerson is actively involved in gang activity as are his two older brothers.

Upon arrest, contact Lt. Fazshout at 800-433-5656 ext. 0964 at Career Criminals/Warrant Unit, Seminole County Sheriff's Office

NOTE: This is a fictional profile; any similarity to an inmate, living or dead, is purely coincidence.

Introduction and Overview

The profile displayed in Box 6.1 provides compelling evidence of the sheer bulk of crime that a single, high-rate offender can commit. Across the nation and abroad, many jurisdictions have initiated systemic efforts to focus criminal justice system resources on the selective targeting of chronic juvenile offenders and career criminals to yield the greatest, most cost-effective reductions in crime and related social problems. These programs have existed under a variety of monikers, including the Habitual Serious and Violent Juvenile Offender Program (HSVJOP); the Serious Habitual Offender Drug Involved Program (SHODI); and the most common, the Serious Habitual Offender Comprehensive Action Program (SHOCAP). The key features of these programs are resource coordination and confidential information sharing among multiple juvenile justice agencies, criminal justice agencies, and social service providers to create dossiers on youth or adults who demonstrate habitual criminal offending and are most at need of community services. In part, the comprehensive efforts to reach repeat offenders were born from the frustration and acknowledgment that many offenders continuously cycled in and out of the criminal justice and social service systems without any collective awareness or oversight.

Most SHOCAP programs target high-risk adolescents with already extensive records of delinquency and related social needs. Once identified, SHOCAP youth are strictly monitored and supervised as they complete court-ordered sanctions and participate in social skills and competency development training. The program is by no means limited to enforcement—religious organizations, welfare agencies, mental health centers, child and family service centers, community-based agencies, schools, police, and the juvenile court pool their resources to reduce antisocial behavior and promote conventional, prosocial behavior (recall the social development model from Chapter 3). In most jurisdictions, youth can be removed from the SHOCAP list and therefore can shed their delinquent label if they remain crime-free for 12 months. In sum, SHOCAP and related policies seek to convert the criminal justice system from a revolving door of leniency and unmet needs to a system of accountability and cost-effective service.

Evaluations of the comprehensive targeting of career criminals have unearthed some problems with program implementation, as well as some ethical dilemmas. At times, it is unclear whether programs should be targeting youth engaged in committing serious violent crimes at high rates or only youth who commit the most serious offenses. For example, a youth could be arrested for armed robbery but have no prior delinquency involvement. Conversely, a youth might accumulate dozens of police contacts for relatively benign forms of delinquency, such as property and status offenses, but never commit acts of violence. Thus, there have been problems in deciding which youth should be included in the program.

The inexact selection of problem youth contributed to a larger issue of poor coordination between the police and prosecutors. Roberta Cronin and her colleagues found that jurisdictions using vertical prosecution, whereby a single prosecutor handled a case from start to finish, provided the continuity needed in taking a case from arrest to conviction. Prosecutors with a greater investment in SHOCAP cases were also less likely to accept plea agreements that avoided the application of recidivism statutes or otherwise more serious charges. A larger and more untenable problem surrounded the ethics of hand-selecting youth as targets of a coordinated system effort (a related civil liberties concern centers on the coordinated sharing of information on private citizens by state agencies). For example, the essence of labeling theory is that official contact with the criminal justice system can solidify and exacerbate the criminal self-image of young offenders. When social service and criminal justice agencies target an individual as a taxing drain on community resources, it sends a clear message that rehabilitation and redemption are doubtful prospects. This is perhaps not the appropriate message to send to an adolescent.[1] For these reasons, programs like SHOCAP have at times been considered controversial.

A more recent initiative toward a comprehensive, system-wide effort to counter career criminals has met with more success. Michael Schumacher and Gwen Kurz have developed a policy based on their book *The 8% Solution: Preventing Serious, Repeat Juvenile Crime*.[2] The authors, who are probation officers in Orange County, California, make a compelling argument for a concentrated effort to stop career juvenile offenders. According to them, young career criminals are fundamentally different from other youth in terms of their offending and psychosocial profile. Unlike critics of SHOCAP policies, who claim that exposure to the juvenile justice system creates a stigmatizing label that tarnishes affected youth, Schumacher and Kurz assert that the pathology of career criminals is evident at first arrest based on risk factors such as a childhood onset of antisocial behavior, family problems (including criminal parents or siblings), problems at school, substance abuse, and gang involvement. Like other scholars, they found that 8% of the juvenile offenders in their jurisdiction accounted for nearly 60% of all criminal cases in the county.

Orange County has since established the 8% Early Intervention Program to serve youth aged 15 years or younger who exhibit at least three risk factors for chronic delinquency. The goals of the program are to increase the structure, supervision, and support for affected youth and their families; hold delinquents legally accountable for their misdeeds; and increase the school attachment of delinquent youth. A larger goal is to create a network of community agencies to foster a healthy environment for at-risk youth. This network provides an assortment of services including transportation, substance abuse counseling, mental health evaluations, employment preparation and job placement, intensive family counseling, and life-skills classes. Preliminary outcomes suggest that many chronic juvenile offenders can be reached, treated, and redirected to a conventional path if salient risk factors are identified early.

SHOCAP and related policies are the umbrella policy stance toward serious and violent juvenile offenders and adult career criminals. The following sections explicate how various components of the criminal justice system, such as police, courts, and corrections, have explicitly focused on the worst types of offenders. For a variety of reasons, the criminal justice system has been largely unsuccessful in reducing crime via the control of career criminals.

The Police and Career Criminals

Because criminal offenders commit crimes of varying seriousness at significantly different rates, law enforcement could best be served by concentrating on offenders at the high end of the offending distribution. In this sense, the police would need to have some preexisting knowledge that an individual offender was a career criminal. This knowledge is easy enough to obtain because officers become well acquainted with high-rate offenders and have access to records bureaus that can provide the rap sheets for all offenders, including the most prolific local criminals. Perusing active warrants and concentrating on chronic offenders and/or persons wanted for serious violent crime is another method of targeting high-rate recidivists. Contrary to most police work—which is reactive—police units with an emphasis on selectively apprehending career criminals must be proactive.

The Repeat Offender Project (ROP) was a specialized police unit in the Washington, D.C., Police Department whose charge was to selectively apprehend career criminals. The unit's mission was to select, apprehend, and contribute to the conviction of criminal offenders who committed five or more Part I Index crimes per week, a parameter that experts ascertained would encompass the 20% most recidivistic offenders. To accomplish this, the ROP (pronounced "rope") unit targeted two types of recidivists: wanted persons with active warrants, who could be arrested on sight; and chronic/dangerous offenders not currently wanted but believed to be currently involved in offending. Information on potential arrest targets originated from official criminal records and "street" sources such as confidential informants, other criminals, and cooperative police agencies involved in information-sharing with the ROP unit.

Police scholars Susan Martin and Lawrence Sherman published three evaluations of ROP. Part of these evaluations included a quasi-experimental, nonequivalent control group design that compared ROP officers to non-ROP officers in terms of their arrest productivity, the dispositions of their arrests, and the prior criminal histories of their arrestees at two time periods. These evaluations furnished some impressive results. Officers in the ROP unit increased the likelihood that serious criminal offenders would be arrested. Indeed, the unit arrested 55% of persons wanted on active warrants, compared to the non-ROP officers who arrested just 9% of the wanted offenders. During both periods of data collection, ROP officers arrested persons whose average arrest histories exceeded the traditional indicator of career criminality, five or more arrests. Similarly, offenders targeted by the ROP had criminal records that contained more serious and violent felonies. Benefits of this program extended beyond the police domain and into the courts. Offenders arrested by the ROP unit were more likely to be prosecuted for a felony, were more likely to be convicted of a felony, and received longer prison sentences than offenders arrested by the traditional police unit. Because ROP officers made fewer arrests, their overall productivity declined; however, the "quality" of their arrests increased because they focused almost exclusively on career criminals.

Specialized units that proactively target career criminals are not without controversy. A civil libertarian argument is that the surveillance of persons suspected to be involved in crime is dubious because that information is largely based on a criminal history for which the individual has already paid some legal price. Fortunately, warrants are issued by the courts and ensure due process measures; thus, there appears to be little downside to aggressively targeting wanted individuals. This does not imply, however, that other suspected recidivists who are not currently with active warrants should be ignored. To the contrary, the ROP evaluations found that many property offenders who were arrested also had extensive records for crimes of violence. Selective apprehension units provide a great opportunity to remove these generalists from the streets.[3]

Despite their promise and potential, specialized police units that target career criminals were not widely adopted nationwide. Part of the reason for this was organizational discontinuity between police departments and prosecutors. Law enforcement officers have always been aware of the hot spots of crime in their jurisdictions and where the most high-rate offenders are likely to be found. However, if officers had not communicated effectively with prosecutors in demonstrating the priority of prosecuting specific offenders, habitual offenders might not have been charged with the necessary zeal and resources. The need for increased communication was bidirectional. For example, charges were often dismissed or reduced by county attorneys because the police investigation lacked important features, information, or evidence that prosecutors needed to ostensibly guarantee conviction. Working separately, the police and the courts made it possible for repeat offenders to fall through the cracks.

The Phoenix, Arizona, ROP improved upon the design of the Washington, D.C., unit by coordinating the efforts and resources of the police and the prosecutor's office. Police officers and prosecutors agreed upon the following nine criteria to identify candidates for ROP targeting: current criminal activity, current substance abuse, current lifestyle, prior probation failure, felony convictions within the past decade, prior juvenile record (i.e., early onset of criminal behavior), past informant activity, family background, and a violent or confrontational modus operandi. By committee, these two criminal justice entities created a roster of the most recidivistic and violent criminals in the Phoenix area. Once a repeat offender was arrested, the police, pretrial services personnel, and the prosecution worked together to build the strongest case possible against the defendant.

An evaluation of the Phoenix ROP found that the program was generally successful in increasing the apprehension and ultimate incarceration of career criminals. Nearly 90% of ROP offenders were convicted, 73% were sentenced to prison, and their average length of sentence was 18 months longer than non-ROP offenders. Most promising was the degree of cooperation and coordination between two commonly disjointed arms of criminal justice, the police and courts. Because of the collective investment from police and judicial officers, defendants could be charged with the most appropriate and potentially serious charges based on their criminal history. Police officers paid attention to details in making arrests that would facilitate later prosecution. Prosecutors, in turn, were more vigilant in convicting chronic offenders of the more serious charges and were less likely to participate in mutually advantageous and expeditious plea bargains. In short, the efficiency and effectiveness of the Phoenix criminal justice system were greatly enhanced by collective attention to the most socially damaging career criminals.[4]

The Courts and Career Criminals

Just as criminal courts of original jurisdiction have been disproportionately busy with the cases in which career criminals are the defendants, appellate courts have reviewed decisions pertaining to a variety of legal issues raised by the state's efforts to control them. These legal issues relate to habitual offender, recidivist, or three-strikes statutes and whether the punishment they impose is proportional and therefore constitutional; dangerousness and its prediction; and the civil commitment of persons who have previously been convicted and punished for acts of sexual violence.[5]

Habitual Offender Statutes

Laws designed to control career criminals have led appellate courts on a meandering odyssey throughout the years. Alternating and at times inconsistent decisions have been established about the constitutionality of punishing chronic criminal offenders with habitual offender laws that require harsher sentences and often life imprisonment. The spirit of the law is to inflict a lifetime achievement penalty for criminals who simply refuse to desist from crime. By definition, habitual offender statutes contain elements of desert and retribution. The letter of the law is more problematic because these statutes result in severe sentences that often exceed the legal seriousness of the instant offense. Thus, jurists have declared that life sentences constitute cruel and unusual punishment if the instant offense was relatively benign (regardless of the severity of the defendant's prior criminal history). The landmark case that addressed the constitutionality of habitual offender laws was *Weems v. United States* in 1910. In that decision, the U.S. Supreme Court decided that criminal punishments must be graduated, proportionate, or commensurate to the seriousness of the underlying crime. The defendant in that case, William Weems, was sentenced to 15 years of hard labor and an assortment of other penalties for falsifying public documents, hardly a grievous offense. Just 2 years later, the U.S. Supreme Court reviewed its first habitual offender law in

Graham v. West Virginia. The Court decided that a life sentence for a repeat property offender (e.g., burglary and grand theft) neither violated double jeopardy provisions in the 5th Amendment nor constituted cruel and unusual punishment.[6]

Habitual offender statutes and related legal issues did not appear on the state-level radar screen until the 1960s. For example, the exclusionary rule was established federally by *Weeks v. United States* in 1914 but not at the state level until *Mapp v. Ohio* in 1961. The proportionality issue for habitual offender statutes was applied to the states via *Robinson v. California* in 1962. The latter part of the 20th century showcased a judiciary unable to reach consensus on the legality of statutes that seek to severely punish recidivists. At issue was the fairness of administering a life sentence for minor felonies regardless of the defendant's record of recurrent convictions and incarceration. In essence, this mirrors the media's inconsistent portrayal of the righteousness of recidivism laws that punish career criminals. In *Rummel v. Estelle* (1980), the U.S. Supreme Court, in a narrow 5:4 decision, affirmed the constitutionality of a Texas law that imposed life imprisonment for three prior felony convictions. The defendant in the case had been convicted of three forgery/fraud cases that yielded meager financial gains between $25 and $125. Nevertheless, the life sentence was imposed.

Hutto v. Davis (1982) explored additional issues in the aggravated sentencing of criminal offenders. First, the U.S. Supreme Court held that two consecutive 20-year prison terms and two fines of $10,000 upon conviction for the distribution of nine ounces of marijuana did not violate the cruel and unusual punishment clause. Moreover, the Court refused to note sentencing disparities for like crimes in the same state and other states. This changed a year later in *Solem v. Helm* (1983), when in a 5:4 decision the Supreme Court held that a life sentence without parole given under a habitual offender law to a person convicted of check fraud for less than $100 was unconstitutional. In the view of the justices, the defendant, who had seven previous nonviolent felony convictions, was treated more harshly than his in-state criminal peers who had committed more serious offenses. Also, the Court ruled that this sentence was harsher than other sentences imposed for similar crimes in other states. In *Harmelin v. Michigan* (1991), the Court ruled (again in a narrow 5:4 opinion) that the 8th Amendment was not violated in noncapital cases that result in a life in prison without parole sentence. The defendant was convicted of possessing 672 grams (24 ounces) of cocaine in Michigan, where possession of more than 650 grams warranted life in prison without parole. In March 2003, the U.S. Supreme Court reviewed two cases originating in California (*Ewing v. California* and *Lockyer v. Andrade*) where 25-years-to-life sentences were administered to chronic offenders whose instant offenses were nominal thefts. The Court affirmed the constitutionality of the sentences, acknowledging that although the sentences were long, so were the criminal records of the recidivists.[7]

The Dangerousness Doctrine

The future dangerousness of serious criminal offenders has also generated considerable legal discourse. The U.S. Supreme Court and lower appellate courts have examined a variety of issues pursuant to the assessment of an offender's future dangerousness as it relates to sentencing issues. Most of these cases sought to ensure that collateral constitutional safeguards were being complied with as the courts examined a defendant's risk of danger to the public.[8] For example, in *Estelle v. Smith* (1981), it was established that states could not compel criminal defendants to submit to a psychiatric evaluation from which a prediction of future dangerousness would be made. In addition, *Vanderbilt v. Collins* (1993) established that only when the defendant requests a mental health defense or a psychiatric examination can potentially aggravating factors about his future dangerousness be raised. Furthermore, the legal acknowledgment that some criminal offenders pose real and substantial risks of danger to other community members justifies an assortment of criminal justice outcomes, ranging from pretrial detention to the death penalty.[9]

The relatively facile manner in which the courts have ruled on dangerousness has not been adopted by the academic community. Criminologists have raised numerous concerns about the concept of dangerousness and its application or feared misapplication. Academicians often assert that dangerousness is too nebulous a concept for the courts to arrive at any consensus about its prediction. As discussed in Chapter 5, it has been argued that dangerousness is a social construction or, at the very least, subject to wildly differing assessments. There is considerable evidence to confirm such a view. Prediction instruments that have been devised to facilitate criminal justice decision making have been found to be largely inaccurate, with false-positive rates in excess of 50%. This means that prediction instruments whose elements include salient criminal history and demographic information cannot meaningfully forecast which offenders will continue to commit crime.[10] Another concern centers on the ethical dilemma raised when prognosticating what criminal offenders might do in the future as a justification for their harsh punishment. Andrew von Hirsch captured this concern succinctly: "No one is clever enough to create a 'fair method' of picking and choosing among defendants convicted of similar criminal acts, and sentencing them on the basis of the crimes they supposedly will commit."[11]

However, not all criminological assessments of the courts' ability to assess dangerousness and appropriately use this factor in sentencing are negative. For example, Marcia and Jan Chaiken examined the ability of the courts in Middlesex County, Massachusetts, and Los Angeles County, California, to identify career criminals for selective prosecution. Several important findings emerged that conflicted with many of the previously raised concerns. Chaiken and Chaiken found that at these two sites, prosecutors were consistent in selecting those who were the most dangerous, frequent, and chronic offenders. Moreover, they found that the best predictors of dangerousness and recidivism were items that could be readily located in criminal records. These were prior convictions for predatory crimes; being on parole, bond, or wanted on warrants when most recently arrested; having a drug problem; and having committed at least three separate transactions of burglary. Similarly, Alan Brantley and Frank Ochberg have developed a rudimentary measure to indicate which prisoners are lethal predators who are most likely to commit serious criminal violence if released from prison. Again, the elements of this scale—history of lethal violence, multiple prior acts of sexual predation, mental abnormality, and legal sanity (i.e., psychopathy)—can be garnered from official records.[12]

Whether academics are comfortable with the courts' use of assessing dangerousness is ultimately not an issue. The U.S. Supreme Court has legally settled the appropriateness of assessing future dangerousness vis-à-vis court functions. In *Barefoot v. Estelle* (1983), the Court rejected the argument, mostly promulgated by academics, that expert testimony about future risks is unreliable. Thus, as long as the other applicable constitutional provisions are followed, future dangerousness will continue to be used in a number of capacities in the criminal courts, including capital sentencing.

Civil Commitment

The case of Leroy Hendricks (*Kansas v. Hendricks*, 1997) catapulted the issue of the civil commitment of criminally dangerous persons to the forefront of academic discussions about the ability of the state to control career criminals. A pedophile with a lengthy criminal history of sexually assaulting children, Hendricks was scheduled for release from prison. After his release, Kansas authorities sought Hendricks's civil commitment under its Sexually Violent Predator Act, which permitted the institutionalization of persons likely to engage in predatory acts of criminal violence brought on by mental abnormality or personality disorders. During his civil commitment trial, Hendricks admitted that he experienced continued urges to sexually abuse children, despite having received extensive treatment for his pedophilia. Moreover, Hendricks stated that whenever he felt stressed out, the urge to molest became uncontrollable. Kansas authorities determined that Hendricks's pedophilia qualified as a mental abnormality and justified his civil commitment. Consequently, Hendricks was civilly committed. The Kansas Supreme Court later invalidated the Sexually Violent Predator Act because Hendricks was not required to suffer from mental illness before the civil commitment was imposed.

The U.S. Supreme Court granted certiorari in the case to assess what constitutes mental abnormality and whether substantive due process and double jeopardy provisions were violated. In a narrow 5:4 decision, the Court found that the Kansas law did not violate due process because there was proof beyond a reasonable doubt that Hendricks had prior sexually violent behavior and a present mental condition that facilitated the likelihood that such violent conduct would reoccur. Civil confinement is permitted so long as the person suffers from an abnormality or personality disorder. Release should occur only if the abnormality or personality disorder abates to such a degree that the person would be safe if released. Yearly reviews of the civilly committed person are required.[13]

The decision galvanized legal scholars and criminologists, who attempted to understand the legality of a civil policy that involuntarily incarcerated violent criminals after they had served sentences imposed by criminal courts.[14] It is important to note that because civil commitment policies are civil and therefore not punitive, the laws are not subject to constitutional concerns such as double jeopardy or ex post facto claims that were addressed in the Hendricks case. The civil commitment ends once the individual demonstrates that he (sexually violent offenders and career criminals are almost always male) no longer suffers from a mental disorder or abnormality. Civil commitment is therefore not a punishment but an opportunity for the treatment of the mentally sick, whose condition and prior conduct pose risks of future violence.

Clearly, the state can have its cake and eat it, too. With civil commitment, the ability of the state to punish violent criminal offenders extends from the criminal justice system, which punishes blameworthiness and mens rea, to the civil world, immune from constitutional challenges, where the incarcerated are viewed as mentally disordered patients. For this reason, academics have fiercely debated this issue. Civil commitment is costly. If civilly committed defendants do not rehabilitate, they will continue to be housed at taxpayers' expense. For some, the policy raises distressing civil liberty and moral questions. In this view, civil commitment is a clever, legalistic effort to continually punish persons who have already been punished criminally. For those who are perhaps rightfully concerned that sexually violent offenders will recidivate, the end may justify the means.

Corrections and Career Criminals

The General Landscape

There is a popular belief that some elusive criminals spend their entire criminal career at-large and never come into contact with the criminal justice system. Partially driving this logic are the highly publicized exploits of notorious offenders, such as serial killers, who operate for years and even decades under the nose of the criminal justice system. It is important to note that these types of offenders have usually been arrested and even imprisoned before their ultimate crime spree. The same logic characterizes all career criminals. Although most of their criminal exploits do not result in criminal justice system intervention, career criminals amass extensive and often mammoth official criminal records with scores of arrests, probation sentences, stints in jail, and commitments to prison. Indeed, getting locked up is a tacitly understood component of a life of crime. For example, the seminal RAND study of 49 incarcerated robbers indicated that 75% of serious offenders have very little difficulty adjusting to prison. Analysis of their records indicated that the amount of time served for prison commitments was extremely low, even for high-rate recidivists. The average time served for a first prison term was 2.4 years, 3.3 years for the second, 3 years for the third, 3.7 years for the fourth, and 5.7 years for the fifth. A recent study of extreme career criminals indicated that the average adult habitual offender was imprisoned more than 3 times during his career. The worst offender amassed more than 25 stints in prison.[15]

Studies by two of the most respected prison experts in the country, Peter Greenwood and Joan Petersilia, have quantified and largely confirmed that serious violent offenders have extensive criminal justice and correctional experiences. Moreover, their analyses suggest a compromise in the political dialogue between those who either argue that the criminal justice system is overly harsh or excessively lenient (recall Chapter 5). Habitual criminals face serious legal consequences throughout their offending career, but the funnel-like structure of the criminal justice system and other structural factors provide numerous opportunities for release and the underenforcement of the law. For example, using official records from the California Department of Justice, Peter Greenwood showed the dispositions and sentencing outcomes of the four violent Index crimes: homicide, forcible rape, robbery, and aggravated assault. For homicide, 10% of cases were released as the criminal complaint was filed and another 10% of cases were rejected at filing. By trial or plea agreement, 75% of murder cases resulted in conviction, and 25% resulted in acquittal or were dismissed. Of the convicted, 77% of homicide offenders were sentenced to prison, 19% were sentenced to jail, and 4% were sentenced to an intermediate sanction. The other crimes had similar rates of dismissal, rejection of charges, and acquittal. Greenwood found that only 44% of forcible rape convictions, 42% of robbery convictions, and a mere 6% of aggravated assault convictions resulted in a prison sentence.

Similarly, in her comprehensive examination of the California prison system and the American criminal justice system, Joan Petersilia found evidence of considerable slack in the state's enforcement and punishment functions. She noted that of 34 million felonies committed during 1990, only 3 million actually entered the criminal justice system. This meant that 91% of serious crimes, disproportionately the activities of career criminals, never entered the system. Thus, even if the prison system severely punishes some high-rate offenders, many others remain at large and continue to offend. The supply of habitual offenders simply exceeds criminal justice system capacities to reduce crime.[16]

In fact, the capacity of the correctional system to punish falls far below what the law permits. State courts are nearly as likely to sentence convicted felons to probation with no time served (32% of all felony sentences) as they are to send felons to prison (40% of all felony sentences). Among felons sentenced to prison, the actual time served is a fraction of the original sentence, even for persons convicted of the most serious crimes. For example, the national average sentence for a violent crime is 89 months, of which only 43 months (48% of the sentence) are actually served. On average, murderers are sentenced to 149-month sentences but serve just 71 months, rapists are sentenced to 117 months but serve just 65 months, kidnappers are sentenced to 104 months but serve only 52 months, and robbers are sentenced to 95 months but serve just 44 months. Perhaps because of this leniency in the prisons, most prisoners reoffend after release from confinement. On average, nearly 70% of prisoners are re-arrested within 3 years, and 47% are convicted of new crimes. Predictably, career criminals are most likely to continue their offending careers after their release from prison. Among recidivists with 11 to 15 career arrests, 79% will be re-arrested within 3 years of prison release. Among offenders with 16 or more career arrests, 82% are re-arrested within 3 years.[17]

At a recent Annual Research and Evaluation Conference partially sponsored by the National Institute of Justice, Michael Block provided a national assessment of whether the criminal justice system appropriately responds to serious criminals. According to Block, the increased use of incarceration in the United States does not reflect its current overuse but, to the contrary, a prior unwillingness to respond appropriately to serious, violent criminals. Using official and victimization estimates from the Uniform Crime Reports and National Crime Victimization Survey, Block estimated that only about 13% of the arrests for Index crimes ended in felony conviction. Overall, about 1 in 100 Index crimes (which are murder, rape, robbery, aggravated assault, larceny, auto theft, burglary, and arson) reported to the police actually result in imprisonment. This varies widely, from 1 in 3 murders to about 3 in 100 for aggravated assault. Block concluded that the recent "get tough" movement in corrections has stemmed from longer prison sentences, not higher levels of imprisonment risk for persons convicted of the most serious crimes. In this view, the correctional system still has not responded punitively enough to serious criminal offenders.[18]

Selective Incapacitation and Its Discontents

Selective incapacitation, the policy that seeks to identify (prospectively, if possible) and incarcerate the most chronic criminals, is the primary criminal justice policy to originate from the career criminal paradigm. Because prison is so costly and so many criminals are not chronic offenders, the incarceration of career offenders offers the most efficient and cost-effective approach to imprisonment and, a priori, the greatest reductions in crime. Selective incapacitation is the central idea behind recent habitual offender statutes, commonly referred to as "three strikes and you're out" or simply three-strikes laws. This section reviews the criminological investigations of this topic, most of them critical, and explicates the central problems with the policy and its effects.

In the light of the ethical controversy over the conceptualization and identification of dangerous persons that was explored in the previous chapter, it is important to note that the very idea of handpicking offenders for imprisonment fundamentally roiled many. Beyond the ethical and ideological concerns was a more pragmatic one: the economic costs of an ever-expanding prison population. Due to the inherent difficulties in accurately identifying chronic offenders for selective incapacitation, prison populations swelled and encompassed more inmates, but not necessarily the most recidivistic ones. The general consensus among researchers was that selective incapacitation policies offered diminishing marginal returns that rapidly increased state expenditures while simultaneously making meager reductions in crime. A study by Thomas Bernard and Richard Ritti demonstrated the fiscal quandaries raised by selective incapacitation. Using the 1945 Philadelphia study with its 627 chronic offenders as baseline information, they postulated that each birth cohort would produce approximately the same number of habitually delinquent boys. Bernard and Ritti calculated that if all of these boys were incarcerated (remember, 6% committed more than 50% of the crime), the incarceration rate would be 6,305 per 100,000 or more than 30 times the current incarceration rate![19] Obviously, state criminal justice systems cannot afford this rate.

Despite the problems with selective incapacitation, imprisonment proliferated across the United States during the latter part of the 20th century. While more and more states busily enacted three-strikes laws to target career criminals, more felons were sentenced to prison, and length of stay in prison increased, something else happened in the 1990s: Crime rates dropped dramatically. This marked a shift in incapacitation research, where the debate transitioned to the relationship between incarceration and crime. Because crime rates were falling so dramatically, was there really a need for enhanced sentencing policies such as three-strikes laws? Moreover, were three-strikes policies actually making matters worse in terms of increasing prison costs and even increasing crime rates?

The research on three-strikes legislation and its effects on criminal justice system expenditures and crime rates is characterized by highly sophisticated quantitative methods and wildly conflicting findings. For example, a recent issue of *Criminology & Public Policy* devoted an entire panel of papers to the topic. Kathleen Auerhahn used simulation modeling to forecast the California prison population through 2030 and arrived at several findings. First, she estimated that by 2030, 50% of the inmates would be "third strikers," offenders sentenced to 25 years to life for their third felony. Second, 80% of the prison population would be sentenced according to the three-strikes laws. Third, the proportion of inmates serving time for violent crimes would decrease to 49% by 2030, whereas the proportion of drug offenders would increase to 30%. Consequently, Auerhahn forecasted a prison population that would become increasingly less dangerous based on instant offense and recommended a policy of "geriatric release" whereby elderly inmates, with their costly medical needs, are released, as they presumably pose little risk to public safety.

In a response essay, Carlisle Moody admonished that the first 2 years of Auerhahn's forecast were completely wrong by comparing the estimates to observed data for those 2 years. Another research article by Tomislav Kovandzic and his colleagues examined the relationship between homicide rates and three-strikes laws in 188 large cities. They found that cities in states that had adopted the legislation experienced 13% to 14% short-term increases and 16% to 24% long-term increases in homicide rates. An unrelated study by Thomas Marvell and Carlisle Moody replicated these results, finding a 10% to 12% short-term and 23% to 29% long-term increase in homicides in states with newly enacted three-strikes laws.[20]

Other studies produced discordant findings. Joanna Shepherd has drawn the opposite conclusion from her research, namely that three-strikes laws significantly decrease crime and thus lend empirical credibility to the promise of selective incapacitation. Specifically, Shepherd found that during the first 2 years after California enacted the legislation, 8 murders, nearly 4,000 aggravated assaults, more than 10,000 robberies, and approximately 385,000 burglaries were deterred. However, larcenies increased by nearly 18,000 during this period. Shepherd's study also offered evidence that the initial fervor over three-strikes legislation was overstated and inaccurate. For example, the average sentence length for felons targeted on second-strike offenses was a mere 4.9 years, suggesting that the felon population was not receiving draconian punishments. Furthermore, Shepherd found that truth-in-sentencing legislation—laws that mandate that inmates serve at least 85% of their sentence and that reduce various forms of sentence reduction—also had crime-saving utility. Using county-level data that covered all 3,054 counties in the United States for the period 1984–1996, Shepherd found that truth-in-sentencing laws decreased murders by 12%, aggravated assaults by 12%, robberies by 24%, rapes by 12%, and larcenies by 3%. However, she also found a displacement effect where burglaries increased by 20% and auto thefts increased by 15%. In terms of fiscal costs to society, truth-in-sentencing laws contributed to a $481 million increase in victim costs for burglary and auto theft but a $5 billion decrease in victim costs for the other offenses. In other words, mandating that felons actually serve the majority of their sentence saved society approximately $4.5 billion annually. Tomislav Kovandzic's empirical assessment of the effects of habitual offender legislation on crime in Florida produced substantively similar findings. Habitual offender laws in that state contributed to reductions in several crimes, including rape, robbery, assault, burglary, larceny, and auto theft.[21]

The renaissance of habitual offender laws created a sense of alarm among some criminologists, who forecasted apocalyptic results for an already stressed criminal justice system. Preliminary empirical research on the topic was conducted too soon after the initiatives took effect; thus, early estimates of three-strikes effects on system overcrowding were exaggerated. A magisterial review by James Austin and his colleagues supported this assessment. In their words,

> From a national perspective, the "three strikes and you're out" movement was largely symbolic. It was not designed to have a significant impact on the criminal justice system. The laws were crafted so that in order to be "struck out" an offender would have to be convicted two or more often three times for very serious but rarely committed crimes . . . consequently, the vast majority of the targeted offender population was already serving long prison terms for these types of crimes. From this perspective, the three strikes law movement is much ado about nothing and is having virtually no impact on current sentencing practices.

More pointedly, Austin and his colleagues advised that the gross errors in predicting the impact of these and other laws by some of the most prestigious researchers underscore how little we know about change within the criminal justice system.[22] It is clear that overall, scholars disagree on whether attempts to use legislation and prison to stop career criminals are counterproductive.[23]

Making Sense of Corrections and Career Criminals

Regardless of its substantive findings, research that attempts to build an empirical bridge between three-strikes legislation, aggregate crime rates, and the daily activities of habitual criminal offenders is potentially problematic. First, even if three-strikes laws dramatically exacerbate violent crime, does it make sense to amend the legislation as some have suggested? Would such a move signal societal acquiescence to career criminals? Logically, it seems that the answer is *yes*. Three-strikes laws seek to toughen the criminal justice system instead of continuing with the generally nonveracious punishments that the system currently administers. As the review by James Austin stated, habitual offender statutes serve to symbolically affirm the public's distaste for serious offenders. Given the political capital of crime, it is doubtful that policy makers will anytime soon amend habitual offender laws because they purportedly upset and antagonize career criminals.

Second, it is important to note that counties, standard metropolitan statistical areas (SMSAs), and states never commit murder, rape, or robbery. In this sense, macrolevel research is ultimately unhelpful in understanding individual-level phenomena, such as the behavior of career criminals. Besides the ecological fallacy of imputing individual action from aggregate information, one should seriously question the substantive value of using state-level legislative information to draw conclusions about the individual-level decisions that result in crime. Hard-core criminal offenders can be people who will abstain from eating and sleeping for several days to participate in their criminal lifestyle. As such, it is uncertain how much we should invest in deterrence research positing that high-rate offenders are well-informed, rational decision makers who will calculatedly adjust their criminal offending according to the prevailing winds of criminal justice policy.[24]

Third, scholars disagree sharply over the contemporaneous relationship between large-scale increases in incarceration and dramatic reductions in crime. To some, the relationship was plain to see. Yet others simply refused to acknowledge an interrelationship between harsher sentencing and punishments, the incapacitation of repeat offenders, and improved public safety. Thomas Marvell and Carlisle Moody have also noticed this trend of academicians denying that prison can reduce crime:

> We have widely circulated these findings, along with the data used, to colleagues who specialize in quantitative analysis. *The most frequent response is that they refuse to believe the results no matter how good the statistical analysis* [italics added]. Behind that contention is the notion, often discussed informally but seldom published, that social scientists can obtain any result desired by manipulating the procedures used. In fact, the wide variety of estimates

concerning the impact of prison populations is taken as good evidence of the malleability of research. The implication . . . is that no matter how thorough the analysis, results are not credible unless they conform with prior expectations.[25]

Correctional policy and practice have meaningfully deterred, incapacitated, and otherwise neutralized thousands of career criminals across the country. In conjunction with changes in the age structure of the population, a booming economy, and more effective social policies, prisons contributed significantly to the falling crime rates of the 1990s. Indeed, a decidedly nonpartisan book on this topic, John Conklin's *Why Crime Rates Fell*, suggested that between 13% and 54% of the crime reduction was the result of the increased use of prison sentences.[26]

The points of dissatisfaction with the prison system are legion. As explained earlier in this chapter, fully 60% of felony convictions in state courts do not result in a prison sentence. For convicted felons sentenced to state prison, the national average is to serve less than half of their actual sentence—this includes those convicted of murder, rape, kidnapping, and armed robbery. While imprisoned, criminal careers do not subside for career criminals; instead, they thrive. For example, Matt DeLisi recently examined the prison misconduct careers of more than 1,000 inmates imprisoned in the southwestern United States. He found that 40% of inmates were habitual or chronic offenders who accumulated more than five official violations, even while incarcerated. Moreover, nearly 8% of inmates amassed more than 30 incidents of misconduct. A small cadre of inmates accounted for 100% of the prison murders, 75% of the prison rapes, 80% of the prison arsons, and 50% of the aggravated assaults occurring behind bars.

In federal prisons, career criminals are among the most violent, problematic, and difficult to manage. Several recent meta-analyses and other summary research have produced consistent findings about the correlates of prison misconduct and subsequent recidivism. The best predictors of continued crime and violence while in prison and after release are onset (itself a proxy of criminal propensity), prison and arrest history, and prior diagnosis of pathology (such as psychopathy).[27] Unfortunately, prison has lost its de facto and de jure punishment capacity for career criminals.

Short of the death penalty, the most serious punishment that the courts can administer is life imprisonment without the possibility of parole. However, even this sanction is problematic. First, in many states, the life imprisonment without parole sanction is not as indefinite as its name implies. These statutes specify a fixed number of years that an inmate must serve before being considered for any reduction. There is considerable state variation in the duration of life imprisonment sentences, as well as the amount of time served. For example, Hawaii mandates a 20-year sentence; Colorado a 40-year sentence; and in states such as Iowa, life imprisonment without parole means that the defendant will die in prison unless the governor commutes the sentence. Federal law permits the Bureau of Prisons to release inmates sentenced to life imprisonment without parole if they are at least 70 years of age and have served a minimum of 30 years—hardly a "life" sentence.[28] Concern with the administrative and health care costs associated with an aging prison population, the overreliance on "good time" to reduce prison sentences, and the potential overuse of executive pardons (recall that the past-governor of Illinois recently commuted all death sentences in the state to life imprisonment) all contribute to a weakened life-without-parole sanction. Empirical research has shown that life sentences without parole equate to approximately 15 years behind bars and that most states reduce life sentences with surprising regularity. Indeed, the improbity of the life imprisonment without parole sanction has been cited as a factor that spurs public support of capital punishment.[29]

Finally, recent deterrence research and surveys of offender views on punishment have shed more light on the criminal justice system's inability to effectively punish high-rate offenders. Generally, deterrence researchers have found that persons who were most likely deterred were those least likely to commit serious crimes in the first place. Chronic offenders, because of their correctional experiences, indicated that the criminal justice system worried them little. Indeed, the worst offenders were generally oblivious to and even emboldened by criminal punishment. In the same way, surveys that examined the punishment viewpoints of criminal offenders indicated that the most active criminals preferred prison to lesser punishments, such as probation. Indeed, prison was viewed as a facile, ostensibly normal experience, whereas community corrections were considered invasive, annoying, and difficult to successfully complete. For instance, Ben Crouch noted that

> prison is preferred by those who already are largely committed to a deviant lifestyle with its attendant trips to jail and prison. For persons deeply involved "in the life," prisons carried only the inconvenience of the sentence, not the added loss of reputation . . . indeed, going to prison may even be a badge of honor for some offenders.[30]

For many career criminals, prison is not a viable crime-control option.

Capital Punishment and Career Criminals

The late criminologist Richard Herrnstein once wrote that

> the average offender is psychologically atypical in various respects, not necessarily to a pathological degree, but enough so that the normal prohibitions against crime are relatively ineffective. In designing public policy, we must bear in mind that a society that successfully keeps 80% to 90% of its population on the right side of the law may find that it needs other measures to deter the remaining 10% to 20%, for reasons that have more to do with individual criminogenic traits than with defects in policy.[31]

One of these "other measures" Herrnstein may have had in mind is capital punishment. The literature on capital punishment is vast, spans many disciplines in the social sciences and humanities, and constitutes one of the most controversial areas in criminology. I have no intention of entering that contentious debate, with the exception of a brief empirical exercise that provides compelling evidence that the death penalty could have profound crime-savings effects when applied to career criminals who have been convicted of murder.

Box 6.2   Official Policy Position of the American Society of
Criminology With Respect to the Death Penalty

"Be it resolved that because social science research has demonstrated the death penalty to be racist in application and social science research has found no consistent evidence of crime deterrence through execution, The American Society of Criminology publicly condemns this form of punishment, and urges its members to use their professional skills in legislatures and courts to seek a speedy abolition of this form of punishment."

—Adopted in November 1989.

Source: http://www.asc41.com/deathpenalty.html

A central issue in death penalty debates centers on the deterrent capacity of the sanction. Historically, most research has shown that capital punishment did not significantly reduce homicide rates, thus questioning the sanction's purpose. That the death penalty does not deter crime is the status quo position in criminology; indeed, it was one of the rationales forwarded by the American Society of Criminology when that organization took an official stand against capital punishment (see Box 6.2). Additional studies, conducted primarily by economists, indicated that the death penalty did indeed have deterrent value and significantly reduced the murder rate.[32] A common limitation of prior work was the use of aggregate-level data to address the decision-making processes of persons who might or might not commit murder. The following empirical demonstration avoids this by using the data from the offending careers of 500 habitual adult offenders.

Of the 500 habitual criminals who appeared in the study "Extreme Career Criminals" published in the *American Journal of Criminal Justice*, 39 had been convicted of murder and sentenced to a nondeath sentence. To assess the crime-savings utility of capital punishment, the offending careers before and after their murder conviction were compared. Had these offenders been sentenced to death and actually executed, their criminal careers would have, of course, ended. Retrospectively examining their offending careers, it was clear that they committed crimes at high rates before and after serving time for a murder conviction. On average, offenders in the sample were arrested for 4 serious violent crimes, defined as murder, rape, robbery, kidnapping, child molestation, or aggravated assault *after* serving time for a murder conviction. Moreover, they averaged 7 arrests for burglary, theft, arson, or auto theft and 29 additional arrests for miscellaneous lesser offenses. These arrests resulted in an average of five additional felony convictions and nearly four additional prison sentences. Had these 39 offenders been executed, 122 arrests for serious violent crimes, 218 arrests for serious property crimes, 863 additional arrests, 144 felony convictions, and 115 prison sentences would have been averted. More distressing than these numbers is the trend that recidivism *increased* for violent and total offending, felony convictions, and prison sentences after the offenders served time for a murder conviction. Only property offending was lower after the homicide event.

Not all of the approximately 3,600 persons on death rows in the United States are necessarily career criminals; however, the preponderance of condemned offenders have extensive arrest and incarceration histories. Although approximately 20,000 people are murdered each year, fewer than 100 people are executed annually. It is probable that a significant amount of serious crime and resultant victimization would be precluded by a more rigorous application of the death penalty insofar as the sanction permanently neutralizes the careers of the most recalcitrant offenders.

Recent events have served to heighten the controversy surrounding the death penalty. Since 1992, the Innocence Project, a nonprofit legal clinic at the Benjamin Cardozo School of Law, has handled cases where postconviction DNA testing could yield conclusive proof of innocence or guilt. To date, 143 offenders have been exonerated. Many of these offenders had been convicted of serious crimes and were sentenced to lengthy prison terms of death. The wrongful conviction of a factually innocent person is abominable; being wrongfully sentenced to death is even more intolerable.

According to the Innocence Project, 12 factors have contributed to wrongful convictions of criminal defendants. In descending order of prevalence, these are mistaken identification, serology inclusion, police misconduct, prosecutorial misconduct, defective or fraudulent science, bad lawyers, errors in microscopic hair matches, false witness testimony, informants and snitches, false confessions, other forensic inclusions, and erroneous DNA inclusions. It is possible that another determinant of wrongful convictions is the zealous (or perhaps overzealous) pursuit of persons already known to the police. Once the case profiles of the 143 exonerated persons are perused, it becomes apparent that a substantial number of them had prior criminal records. Some were chronic offenders. Police and prosecutorial misconduct have been cited as causes of wrongful convictions. Were these criminal justice agents motivated to dispose of career criminals by probabilistically linking them to crimes? Obviously, this discussion is purely speculative. But it is certainly possible that innocent defendants who also happen to be repeat offenders could erroneously become implicated in capital crimes. For example, as mentioned in Chapter 5, one of the individuals who was found to be wrongfully convicted of murder had previously been convicted of homicide on two separate occasions. Whether the criminal justice system plays "catch up" with career offenders and wrongfully implicates them in crimes is unsettled. Fortunately, the Innocence Project exists to catch potential miscarriages of justice.[33]

In my opinion, the state should assume the function that the Innocence Project has performed by conducting, where applicable, tests of DNA evidence that could exonerate or affirm the guilt of criminal defendants. Miscarriages of justice are not merely the concern of watchdog groups. Indeed, they should concern everyone. More important, capital punishment procedures must be fixed when considering the use of capital punishment as a strategy to stop career criminals.

Notes

1. Cronin, R. C., Bourque, B. B., Gragg, F. E., Mell, J. M., & McGrady, A. A. (1988). *Evaluation of the habitual serious and violent juvenile offender program: Final report.* Washington, DC: U.S. Department of Justice, Office of Justice Programs, Office of Juvenile Justice and Delinquency Prevention; Krisberg, B., & Howell, J. C. (1998). The impact of the juvenile justice system and prospects for graduated sanctions in a comprehensive strategy. In R. Loeber & D. P. Farrington (Eds.), *Serious & violent juvenile offenders: Risk factors and successful interventions* (pp. 346-366). Thousand Oaks, CA: Sage.

2. Schumacher, M., & Kurz, G. A. (1999). *The 8% solution: Preventing serious, repeat juvenile crime.* Thousand Oaks, CA: Sage; *The 8% solution.* (2001, November 21). OJJDP Fact Sheet No. 39. Washington, DC: U.S. Department of Justice, Office of Justice Programs, Office of Juvenile Justice and Delinquency Prevention.

3. Martin, S. E. (1986). Policing career criminals: An examination of an innovative crime control program. *Journal of Criminal Law & Criminology, 77,* 1159-1182; Martin, S. E., & Sherman, L. W. (1986). Selective apprehension: A police strategy for repeat offenders. *Criminology, 24,* 155-174; Martin, S. E., & Sherman, L. W. (1986). Catching career criminals: Proactive policing and selective apprehension. *Justice Quarterly, 3,* 171-192.

4. Abrahamse, A. F., Ebener, P. A., Greenwood, P. W., Fitzgerald, N., & Kosin, T. E. (1991). An experimental evaluation of the Phoenix repeat offender program. *Justice Quarterly, 8,* 141-168.

5. A tangential but importantly related issue in the courts' role in controlling career criminals is the waiver or transfer of juvenile defendants to adult criminal courts. Primarily, there are three ways that juveniles can legally be prosecuted as adults: a judicial waiver, in which the judge has the discretion to transfer; a prosecutorial waiver, in which the prosecutor has the discretion to transfer; and a legislative waiver, in which the decision to transfer is statutory, based on offense seriousness and criminal history of the delinquent. Unfortunately, the consequences of transferring juveniles to criminal court are mostly negative in that the adult incarceration of adolescents significantly increases recidivism; see Fagan, J., & Zimring, F. E. (Eds.). (2000). *The changing borders of juvenile justice: Transfer of adolescents to the criminal court.* Chicago: University of Chicago Press; Winner, L., Lanza-Kaduce, L., Bishop, D. M., & Frazier, C. E. (1997). The transfer of juveniles to criminal court: Reexamining recidivism over the long term. *Crime & Delinquency, 43,* 548-563; Thomas, C. W., & Bishop, D. M. (1984). The effect of formal and informal sanctions on delinquency: A longitudinal comparison of labeling and deterrence theories. *Journal of Criminal Law & Criminology, 75,* 1222-1245. In part based on these findings, efforts have been made to better integrate formerly incarcerated violent adolescents into society by providing assorted skills, resources, and social support. An evaluation of violent juvenile offenders from Boston, Detroit,

Memphis, and Newark showed that those who received reintegration treatments were significantly less likely to recidivate and remained crime-free for longer periods than controls. See Fagan, J. A. (1990). Treatment and reintegration of violent juvenile offenders: Experimental results. *Justice Quarterly, 7*, 233-264.

6. Other early case law that examined this issue includes *O'Neil v. Vermont*, 144 U.S. 323 (1892); *Howard v. Fleming*, 191 U.S. 126 (1903); *Weems v. United States*, 217 U.S. 349 (1910); *Graham v. West Virginia*, 224 U.S. 616 (1912). An outstanding essay that explores the historical jurisprudence of habitual offender statutes is Zeigler, F. A., & del Carmen, R. V. (1996). Constitutional issues arising from "three strikes and you're out" legislation. In D. Shichor & D. K. Sechrest (Eds.), *Three strikes and you're out: Vengeance as public policy* (pp. 3-24). Thousand Oaks, CA: Sage.

7. *Weeks v. United States*, 232 U.S. 383 (1914); *Mapp v. Ohio*, 367 U.S. 643 (1961); *Robinson v. California*, 370 U.S. 660 (1962); *Rummel v. Estelle*, 445 U.S. 263 (1980); *Hutto v. Davis*, 454 U.S. 370 (1982); *Solem v. Helm*, 463 U.S. 277 (1983); *Harmelin v. Michigan*, 501 U.S. 957 (1991). *Ewing v. California*, 01-6978, and *Lockyer v. Andrade*, 01-1127, in Mears, B. (2003). *Supreme Court upholds long sentences under 3-strikes-you're-out law*. Retrieved October 22, 2003, from http:www.cnn.com/2003/LAW/03/05/scouts.three.strikes/

8. *Estelle v. Smith*, 451 U.S. 454 (1981); *Vanderbilt v. Collins*, 994 F. 2nd 189 (5th Circuit) (1993); *Ake v. Oklahoma*, 470 U.S. 68 (1985); *Barefoot v. Estelle*, 463 U.S. 880 (1983); *Powell v. Texas*, 492 U.S. 680 (1989).

9. *United States v. Salerno*, 481 U.S. 739 (1987); *Jurek v. Texas*, 428 U.S. 262 (1976); *Simmons v. South Carolina*, 512 U.S. 154 (1994).

10. Although initially promising, findings in the following were dampened by subsequent analyses: Greenwood, P. W., & Abrahamse, A. (1982). *Selective incapacitation*. Santa Monica, CA: RAND. For examples, see Cohen, J. (1983). Incapacitation as a strategy for crime control: Possibilities and pitfalls. In M. Tonry & N. Morris (Eds.), *Crime and justice: An annual review of research* (Vol. 5, pp. 1-84). Chicago: University of Chicago Press; Visher, C. A. (1986). The RAND inmate survey: A reanalysis. In A. Blumstein et al. (Eds.), *Criminal careers and "career criminals"* (pp. 161-211). Washington, DC: National Academy Press; von Hirsch, A. (1985). *Past or future crimes: Deservedness and dangerousness in the sentencing of criminals*. New Brunswick, NJ: Rutgers University Press. For a recent update and explication of the prediction literature, see DeLisi, M. (2001). Scaling archetypal criminals. *American Journal of Criminal Justice, 26*, 77-92.

11. von Hirsch, A. (1984). The ethics of selective incapacitation: Observations on the contemporary debate. *Crime & Delinquency, 30*, 175-194 (p. 191). For other works that critically evaluated the ethical problems with attempts to predict criminal dangerousness, see Feld, B. C. (1983). Delinquent careers and criminal policy: Just deserts and the waiver policy. *Criminology, 21*, 195-212; Mathiesen, T. (1998). Selective incapacitation revisited. *Law & Human Behavior, 22*, 455-469; Polk, K., &

Gibbons, D. C. (1988). Polk, K., & Gibbons, D. C. (1988). The uses of criminology, the rehabilitative ideal, and justice. *Crime & Delinquency, 34,* 263-276. Zimring, F. E., & Hawkins, G. (1986). Dangerousness and criminal justice. *Michigan Law Review, 85,* 481-509; Zimring, F. E., & Hawkins, G. (1995). *Incapacitation: Penal confinement and the restraint of crime.* New York: Oxford University Press.

12.   Chaiken, M. R., & Chaiken, J. M. (2004). Priority prosecution of high-rate dangerous offenders. In B. W. Hancock & P. M. Sharp (Eds.), *Public policy, crime, and criminal justice* (3rd ed., pp. 231-243). Upper Saddle River, NJ: Prentice Hall; Brantley, A. C., & Ochberg, F. M. (2003). Lethal predators and future dangerousness. *FBI Law Enforcement Bulletin, 72,* 16-22.

13.   *Kansas v. Hendricks,* 521 U.S. 346 (1997).

14.   Entire special issues on sexually violent offenders, their control, and civil commitment occasionally appeared in academic journals, including *Behavioral Sciences and the Law* and *Psychology, Public Policy & Law.* For examples of this research, see Becker, J. V., Stinson, J., Tromp, S., & Messer, G. (2003). Characteristics of individuals petitioned for civil commitment. *International Journal of Offender Therapy & Comparative Criminology, 47,* 185-195; Erickson, P. E. (2002). The legal standard of volitional impairment: An analysis of substantive due process and the United States Supreme Court's decision in Kansas v. Hendricks. *Journal of Criminal Justice, 30,* 1-10; Janus, E. S. (2000). Sexual predator commitment laws: Lessons for law and the behavioral sciences. *Behavioral Sciences & the Law, 18,* 5-21; Simon, J. (1998). Managing the monstrous: Sex offenders and the new penology. *Psychology, Public Policy & Law, 4,* 452-467.

15.   Petersilia, J., Greenwood, P. W., & Lavin, M. (1978). *Criminal careers of habitual felons.* Santa Monica, CA: RAND; DeLisi, M. (2001). Extreme career criminals. *American Journal of Criminal Justice, 25,* 239-252.

16.   Greenwood, P. W. (1990). The violent offender in the criminal justice system. In N. A. Weiner, M. A. Zahn, & R. J. Sagi (Eds.), *Violence: Patterns, causes, public policy* (pp. 339-350). Fort Worth, TX: Harcourt Brace College Publishers; Petersilia, J. (1992). California's prison policy: Causes, costs, and consequences. *The Prison Journal, 72,* 8-36.

17.   Durose, M. R., & Langan, P. A. (2003, June). *Felony sentences in state courts, 2000.* Bulletin. Washington, DC: U.S. Department of Justice, Office of Justice Programs, Bureau of Justice Statistics; Greenfeld, L. A. (1995, April). *Prison sentences and time served for violence.* Selected findings. Washington, DC: U.S. Department of Justice, Office of Justice Programs, Bureau of Justice Statistics; Langan, P. A., & Levin, D. J. (2002, June). *Recidivism of prisoners released in 1994.* Special report. Washington, DC: U.S. Department of Justice, Office of Justice Programs, Bureau of Justice Statistics.

18.   Block, M. K. (1996). Supply side imprisonment policy. *Two views on imprisonment policies.* Research report. Washington, DC: U.S. Department of Justice, Office of Justice Programs, National Institute of Justice. Block's research does not

align with the conventional wisdom in criminology, even though it presents a similar correctional picture as Greenwood and Petersilia's work. The more popular view that laments the use of imprisonment in the United States was presented by Professor Franklin Zimring in the alternate presentation titled "Lethal Violence and the Overreach of American Imprisonment."

19.   Bernard, T. J., & Ritti, R. R. (1991). The Philadelphia birth cohort and selective incapacitation. *Journal of Research in Crime and Delinquency, 28,* 33-54. For studies on selective incapacitation, see Barnett, A., & Lofaso, A. J. (1985). Selective incapacitation and the Philadelphia cohort data. *Journal of Quantitative Criminology, 1,* 3-36; Gottfredson, S. D., & Gottfredson, D. M. (1994). Behavioral prediction and the problem of incapacitation. *Criminology, 32,* 441-474; Greenberg, D. F. (1975). The incapacitative effect of imprisonment: Some estimates. *Law & Society Review, 9,* 541-580; Van Dine, S., Conrad, J. P., & Dinitz, S. (1979). *Restraining the wicked: The incapacitation of the dangerous criminal.* Lexington, MA: Lexington Books; Zimring, F. E., & Hawkins, G. (1988). The new mathematics of imprisonment. *Crime & Delinquency, 34,* 425-436.

20.   Auerhahn, K. (2002). Selective incapacitation, three strikes, and the problem of aging prison populations: Using simulation modeling to see the future. *Criminology & Public Policy, 3,* 353-388; Moody, C. E. (2002). Simulation modeling and policy analysis. *Criminology & Public Policy, 3,* 393-398; Kovandzic, T. V., Sloan, J. J. III, & Vieraitis, L. M. (2002). Unintended political consequences of politically popular sentencing policy: The homicide promoting effects of "three strikes" in U.S. cities (1980-1999). *Criminology & Public Policy, 3,* 399-424; Marvell, T. B., & Moody, C. E. (2001). The lethal effects of three-strikes laws. *Journal of Legal Studies, 30,* 89-106. Beyond three strikes, another study found that imprisonment had a weak effect on crime yet many important factors; see DeFina, R. H., & Arvanites, T. M. (2002). The weak effect of imprisonment on crime, 1971-1998. *Social Science Quarterly, 83,* 635-653.

21.   Shepherd, J. M. (2002). Fear of the first strike: The full deterrent effect of California's two- and three-strikes legislation. *Journal of Legal Studies, 31,* 159-201; Shepherd, J. M. (2002). Police, prosecutors, criminals, and determinate sentencing: The truth about truth-in-sentencing laws. *Journal of Law and Economics, 45,* 509-534; Kovandzic, T. V. (2001). The impact of Florida's habitual offender law on crime. *Criminology, 39,* 179-204.

22.   Austin, J., Clark, J., Hardyman, P., & Henry, D. A. (1999). The impact of "three strikes and you're out." *Punishment and Society, 1,* 131-162 (pp. 138-142, 131).

23.   For examples of studies that were not supportive of three-strikes and recidivism statutes, see Clark, J., Austin, J., & Henry, D. A. (1997, September). *"Three strikes and you're out": A review of state legislation.* Research in brief. Washington, DC: U.S. Department of Justice, Office of Justice Programs, National Institute of Justice; Kunselman, J. C., & Vito, G. F. (2002). Questioning mandatory sentencing efficiency: A case study of persistent felony offender rapists in

Kentucky. *American Journal of Criminal Justice, 27,* 53-68; Meehan, K. E. (2000). California's three-strikes law: The first six years. *Corrections Management Quarterly, 4,* 22-33; Vitiello, M. (1997). Three strikes: Can we return to rationality? *Journal of Criminal Law and Criminology, 87,* 395-481; Zimring, F. E., Hawkins, G., & Kamin, S. (2001). *Punishment and democracy: Three strikes and you're out in California.* New York: Oxford University Press. For examples of supporting research, see DiIulio, J. J., & Piehl, A. M. (1991, Fall). Does prison pay? The stormy national debate over the cost-effectiveness of imprisonment. *Brookings Review,* 28-35; La Course, D. (1994). Three strikes is working in Washington. *Journal of Interpersonal Violence, 9,* 421-424; Levitt, S. D. (1996). The effect of prison population size on crime rates: Evidence from prison overcrowding litigation. *Quarterly Journal of Economics, 111,* 319-351; Piehl, A. M., & DiIulio, J. J. (1995, Winter). Does prison pay? Revisited: Returning to the crime scene. *Brookings Review,* 20-25.

24. An outstanding qualitative look at the lifestyles and decision-making processes of serious criminal offenders is Hochstetler, A. (2001). Opportunities and decisions: Interactional dynamics in robbery and burglary groups. *Criminology, 39,* 737-764.

25. Marvell, T. B., & Moody, C. E. (1997). The impact of prison growth on homicide. *Homicide Studies, 1,* 205-233 (p. 221).

26. Conklin, J. E. (2003). *Why crime rates fell.* Boston: Allyn & Bacon. This work masterfully reviews the literature on the prison-crime relationship and many of the issues relating to the control of career criminals. It also presents a sobering look at the role that political ideology has in influencing the research of criminologists.

27. DeLisi, M. (2003). Criminal careers behind bars. *Behavioral Sciences & the Law, 21,* 653-669; Allender, D. M., & Marcell, F. (2003). Career criminals, security threat groups, and prison gangs: An interrelated threat. *FBI Law Enforcement Bulletin, 72,* 8-12; Benda, B. B., Corwyn, R. F., & Toombs, N. J. (2001). Recidivism among adolescent serious offenders: Prediction of entry into the correctional system for adults. *Criminal Justice & Behavior, 28,* 588-613; Cottle, C. C., Lee, R. J., & Heilbrun, K. (2001). The prediction of criminal recidivism in juveniles: A meta-analysis. *Criminal Justice & Behavior, 28,* 367-394; Kroner, D. G., & Mills, J. F. (2001). The accuracy of five risk appraisal instruments in predicting institutional misconduct and new convictions. *Criminal Justice & Behavior, 28,* 471-489; Loza, W. (2003). Predicting violent and nonviolent recidivism of incarcerated male offenders. *Aggression and Violent Behavior, 8,* 175-203; Walters, G. D. (2003). Predicting institutional adjustment and recidivism with the psychopathy checklist factor scores: A meta-analysis. *Law & Human Behavior, 27,* 541-558.

28. Sabol, W. J., & McGready, J. (1999, June). *Time served in prison by federal offenders, 1986-1997.* Special report. Washington, DC: U.S. Department of Justice, Office of Justice Programs, Bureau of Justice Statistics.

29. Lane, J. (1993). Is there life without parole? A capital defendant's right to a meaningful alternative sentence. *Loyola of Los Angeles Law Review, 26,* 327-356;

Cheatwood, D. (1988). The life-without-parole sanction: Its current status and a research agenda. *Crime & Delinquency, 34,* 43-59; McGarrell, E., & Sandys, M. (1996). The misperception of public opinion toward capital punishment: Examining the spuriousness explanation of death penalty support. *American Behavioral Scientist, 39,* 500-513.

30. Pogarsky, G. (2002). Identifying "deterrable" offenders: Implications for research on deterrence. *Justice Quarterly, 19,* 431-452; Piquero, A. R., & Pogarsky, G. (2002). Beyond Stafford and Warr's reconceptualization of deterrence: Personal and vicarious experiences, impulsivity, and offending behavior. *Journal of Research in Crime and Delinquency, 39,* 153-186; Crouch, B. M. (1993). Is incarceration really worse? Analysis of offenders' preferences for prison over probation. *Justice Quarterly, 10,* 67-88 (p. 84); Petersilia, J., & Deschenes, E. P. (1994a). Perceptions of punishment: Inmates and staff rank the severity of prison versus intermediate sanctions. *The Prison Journal, 74,* 306-328; Petersilia, J., & Deschenes, E. P. (1994b). What punishes? Inmates rank the severity of prison vs. intermediate sanctions. *Federal Probation, 58,* 3-8; Wood, P. B., & May, D. C. (2003). Racial differences in perceptions of the severity of sanctions: A comparison of prison with alternatives. *Justice Quarterly, 20,* 605-632.

31. Herrnstein, R. J. (1995). Criminogenic traits. In J. Q. Wilson & J. Petersilia (Eds.), *Crime* (pp. 39-64). San Francisco: ICS Press (pp. 39-40).

32. A recent synthesis of this literature appears in Dezhbakhsh, H., Rubin, P. H., & Shepherd, J. M. (2003). Does capital punishment have a deterrent effect? New evidence from postmoratorium panel data. *American Law and Economics Review, 5,* 344-376. A respected volume on the topic is Bedau, H. A. (Ed.). (1997). *The death penalty in America: Current controversies.* New York: Oxford University Press.

33. Readers should consult the organization website for more information on their mission and the profiles of the 143 persons exonerated to date (www.inno cenceproject.org). Additional issues about wrongful conviction appear in Scheck, B., Neufeld, P., & Dwyer, J. (2001). *Actual innocence: When justice goes wrong and how to make it right.* New York: Signet.

7

Conclusion: Do We Have the Will to Stop Career Criminals?

Do we simply turn our heads, and look the other way?

—Elvis Presley, "In the Ghetto"

Overview

In a way, the crime problem in a society is the career criminal problem because about 5% of the offenders account for more than half of the total crime and delinquency affecting the population. This appears to be a resilient feature of disparate societies across the globe. For instance, one of the most authoritative works on career criminals to emerge in recent years is Terrie Moffitt's developmental taxonomy with its two archetypal offender groups: adolescence-limited and life-course persistent. The latter group is the latest moniker for career criminals and represents all of the negative characteristics that the worst offenders embody. In fact, scholars have furnished empirical support for Moffitt's life-course persistent offender group by using an array of data sources and research methods. Specifically, these seriously antisocial individuals have been found in general population samples from the Netherlands; large cohorts of African Americans from the United States; a sample of parolees from Buffalo, New York; a sample of arrestees from Colorado; a Swedish birth cohort; the Dunedin (New Zealand) Multidisciplinary Health and Development Study; and a sample of offenders from Colombia, South America.[1]

Unfortunately, all of these places suffer from the actions of a subset of the population whose entire life histories are characterized by a protean infliction of harm onto others. Across contexts, these offenders demonstrate an overt unwillingness to comply with conventional norms and socially coexist with others. School and the responsibilities inherent in education are rejected. Work is viewed as an arduous waste of time. Personal relationships and enduring friendships are shunned because they presumably pale to the fleeting excitement of social interaction with no involvement. Chronic offenders instead spend their days immersed in vice and malaise.[2] At minimum, career criminals cost society more than $1 million in terms of victim costs and criminal justice expenditures. The most frequent offenders among them generate costs exceeding $10 million each. Estimates of the assorted costs posed by career criminals only begin to address this social impact. For instance, Mark Cohen and his colleagues recently found that citizens' willingness to pay for programs that would reduce serious crimes are 1.5 to 10 times higher than previous estimates of the costs of crime.[3] People are beleaguered by crime, especially the recurrent exploits of habitual offenders. However, until something meaningful is done, society will continue to spend millions of dollars to, in effect, pay for its own ruination at the hands of career criminals.

Although the empirical evidence of career criminals is unassailable, this knowledge has not translated well into developing policies to effectively control criminal behavior. Most visible has been the failure to produce prediction instruments that can accurately identify career criminals early enough to forestall their offending. Despite decades of research toward the accurate prediction of future criminal conduct and dangerousness, ethical concerns and methodological problems remain, and more research is needed. This does not mean that the knowledge produced in this area is without use, however. It is axiomatic that the greatest predictor of one's future conduct is one's past conduct. If one knows the age when an offender first committed antisocial behavior, the number of times an individual has been arrested and imprisoned, and the frequency with which an individual commits acts of predation against others, then one can make a fairly accurate prediction whether an offender is likely to reoffend. These assessments should and will continue to be used, except for selective incapacitation purposes. My hope is that the risk-factor paradigm will fare as well in criminal justice as it has fared in prevention.[4]

It is easy to see why career criminals and the handling of them are such divisive issues that result in such heated academic debates. Because their pathology is significantly heritable, there is compelling truth to the idea that habitual criminals are "bad seeds" who were simply bad from the start. Indeed, recent research suggests that one of the most controversial theories of crime, self-control theory, is likely to become even more hotly contested. A growing number of scholars are noting the diagnostic overlap between the theorized elements of low self-control and more psychologically and biologically based constructs like psychopathy and attention deficit hyperactivity disorder (ADHD).[5] Although Gottfredson and Hirschi clearly expressed that socialization processes create self-control, others have surmised that self-control might itself be a biologically based phenomenon that predates socialization. If about 80% of the variation in ADHD is genetic, could it also be the case that persons with low self-control were simply born that way? Future research will explore this question, and it is my prediction that self-control theory will become increasingly aligned with nonsociological propensity approaches.

This synthesis will hopefully result in a definitive theoretical explanation for habitual criminality. Because the etiology of career criminality is mostly environmental, we are faced with the continued failure of social policies to positively redirect the trajectories of at-risk families and their children. Despite all of the research and resources focused on the treatment of chronic delinquents, the same formula of 5% causing more than 50% of the problems persists.

Policy recommendations often appear as afterthoughts in concluding chapters. This is not the case here. We must truly invest in, not merely pay lip service to, two complementary yet distinct public policies: prevention and retributive justice. Attention paid to one at the expense of the other will not meaningfully reduce the prevalence of career criminals. Fortunately, prevention and retributive criminal justice offer much to liberals and conservatives and, in the spirit of feasible political compromise, force both ends of the political spectrum to face facts. Policy recommendations appear below, followed by the political feasibility of their implementation.

Prevention and the Conservative Compromise

Unfortunately, prevention has only recently appeared on the criminological radar screen. For example, the Blueprints for Violence Prevention Program, created by scholars at the Center for the Study and Prevention of Violence at the University of Colorado, was not initiated until 1996. Tellingly, less than 50 model and promising programs have been identified across the United States, suggesting that prevention has not been a viable part of public policy. Similarly, the flagship journal *Prevention Science* was not founded until 2000. Prior to that date, prevention was only an ancillary topic located within a variety of disciplines in the fields of medicine, human development, psychiatry, and psychology.

Perhaps one reason why prevention has not been integral to criminology is the generally poor reputation of treatment. In the 1970s, a series of works appeared that seriously questioned the performance of rehabilitation programs, culminating in Robert Martinson's assessment that "nothing works" to transform criminal offenders into law-abiding citizens. In his well-known, wry assessment of treatment, Michael Gottfredson declared that the conventional wisdom in criminology was that treatment and rehabilitation programs were simply ineffective. The "nothing works" doctrine was part hyperbole, however, because even Martinson and his colleagues found that many programs worked some of the time for some offenders. Over the years, the "nothing works" doctrine has been softened by subsequent quantitative reviews of the literature that have found that treatment can indeed work in reducing recidivism, although the treatment effects are relatively low overall. For example, Frank Cullen, an influential criminologist and rehabilitation enthusiast, concluded that approximately 45% of offenders who receive treatment recidivate, compared to 55% for offenders who do not.[6] That is not very promising.

In the absence of an earnest, comprehensive prevention campaign, the typical societal response to career criminals has been the delayed application of largely ineffectual criminal justice system policies. In her review of the promise of prevention as it relates to neurobiological research, Diana Fishbein offered a sadly accurate conclusion:

> As a result of the ineffective, unidimensional approaches of the past, we are now defaulting to the mental health and criminal justice systems with troubled individuals. Rather than ignoring the warning signs in childhood and waiting until adulthood to put these systems into motion, spending billions

of dollars for legal remedies that do not produce favorable outcomes, *the provision of sorely needed services and interventions to high risk individuals can yield far greater benefits* [italics added].[7]

Clearly, waiting to treat persons with multiple problems has not worked.

As reviewed in Chapter 3, the alternative is to intervene early in the lives of at-risk families to improve the health and development of parents and children. *At-risk* generally applies (but is not limited) to teenage mothers with limited human and social resources. Prevention programs can provide an assortment of benefits to pregnant women and their children. These include standard medical care, the prescription of prenatal vitamins, consultation with nurses and other professionals, and treatment for problem behaviors such as smoking, substance abuse, and other risky behaviors. Because teenage mothers legally should still be in school, intervention programs can assist them in finishing high school, continuing their education, and garnering life and other social skills to increase their employability. Fathers must become involved in the lives of their children and families, in addition to participating in conventional activities such as school and work. Taken together, prevention programs can bolster the health and competence of adolescent mothers, which in turn increase the life chances of their children.

Many research programs suggest that getting involved in the lives of at-risk mothers-to-be yields enormous dividends. With the help of medical and other professional service providers, impoverished teenage mothers improve their diets, reduce or quit smoking, benefit from greatly enhanced medical care, develop greater social support networks of family and friends, and experience significantly fewer pregnancy and delivery problems. This equates to reductions in preeclampsia, fewer premature births, and higher birth weights. The interaction between a healthy mother and child decreases the likelihood of abusive parenting, contributes to safer homes, and promotes the cognitive development of children. For the low-income, young, and unmarried women who received these interventions, the 15 years after the delivery of their first child were far different than they would have been otherwise. These women were less likely to engage in criminal conduct and become involved in the criminal justice system, less likely to need or receive public assistance, and more likely to have the skills to be independent, successful adults. In other words, healthy moms were much more likely to produce healthy, social children.

Children whose mothers were healthy throughout their pregnancies were significantly less likely to suffer from neuropsychological deficits that impair emotional and behavioral regulation and cognition. Again, the longitudinal benefits of this are great. Children who are emotionally and behaviorally equipped for competence in school are likely to mature into competent, prosocial adults who are ready and able to face responsibility. Thus, they are less likely to run away from home, have fewer substance abuse problems, are less sexually promiscuous, and are less likely to be arrested, convicted, and punished for criminal behavior.

Prevention must occur during the early elementary school years (before approximately age 10); otherwise, it becomes increasingly more difficult to reduce negative behaviors and promote healthy ones. Successful prevention programs possess elements that should be replicated by developing programs. First, because the origins of career criminality are congenital and sociological, interventions should be multidimensional and contain cognitive, behavioral, affective, and medical components. Similarly, professionals should educate program participants on the reasons for the program, perhaps even sharing the long-term, successful consequences of other programs. People are more likely to be receptive to prevention if they know the academic and concrete reasons for it. Second, because social institutions interact to promote or reduce problem behaviors, prevention programs should target youth, parents, families, teachers, and other socialization agents to create a social support web. Programs that narrowly focus on one institutional domain will not work. Third, programs should have a developmental focus to target problem behaviors and other issues that occur at various life stages. A genuine investment made by program and client must exist. Short-lived applications of parenting or other skills quickly lose their preventative value. True prevention should be fairly intense in application and should offer the breadth of services needed by people with multiple and severe problems. Finally, prevention programs must follow respondents over time to evaluate long-term effectiveness.[8]

Why haven't we meaningfully invested in prevention? Although there are many answers to this question, conservative political leaders and their voting constituents are one source of opposition to the prevention programs described above. Traditionally, conservatives are committed to a streamlined government that provides only those services that its citizens cannot provide for themselves, such as military defense. From this perspective, the governmental largesse that proliferated with the War on

Poverty and other social programs was doubly unnecessary and bad. First, citizens' tax dollars were required to subsidize these programs; and, second, competent adults should obtain these services on their own. Conservatives, by and large, believe that it is patently unfair to expect law-abiding, "non–risk factor" people help pay for the child-rearing, educational, and medical needs of persons who cannot care for themselves. The unfairness and lack of reciprocity inherent in prevention programs are partially why welfare and the role that the government should lead in private lives are such hotly contested issues.

The conservative indignation against social policies that provide rudimentary skills and services to persons in need may be justified, but it should not prevent the widespread implementation of prevention programs. There is simply too much at stake not to intervene. According to David Olds, the Nurse-Family Partnership program—the sine qua non of prevention success—costs a meager $8,000 per family for nearly 3 years of services. If the costs are shared, such as by Medicaid, Temporary Assistance to Needy Families, and the Maternal and Child Health Block-Grants, then prevention programs do not overburden any single source.[9] Recall that, on average, career criminals inflict social costs of more than $1 million per offender. Thus, in fiscal terms, prevention is well worth the investment because it forestalls or precludes later spending and the need for additional largesse.

Beyond the topic of tax dollars, conservatives need to compromise and embrace prevention for humanistic reasons. Every child born to an indigent, teenage mother who receives comprehensive prevention services is much less likely to become an unproductive and dangerous societal burden. Their lives are worth saving from a lifetime of malaise and antisocial behavior. Furthermore, the lives of their potential future victims, as well as the lives of their victims' families and friends, are also worth saving. Scientifically sound prevention programs like those discussed in this book help to prevent career criminals from developing and constitute a tremendous "front-end" policy opportunity.

Retributive Justice and the Liberal Compromise

Even if societies were to increase their investment in prevention programs tenfold, the career criminal problem would not disappear. Front-end policy approaches are only half of the solution—the other half is the responsibility of the criminal justice system. Indeed, the criminal justice system could more effectively contain and control career criminals, which would result in sizable reductions in crime. Like prevention, the systemic Serious Habitual Offender Comprehensive Action Program (SHOCAP) approach, whereby police, courts, corrections, and social service providers share information and coordinate their efforts to target the worst offenders, has been under-utilized. Youth who recurrently commit offenses of extreme violence (e.g., murder, rape, armed robbery, and abduction) are already on the career criminal trajectory. Serious and violent juvenile offenders aged 15 or 16 are about a decade into their antisocial career. At the very least, these types of juvenile offenders should be prosecuted, convicted, and punished accordingly. A well-coordinated and resourced comprehensive program can provide juvenile justice and service providers with the necessary tools to sensibly and cost-effectively select the worst juvenile offenders for serious punishment. I am happy to report that such an effort has already been initiated. Since 1993, the federal Office of Juvenile Justice and Delinquency Prevention has established a comprehensive strategy for addressing the challenges posed by serious, violent, and chronic juvenile offenders.[10] It offers an appropriate balance of prevention, rehabilitation, and social control measures that hopefully will curb burgeoning criminal careers.

The youthfulness of juvenile delinquents—even the most violent and remorseless ones—occasionally makes it difficult to treat them as harshly as the law allows. This moral concern should not apply to unremitting adult career criminals who have for decades committed repeated violations of the law. Unfortunately, the retributive policies designed to stop them have been adulterated by indecision, politics, and other diffuse influences, namely the conflicting images of the news media and the small but vocal ideas of partisan academics.

Separate from the substantive ethical concerns discussed in Chapter 5, residual sentiment within criminology perpetuates the ideas that career criminals are more fiction than threat and that tough-minded criminal justice policies are the real menace. Two quotations directly address this issue. David Gelernter suggested that

> the community at large favors the death penalty, but intellectuals and the cultural elite tend to oppose it. This is not because they abhor killing more than other people do, but because the death penalty represents absolute speech from a position of moral certainty, and doubt is the black-lung disease of the intelligentsia, an occupational hazard now inflicted on the culture as a whole.

Contrast that with statements from Edwin Sutherland, the patriarch of American criminology:

> The problem of the death penalty is important primarily because it is an issue on which those who wish to act on the basis of prejudice, magic, and common sense confront those who wish to act on the basis of a scientific understanding of the processes at work in the causation of crime.[11]

It is interesting that propensity theories are often impugned for being simplistic and advancing the commonsense notion that violent criminals are simply bad. Just as in Sutherland's day, some go to great lengths and use their considerable rhetorical discourse to demonize efforts to stop the worst criminals.

Still, career criminals are able to accrue hundreds of arrests, dozens of convictions, and multiple stints in prison because of a nationwide trend of adulterated criminal justice and underenforcement of the law. Friedrich Nietzsche once wrote that "there is a point in the history of society when it becomes so pathologically soft and tender that among other things it sides even with those who harm it, criminals, and does this quite seriously and honestly."[12] We must not reach this point. Thankfully, the overwhelming majority of criminologists and criminal justice professionals do not partake in the gamesmanship that extends endless solicitude to wrongdoers and patronizes justifiable public concern, fear, and outrage over career criminals.

The liberal camp must relent and stop haranguing criminal justice; otherwise, the two-pronged approach toward reducing career criminals is not possible. Just as conservatives need to acknowledge that we do not live in a perfect world where all citizens successfully care for themselves, liberals need to face facts about career criminals. Those who victimize others are the aggressors, not the victims. As such, empathy should be reserved for the specific victims of career criminals and the public writ large whose moral sentiments have been outraged. Adam Smith once stated that mercy to the guilty is cruelty to the innocent; the Left must learn this lesson or the criminal justice system cannot successfully neutralize career criminals.

Conclusion

As someone who has interviewed hundreds of career criminals—and studied their implausibly lengthy criminal records; the overlapping nature of their pathological substance abuse, mental health, and life problems; and the overall wreckage of their lives—I am continually struck by them. It was obvious to the offenders themselves that the latest round of court-ordered treatment or conditions of their probation or parole were a waste of time. Rehabilitation means to restore to a prior condition of good health, yet most career criminals have never experienced a healthy, prosocial life in the first place. Like Sisyphus eternally pushing the stone uphill, the revolving door of the criminal justice system spins for naught.

There is a genuine chance that prevention efforts will move to the fore-front of criminology. The remarkable results that many programs have produced will become increasingly disseminated by academics, and hopefully this book will be useful in this regard. Because prevention provides so much bang for the buck, it is palatable to citizens across the political spectrum. The costs of implementation can in no way compare to the enormous costs of ignoring the warning signs and risk factors. This chapter began with a quote from perhaps an unusual source, one of Elvis Presley's chart-topping hits. If we continue to "turn our heads, and look the other way," today's disadvantaged and impoverished children could mature into criminal offenders.

That the criminal justice system will be permitted to get as tough as it needs to be to stop the worst offenders is less clear. At this writing, a criminal defendant in Washington had pleaded guilty to 48 counts of first-degree murder in exchange for multiple life sentences. This plea closes the vile saga of the Green River Killer but also spares the life of the murderer. For many, this defendant's dodging of the death penalty is a disgrace. No sooner was the decision rendered than the media and other social commentators theorized that because a 48-time killer was spared the ultimate sanction, it is doubtful that future killers with lower body counts will or should have to face capital punishment. Thus, a plea agreement for the most prolific serial killer in American history immediately morphs into a heated dialogue over our harshest punishment. Also in the public policy winds at this writing is political wrangling between Republicans and Democrats. Republicans want a national Amber Alert system passed in conjunction with policies that would deny pretrial release to child rapists and abductors, eliminate the statute of limitations on child abductions and sex crimes, allow judges to extend to life the supervised term of released sex offenders, and require life sentences for twice-convicted sex offenders. Democrats view these latter policies as draconian infringements on civil liberties.[13]

Dennis Stevens once conducted a survey that explored the opinions of prison inmates about the death penalty. A few interesting findings emerged. Inmates with more extensive histories of violence were the greatest advocates of the death penalty—so long as it applied to other offenders. Inmates were generally reluctant to report that their violent crimes warranted a death sentence. This is not surprising, given that serious offenders tend to disassociate themselves from any responsibility for their conduct. Inmates did not believe that the death penalty had much deterrent value. However, inmates also provided a more novel rationale for the death penalty. According to them, certain offenders are so violent, so unrepentant, so immune to redemption, and so vile that the death penalty is itself an opportunity to "get rid of the low-life."[14]

We would be foolish to turn our heads and look the other way instead of helping impoverished families and children. In the same way, we must not shirk from our obligation to pass moral and legal judgment on career criminals, a group whose existence is characteristic of nearly all societies and whose pathology cannot be exaggerated.

Notes

1. Donker, A. G., Smeenk, W. H., van der Laan, P. H., & Verhulst, F. C. (2003). Individual stability of antisocial behavior from childhood to adulthood: Testing the stability postulate of Moffitt's developmental theory. *Criminology, 41,* 593-610; Piquero, A. R., & White, N. A. (2003). On the relationship between cognitive abilities and life-course persistent offending among a sample of African Americans: A longitudinal test of Moffitt's hypothesis. *Journal of Criminal Justice, 31,* 399-409; Mazerolle, P., & Maahs, J. (2002). *Developmental theory and battering incidents: Examining the relationship between discrete offender groups and intimate partner violence.* Final report. Washington, DC: U.S. Department of Justice, Office of Justice Programs, National Institute of Justice; DeLisi, M. (2001). Scaling archetypal criminals. *American Journal of Criminal Justice, 26,* 77-92; Kratzer, L., & Hodgins, S. (1999). A typology of offenders: A test of Moffitt's theory among males and females from childhood to age 30. *Criminal Behavior and Mental Health, 9,* 57-73; Bartusch, D. J., Lynam, D. R., Moffitt, T. E., & Silva, P. A. (1997). Is age important? Testing a general versus a developmental theory of antisocial behavior. *Criminology, 35,* 13-48; Klevens, J., Restrepo, O., Roca, J., & Martinez, A. (2000). Comparison of offenders with early- and late-starting antisocial behavior in Colombia. *International Journal of Offender Therapy and Comparative Criminology, 44,* 194-203.

2. From a variety of perspectives, an impressively large literature illustrates the general malaise that typifies the lives of career delinquents. For examples, see

Elliott, D. S., Huizinga, D., & Menard, S. (1989). *Multiple problem youth: Delinquency, substance use and mental health problems.* New York: Springer-Verlag; Huizinga, D., Loeber, R., Thornberry, T. P., & Cothern, L. (2000, November). *Co-occurrence of delinquency and other problem behaviors.* Juvenile Justice Bulletin. Washington, DC: U.S. Department of Justice, Office of Justice Programs, Office of Juvenile Justice and Delinquency Prevention; McCord, J. (2001). Psychosocial contributions to psychopathy and violence. In A. Raine & J. Sanmartin (Eds.), *Violence and psychopathy* (pp. 141-169). New York: Kluwer Academic/Plenum Publishers; Najaka, S. S., Gottfredson, D. C., & Wilson, D. B. (2002). A meta-analytic inquiry into the relationship between selected risk factors and problem behavior. *Prevention Science, 2,* 257-271; Woodward, L. J., Fergusson, D. M., & Horwood, L. J. (2002). Romantic relationships of young people with childhood and adolescent onset antisocial behavior problems. *Journal of Abnormal Child Psychology, 30,* 231-243.

3.   Cohen, M. A. (1998). The monetary value of saving a high-risk youth. *Journal of Quantitative Criminology, 14,* 5-33; Cohen, M. A., Rust, R. T., Steen, S., & Tidd, S. T. (2004). Willingness-to-pay for crime control programs. *Criminology, 42,* 89-110; DeLisi, M., & Gatling, J. M. (2003). Who pays for a life of crime? An empirical assessment of the assorted victimization costs posed by career criminals. *Criminal Justice Studies: A Critical Journal of Crime, Law & Society, 16, 283-293.*

4.   On the prevention of serious and violent criminal offenders, see Jones, D., Dodge, K. A., Foster, E. M., Nix, R., & Conduct Problems Prevention Research Group. (2002). Early identification of children at risk for costly mental health service use. *Prevention Science, 3,* 247-256; Olds, D. L. (2002). Prenatal and infancy home visiting by nurses: From randomized trials to community replication. *Prevention Science, 3,* 153-172; Patterson, G. R., Dishion, T. J., & Yoerger, K. (2000). Adolescent growth in new forms of problem behavior: Macro- and micro-peer dynamics. *Prevention Science, 1,* 3-13.

5.   DeLisi, M. (2003). Self-control pathology: The elephant in the living room. *Advances in Criminological Theory, 12,* 21-38; Pratt, T. C., Cullen, F. T., Blevins, K. R., Daigle, L., & Unnever, J. D. (2002). The relationship of attention deficit hyperactivity disorder to crime and delinquency: A meta-analysis. *International Journal of Police Science & Management, 4,* 344-360; Unnever, J. D., Cullen, F. T., & Pratt, T. C. (2003). Parental management, ADHD, and delinquent involvement: Reassessing Gottfredson and Hirschi's general theory. *Justice Quarterly, 20,* 471-500; Wiebe, R. P. (2003). Reconciling psychopathy and low self-control. *Justice Quarterly, 20,* 297-336.

6.   Martinson, R. (1974). What works? Questions and answers about prison reform. *The Public Interest, 35,* 22-54; Lipton, D., Martinson, R., & Wilks, J. (1975). *The effectiveness of correctional treatment: A survey of treatment evaluation studies.* New York: Praeger; Gottfredson, M. R. (1979). Treatment destruction techniques. *Journal of Research in Crime and Delinquency, 16,* 39-54; Cullen, F. T. (2002). Rehabilitation and treatment programs. In J. Q. Wilson & J. Petersilia (Eds.),

Crime: Public policies for crime control (pp. 253-290). Oakland, CA: Institute for Contemporary Studies Press.

7. Fishbein, D. (2000). The importance of neurobiological research to the prevention of psychopathology. *Prevention Science, 1,* 89-106 (p. 102).

8. For a masterful review of the qualities of effective prevention programs, see Webster-Stratton, C., & Taylor, T. (2001). Nipping early risk factors in the bud: Preventing substance abuse, delinquency, and violence in adolescence through interventions targeted at young children (0-8 years). *Prevention Science, 2,* 165-192.

9. Olds, D. L. (2002). Prenatal and infancy home visiting by nurses: From randomized trials to community replication. *Prevention Science, 3,* 153-172.

10. Howell, J. C. (2003). Diffusing research into practice using the comprehensive strategy for serious, violent, and chronic juvenile offenders. *Youth Violence and Juvenile Justice, 1,* 219-245.

11. Gelernter, D. (2001). What do murderers deserve? In H. Tischler (Ed.), *Debating points: Crime and corrections* (pp. 13-20). Upper Saddle River, NJ: Prentice Hall; Sutherland, E. (1925). Murder and the death penalty. *Journal of Criminal Law and Criminology, 15,* 522-529.

12. Nietzsche, F. (1966). *Beyond good and evil.* New York: Vintage Books.

13. Associated Press. (2003). Stand-alone Amber Alert bill fails in House. Retrieved March 27, 2003, from http://www.cnn.com/2003/ALLPOLITICS/03/26/amber.alert.ap/index/html. During this same time, a child advocacy group titled Parents for Megan's Law conducted a nationwide study of state monitoring of released sex offenders. They found that, nationally, 25% of sex offenders were unaccounted for. In some states, the proportion of sex offenders with whereabouts unknown was 50%. See Associated Press. (2003). Survey: States losing sex offenders. Retrieved February 6, 2003, from http://www.msnbc.com/news/869586 .asp?0dm=C216N

14. Stevens, D. J. (1992). Research note: The death sentence and inmate attitudes. *Crime & Delinquency, 38,* 272-279.

Index

About the Author

Matt DeLisi (Ph.D., University of Colorado, 2000) is Assistant Professor in the Department of Sociology and Coordinator of the Criminal Justice Studies Program at Iowa State University. His primary areas of study are career criminals and self-control theory, and his research has appeared in *Advances in Criminological Theory; American Journal of Criminal Justice; Behavioral Sciences and the Law; Crime and Criminal Justice International; Criminal Justice Policy Review; Criminal Justice Review; Criminal Justice Studies: A Critical Journal of Crime, Law and Society; Encyclopedia of Juvenile Justice; International Journal of Offender Therapy and Comparative Criminology; Journal of Criminal Justice; Justice Quarterly; Pakistan Journal of Social Science; The Social Science Journal; The Justice Professional*; and *Women and Criminal Justice*. Dr. DeLisi is a member of both the Academy of Criminal Justice Sciences and American Society of Criminology and has delivered nearly 20 presentations to professional criminal justice and social science organizations.